THOMAS ANNAN
OF GLASGOW

Thomas Annan of Glasgow

Pioneer of the Documentary Photograph

Lionel Gossman

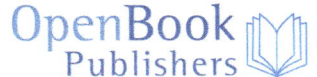

http://www.openbookpublishers.com

©2015 Lionel Gossman

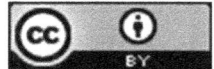

This work is licensed under a Creative Commons Attribution 4.0 International license (CC BY 4.0). This license allows you to share, copy, distribute and transmit the work; to adapt the work and to make commercial use of the work providing attribution is made to the author (but not in any way that suggests that he endorses you or your use of the work). Attribution should include the following information:

Gossman, Lionel. *Thomas Annan of Glasgow: Pioneer of the Documentary Photograph*. Cambridge, UK: Open Book Publishers, 2015. http://dx.doi.org/10.11647/OBP.0057

Please see the list of illustrations for attribution relating to individual images. Every effort has been made to identify and contact copyright holders and any omission or error will be corrected if notification is made to the publisher. For information about the rights of the Wikimedia Commons images, please refer to the Wikimedia website (the relevant links are listed in the list of illustrations).

In order to access detailed and updated information on the license, please visit http://www.openbookpublishers.com/isbn/9781783741274#copyright

Further details about CC BY licenses are available at http://creativecommons.org/licenses/by/4.0

All the external links were active on 18/05/2015 unless otherwise stated.

Digital material and resources associated with this volume are available at http://www.openbookpublishers.com/isbn/9781783741274#resources

ISBN Paperback: 978-1-78374-127-4
ISBN Hardback: 978-1-78374-128-1
ISBN Digital (PDF): 978-1-78374-129-8
ISBN Digital ebook (epub): 978-1-78374-130-4
ISBN Digital ebook (mobi): 978-1-78374-131-1
DOI: 10.11647/OBP.0057

Cover image: Thomas Annan, "Close, No. 46 Saltmarket," from *Glasgow Improvements Act 1866. Photographs of Streets, Closes &c. Taken 1866-71*, Plate 22. Albumen Print. Princeton University Library, Department of Rare Books and Special Collections.

All paper used by Open Book Publishers is SFI (Sustainable Forestry Initiative), PEFC (Programme for the Endorsement of Forest Certification Schemes) and Forest Stewardship Council(r)(FSC(r) certified.

Printed in the United Kingdom and United States by Lightning Source
for Open Book Publishers (Cambridge, UK).

In his battle against Time, that enemy of our precarious existence [. . .], it was in photography, also born of an age-old longing to halt the moment, to wrest it from the flux of "durée" in order to "fix" it forever in a semblance of eternity, that Proust found his best ally.

— Brassaï[1]

Contents

Prefatory Note and Acknowledgments ix

1. Introduction 1
2. Paintings 25
3. Portraits 39
4. Landscapes 49
5. The Built Environment 67
6. *The Old Closes and Streets of Glasgow* 89
7. Epilogue 125

Endnotes 127
List of Illustrations 163
Index of Names 177

Prefatory Note and Acknowledgments

When I graduated from Glasgow University in 1951, my parents followed the then common practice of having a graduation portrait made of me dressed in (rented) academic gown and holding my diploma. To this end I was sent off to the studio of T. & R. Annan in Sauchiehall Street in the heart of the city. Some years later I became aware of the most admired of the photographic works of Thomas Annan, who had founded the firm in the 1850s, namely his still quite frequently discussed and reproduced images of the slums of Glasgow (*The Old Closes and Streets of Glasgow*, 1871). But it was only in the spring of 2014 that, thanks to Julie Mellby, Princeton University's Graphic Arts librarian, I learned of the treasure trove of early photographic albums by Annan in Princeton's Graphic Arts Collection.[2] Julie urged me to write an article for the *Princeton University Library Chronicle* with a view to acquainting the Friends of the Library, for whom the *Chronicle* is primarily intended, with these unusual and rare works—available only in microform even in most leading University libraries—and with Annan's achievement as a photographer. As a native Glaswegian, I could hardly pass up the opportunity of spreading the word about Annan, even though, as a retired professor of French literature, I was also acutely conscious of my limited familiarity with the history of photography and with the major issues in the field. As my interest in the topic broadened, however, what was to have been a short essay of 20-30 pages grew into a considerably longer study—one, moreover, for which I collected many illustrations. Since neither the longer study nor the large number of illustrations I had selected could be accommodated by the *Chronicle* (even in the form of an online portfolio), it became necessary to restrict the *Chronicle* essay to a single work of Annan's and to seek other publishing opportunities for the full study. Open Book Publishers was an obvious choice for me. Since my retirement in 1999, I have worked with this innovative publisher on four books and I enthusiastically support the company's Open Access policy.

The chief purpose of these brief prefatory remarks is to acknowledge with gratitude both the unfailing support of my colleagues at Princeton— Julie Mellby, Gretchen Oberfranc, the editor of the *Princeton University Library Chronicle*, and Steve Ferguson, the Curator of Rare Books and Acting Associate University Librarian for Rare Books and Special Collections—and the invaluable advice and assistance I have received from leading experts in the field, notably Ray McKenzie, recently retired from the faculty of the Glasgow School of Art, Tom Normand of the University of St. Andrews, and Roddy Simpson, Honorary Research Fellow in the School of Culture and Creative Arts at the University of Glasgow. I am also much indebted to helpful librarians at Glasgow University Library, St. Andrews University Library, Princeton University Library and the Mitchell Library in Glasgow. I would like to offer special thanks to Mary Clare Altenhof and her staff at the Fine Arts Library of Harvard University for their assistance, encouragement and interest in the project, and to curators at the National Portrait Gallery in London, the photographic collection at St. Andrews University, the Capital Collections of the City of Edinburgh Council, the City Art Centre in Edinburgh, the Glasgow Museums and the Perth Museum and Art Gallery for generously permitting me to use, at no cost, reproductions of artworks in their collections. I am also glad of the opportunity to record my appreciation of the liberal policy in accordance with which the British Library, the Victoria and Albert Museum, the Library of Congress and the Metropolitan Museum of Art in New York permit the use, for non-commercial purposes, of images posted on their websites.

Finally, I am greatly indebted, as on previous occasions, to Alessandra Tosi of Open Book Publishers for her tireless collaboration and sound advice, to her assistant Bianca Gualandi, who worked heroically on the illustrations, to my copy-editor Ben Fried, and to Stephen Bann, one of the readers of the manuscript, for some stimulating suggestions. OBP joins with me in thanking the University Committee on Research in the Humanities and Social Sciences at Princeton for their continued support.

Lionel Gossman, Princeton, April 2015

1. Introduction

Victorian Scotland was the site of an astonishing florescence of photography, and Thomas Annan was one of an impressive cohort of Scottish masters of the young medium. Born in 1829 into a farming and flax-spinning family in Dairsie, Fife, in the East of Scotland, he left home at the age of fifteen to join the staff of the local *Fife Herald* newspaper, based in the nearby county capital of Cupar, as an apprentice lithographic engraver. Having completed his projected seven-year apprenticeship in four years, he moved to the then rapidly expanding and industrializing city of Glasgow in the West of Scotland, where, on the strength of a glowing reference from the *Herald*, he obtained a position in the large lithographic establishment of Joseph Swan, who had set up in the city in 1818 and developed a thriving business in illustrations for mechanical inventions, maps for street directories, book-plates, and, not least, books on Scottish scenes illustrated by engravings of landscape paintings. Over the next six years Annan honed his engraving skills at Swan's.[3]

In 1855, still in his mid-twenties, Thomas Annan decided to set up in business on his own. By this time, however, the rapid rise of photography on a commercial scale had led to a drop-off in the lithographic trade. In addition, Annan may well have doubted that he could compete in lithography with his former employer's well-established company. It was probably for both reasons that he decided to switch fields and explore the possibilities of photography.

Despite its huge initial success, especially in Continental Europe and the United States (Britain was the only country where its use was restricted by a patent), Louis Daguerre's "daguerreotype," which had been invented around 1835-1837 and publicized in 1839, had begun to give way to a completely different photographic process discovered in 1835 and much

http://dx.doi.org/10.11647/OBP.0057.01

improved in 1841 by the Englishman William Henry Fox Talbot. Unlike the daguerreotype, which had no negative and produced only a single image, albeit an extremely precise and detailed one, Talbot's "calotype" allowed for the production of multiple images from a single negative.[4] In addition, some photographers and critics preferred it because they believed it gave more scope to the photographer than the daguerreotype, which in their view was in fact too precise and detailed and thus "could not record the sentiments of the mind"[5] (i.e. the daguerreotype left no room for the insights and imagination of the photographer).

Among the earliest practitioners of the calotype, besides Talbot himself (Figs. 1:1-3), was the Scottish team of the respected landscape painter David Octavius Hill (Figs. 1:4-7) and his associate Robert Adamson, a young chemist and engineer from St. Andrews, who together set up a photographic studio in 1843 at Rock House at the southwestern entrance to Calton Hill in Edinburgh. Their international renown was soon such that a succession of notables stopped by the studio to have photographic portraits taken—among them, in 1844, the King of Saxony, Friedrich August II, on a tour of Great Britain with his personal physician, Carl Gustav Carus, a friend of Goethe and a gifted Romantic painter in his own right. "We found a large number of artworks hanging on the walls—landscapes, photographs of buildings, portraits," Carus reported. "Much of this was entrancing. Ever since, such unmediated imprintings [*Abformungen*] of nature have given me much to think about."[6] The photographs of Hill and Adamson, mostly taken in the 1840s (Adamson died in 1848 at the young age of 27), are now considered classics of early photography—"the earliest and most brilliant works bearing witness to the young medium," in the words of a recent German scholar (Figs. 1:8-15).

The two men worked as a team and Hill's photographic production flagged after Adamson's premature death, so much so that on his own death many years later, in 1870, as the eminent photographic collector and historian Helmut Gernsheim noted, "neither newspapers nor art journals referred to his photographic work. More surprisingly still, no photographic journal even mentioned his death." It took James Craig Annan, Thomas Annan's son and partner, to rescue the man his father admired deeply from oblivion. "Today," as a result, "David Octavius Hill and Robert Adamson are universally accorded first place in the annals of photography," on account of "the artistic spirit with which their photographs are imbued. [. . .] It is indeed astonishing that in its very first years the new art should have reached its highest peak in the magnificent achievements of these two Scottish photographers."[7]

Inspired in part by Hill and Adamson, and aided by the fact that, thanks to the intervention of the Principal of St. Andrews University, Sir David Brewster, a physicist, close friend and collaborator of Talbot, the latter's patents did not apply in Scotland, other Scots took up photography professionally. In 1849, Thomas Rodger, a nineteen-year-old former chemistry assistant to the St. Andrews surgeon John Adamson—himself an accomplished amateur photographer from whom his younger brother Robert, David Octavius Hill's partner, had received his earliest instruction in the new medium—opened a studio in St. Andrews. A modern plaque outside the building where the studio was located (today the Careers Centre of the University of St. Andrews) reads: "The first professional photographer in St. Andrews, he was taught the calotype process by Dr. John Adamson, who induced him to make it his life's work. His pictorial record of the town, its people, the fisher folk and eminent visitors, brought him great fame. His favour with visiting royalty gave him journeys to London on Royal Photographic missions. He built this house and in it the first photographic studio in the town. Brewster, the Adamsons, and Rodger made St. Andrews a world centre of photography." (Figs. 1:16-17)

After a brief career as a painter of portrait miniatures catering to the wealthy families of the northeast of Scotland, George Washington Wilson set up a studio in Aberdeen in 1852 and ventured into portrait photography. From these early beginnings, aided by technical and commercial acumen, as well as by a contract to photograph the Royal Family while documenting the construction of Balmoral Castle in 1854-1855, Wilson soon established himself as one of Scotland's premier photographers. In 1863 he took a now iconic photograph of Queen Victoria with her faithful servant John Brown at Balmoral (Fig. 1:18), and in the single year 1864-1865, his company produced 553,331 prints of portraits and landscapes.

Landscapes in particular were his forte; by the 1880s, the company claimed to offer 10,000 views of Scottish scenes (Figs. 1:19-20).[8]

Around the same time that Wilson was setting up in Aberdeen (1851), James Valentine opened a photographic portrait studio in his family's engraving and stationary business in Dundee. By 1855 he claimed to be building one of the largest photographic glasshouses in the kingdom. Though on rare occasions his work came strikingly close to Annan's images of the slums of Glasgow (Fig. 1:21), Valentine's reputation rested on his photographs of landscapes and ancient (often ruined) buildings. In 1868 he received an appointment as Royal Photographer and a commission from the Queen to photograph a set of forty views of Highland scenery. The Valentine business ultimately developed into a considerable international operation, occupying a five-story factory building and producing picture postcards of town, countryside, and celebrated buildings not only for the crowds of tourists visiting Scotland in the nineteenth century—the heyday of "Ossian" (James Macpherson), Walter Scott and other Scottish writers, such as James Hogg (the "Ettrick Shepherd") and Robert Burns—but for travellers in many other parts of the world, such as Norway, Jamaica, Tangiers, Morocco, Madeira and New Zealand, well into the twentieth century. As early as the mid-1870s an elaborate works had already been built in the gardens of two adjoining villas in Dundee. It soon covered the whole site and employed over 100 people. In the *British Journal of Photography* for 12 March 1886, the Valentine Dundee establishment was described as one of the largest and most comprehensively equipped in the kingdom (Figs. 1:22-23).[9]

Other Scots who made a name for themselves internationally, often for work executed abroad, include Edinburgh-born John Thomson, known for his photographs of the Far East and for his popular *Street Life in London* (1876-1877), to which we shall have occasion to refer later; Alexander Gardner, who emigrated to the United States in 1856 at the age of 35 and was responsible for many of the great Civil War photographs (some wrongly attributed to his employer, Matthew Brady) as well as for a number of celebrated and widely reproduced portraits of Lincoln; William Carrick and John MacGregor, classic photographers of mid- to late-nineteenth-century Russia; Robert Macpherson, known for his photographs of ancient and Renaissance Rome and the first photographer permitted to take pictures in the Vatican; William Notman of Paisley, who in the same year that Gardner, also from Paisley, left for the United States, emigrated to Canada and established flourishing professional photographic studios first in Montreal, then in Toronto and Halifax, where he produced well-regarded individual and group portraits for customers of all classes. In 1858 he was commissioned by the Grand Trunk Railway to photograph the construction of Montreal's Victoria Bridge, and in the 1870s and 80s he sent photographers across Canada to record the building of the Canadian Pacific Railway, the rise of the western cities, and the life of the Plains and Coastal Indians. On the occasion of the official inauguration of the Victoria Bridge by the Prince of Wales, in 1860, he presented the future Edward VII, then still a student at Christ Church, Oxford, with a handsome album of his photographs, the so-called Maple Box Portfolio. Its acceptance by the Royal Family permitted Notman to describe himself on an advertising pamphlet of 1867 as "Photographer to the Queen." He subsequently opened studios in a dozen other Canadian cities as well as in Boston and Albany, N.Y. In 1873 alone, his firm created 14,000 images (Figs. 1:24-32).[10]

Less well remembered today, but highly successful in their time, were Horatio Ross, from an old landowning family in the North of Scotland, who made a name for himself as a photographer of country sports; John Moffat of Aberdeen, who opened a photographic studio on Princes Street in Edinburgh in 1857 that continued in operation until the 1960s; and Archibald Burns, a landscape photographer who worked from David Octavius Hill's Rock House on Edinburgh's Calton Hill, which he shared briefly with the Annan family in 1871. The author of a collection of photographs of old Edinburgh, published in 1868 as *Picturesque "Bits" of old Edinburgh*, Burns was commissioned in 1871 by the Edinburgh Improvement Trust to take photographs of the old closes between the University and Cowgate that were about to be demolished (Figs. 1:33-35). We shall have occasion to refer to Burns's work when discussing the photographs of *The Old Closes and Streets of Glasgow*, which the Glasgow City Improvement Trust had commissioned Annan to take three years earlier. Even in the then relatively inaccessible small town of Largs, described in *The Photographic Studios of Europe* (1888) as "a fishing village" and "modest little watering place" on the Firth of Clyde, one John Fergus had set up as a self-described "photo artist" and, despite the remoteness of the location (clients from England had first to travel north to Glasgow, take a train to Wemyss Bay, and then board a steamer for the trip down the Firth of Clyde to Largs), succeeded in attracting a sophisticated clientele from all over Britain for his widely admired portraits (Figs. 1:36-37).[11]

Many amateurs were also drawn to photography, especially in Scotland, where the patents on common photographic processes that had been taken out in England did not apply for a time and where costs were thus somewhat reduced.[12] Of these non-professionals, one who still figures in studies of photography was the remarkable Clementina Elphinstone Fleeming (1822-1865), better known by her married name as Clementina, Lady Hawarden. Born and raised at Cumbernauld House near Glasgow, the daughter of a distinguished Scottish father, the Hon. Charles Elphinstone Fleeming, M.P. for Stirlingshire, and a Spanish mother, she produced hundreds of highly original and imaginative images that won silver medals in 1863 and 1864 when they were exhibited at the Photographic Society in London (Figs. 1:36-37).[13] Thomas Keith of Aberdeen was best known as a surgeon who pioneered new procedures in ovarian surgery, worked with Sir James Young Simpson to develop anesthetics, and was one of the first to introduce Lister's antiseptic techniques in his professional work. He made the results of his surgical practice known in several books on "ovariotomy" in the 1860s. However, he was also a keen amateur photographer for several years, between 1852 and 1857, and he produced a number of urban scenes, using Gustave Le Gray's waxed paper process, that could be said to anticipate those of Burns and Annan (Figs. 1:38-39).[14]

The success of pioneers like Hill and Adamson and the growing number of contemporaries taking up photography as a viable profession—about thirty studios appear to have opened in Glasgow alone in the 1850s—may well have encouraged Thomas Annan to abandon the engraving business in 1855 and set up in Glasgow, with a partner, as a "collodion calotypist." It may even be that Hill himself encouraged Annan to make this move—in which he had been preceded in 1852 by one of the earliest Glasgow commercial photographers, John Urie of Paisley, who also started out as an engraver—for it has been speculated that the Annan family, living not far from St. Andrews, may have known the Adamsons and that Thomas Annan could have been aware, when he was still an apprentice engraver in Cupar, of the Hill-Adamson partnership. "My father [. . .] had an intense admiration and appreciation of Hill as a man and as an artist," James Craig Annan recalled in a 1945 letter, written toward the end of his life, to Helmut Gernsheim, the celebrated historian of photography.[15]

Be that as it may, by 1857 Annan had dissolved his partnership and founded his own firm in Woodlands Road in the fast-developing West End of Glasgow. This practice was soon successful enough to warrant the establishment of a studio at 116 Sauchiehall Street in the heart of the modern city, as well as a photographic printing works in nearby Hamilton, where the air was cleaner and whither in 1859 he also moved his family. Appropriately enough, their new home was given the name Talbot Cottage. Annan quickly made a considerable reputation for himself both as a skilful and meticulous printer from negatives supplied by others and as a fine photographer in his own right. In general, he was quick to adopt the latest technical innovations in photography. Thus by making use of Sir Joseph Wilson Swan's carbon process, the Scottish rights for which he characteristically had the foresight to purchase in 1866, Annan was able to move into the "permanent" photography that made book illustration a practical proposition. Previous, silver-based processes had had a tendency to discolor and fade. The carbon process ensured stability of the image. To maximize benefits from the acquisition of the rights to the carbon process, an extensive new printing establishment was opened in Lenzie, six miles northeast of Glasgow city center. It was there that Annan printed the negatives for the second set of albums of what is now his best-known work, *The Old Closes and Streets of Glasgow*, the first set of which had been produced as albumen prints in 1871. In 1883 he travelled to Austria where, on payment of a considerable sum, he arranged for his son James Craig Annan to learn another "permanent" process, the new technique of photogravure, from its inventor, Karl Klič. He also purchased the British rights to Klič's invention, which James Craig Annan, who was to achieve greater renown than his father, put to good use in later years, not least in an updated and much expanded photogravure version, published in 350 copies in 1891 under the title *University of Glasgow Old and New*, of his father's 1871 *Memorials of the Old College of Glasgow*. James Craig Annan also issued a revised and somewhat expanded photogravure edition in 1900 of his father's *The Old Closes and Streets of Glasgow*, in a similarly limited number of copies.

Like most professional photographers, Annan practiced all the genres for which there was a market: photographic reproductions of paintings, which the public increasingly preferred to engravings; portraits, including the popular and relatively inexpensive new carte-de-visite (2⅛ x 3½ inches) and cabinet (4½ x 6½ inches) formats; landscapes, much in demand in Scotland as waves of tourists swept over the country to view the sites made famous by the novels and poems of Walter Scott; photographs of buildings and public works, usually commissioned by well-to-do property owners or local authorities—the field of activity for which Annan is best remembered and by which he is chiefly represented in Princeton's collections; as well as photographs of machinery and the modern triumphs of industry and engineering. The work he displayed at exhibitions in Edinburgh (1858 and 1864), Glasgow (1859), London (1861, 1863, 1864) and Dublin (1865) included samples from all those fields—numerous photographs of paintings, sculptures and buildings of note, portraits (sometimes photographed from paintings), countless landscapes, several images of machinery and one (displayed, appropriately enough, in the Glasgow show of 1859) of the Clyde-built S.S. "United Kingdom," launched in 1857 to inaugurate the Anchor Line of Glasgow's transatlantic service to Montreal.[16] On his business card in 1861 Annan listed among the kinds of work his firm was equipped to undertake "photographs of engravings and architectural drawings," of "ships taken when on the stocks or when launched or from paintings," of "engines and machinery," together with "'Cartes de Visite' and large portraits," and photographs of "groups taken out of doors, volunteers, cricket clubs, &c, views of gentlemen's seats and every variety of landscape subjects."[17] An important point, to which we shall return, is that, for the more than twenty books and albums in which his photographs appear, Annan was always *commissioned* to provide illustrations—and nothing more. He himself virtually never contextualized his own photographs. There is usually a text—though not in at least one crucial case—but it is always the work of somebody else: the person or persons who had the idea for the book in the first place, or a representative of the agency that commissioned the photographs, or the author whose work the publisher engaged Annan to illustrate. As we shall see, this can have the liberating effect of placing the modern viewer in the position of directly interpreting the images without having to take the photographer's own expressed understanding of them into account. What Virginia Woolf once wrote of Jane Austen's novels—"she stimulates us to supply what is not there"[18]—might well be said of the photographs that were brought together and published as *The Old Closes and Streets of Glasgow*.

In the following pages, I aim to provide an overview of Annan's work, taking account of the holdings in the Graphic Arts Collection of Princeton's Firestone Library, but not limiting myself to them. For the sake of convenience, I shall survey in turn the four major genres in which he was active: photographs of paintings, portraits, landscapes, and the built environment. My choice of category may at times seem arbitrary: Annan's *Views on the Line of the Loch Katrine Water Works* (1859), for instance, could have been discussed under "The Built Environment" instead of under "Landscapes," since the photographer's subject was a major engineering work *in* a celebrated landscape. A category comprising "Art Works" would have accommodated many photographs of ancient buildings and sculptures that do not fit the category of "Paintings" and are included here instead in the chapters on "Landscapes" and "The Built Environment." In addition, certain categories, notably "Portraits," are dealt with quite briefly, while others, such as "The Built Environment," are discussed at considerable length. However, I believe my treatment of the different categories reflects the significance of Annan's work in and contribution to each. A final section of the book, longer than the others, is devoted to the photographer's most widely recognized achievement, the album known as *The Old Closes and Streets of Glasgow*.

While my primary aim in this short study is to offer a broad presentation of Annan's activity as a photographer, his involvement in the life of the city where he set up his studio and printing works was so considerable that it has proved impossible to separate his work from the extraordinary history of Glasgow in the nineteenth century. It is my earnest hope that the photographer and the city are as connected in what follows as they were in Thomas Annan's career.

Introduction 9

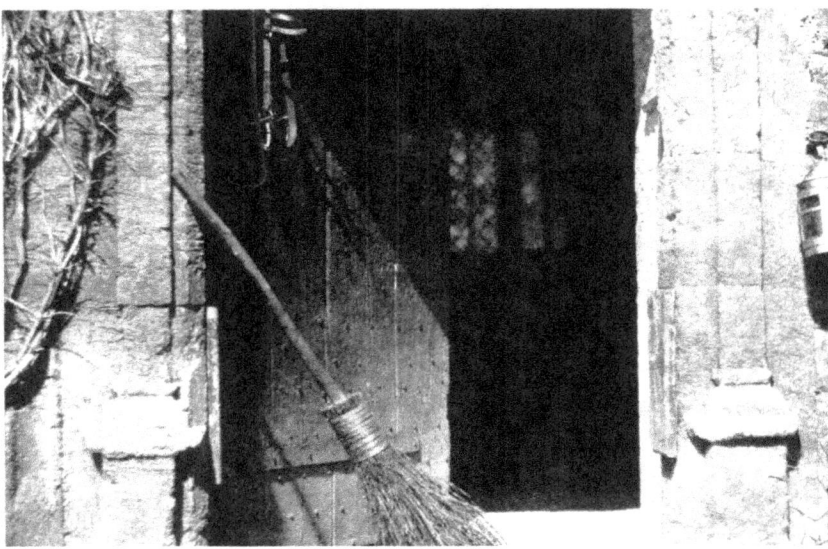

1:1 William Henry Fox Talbot, "The Open Door," from *The Pencil of Nature* (London: Longman, Brown, Green & Longmans, 1844), Plate VI. Salted paper print. Rare Book Division, Department of Rare Books and Special Collections, Princeton University Library.

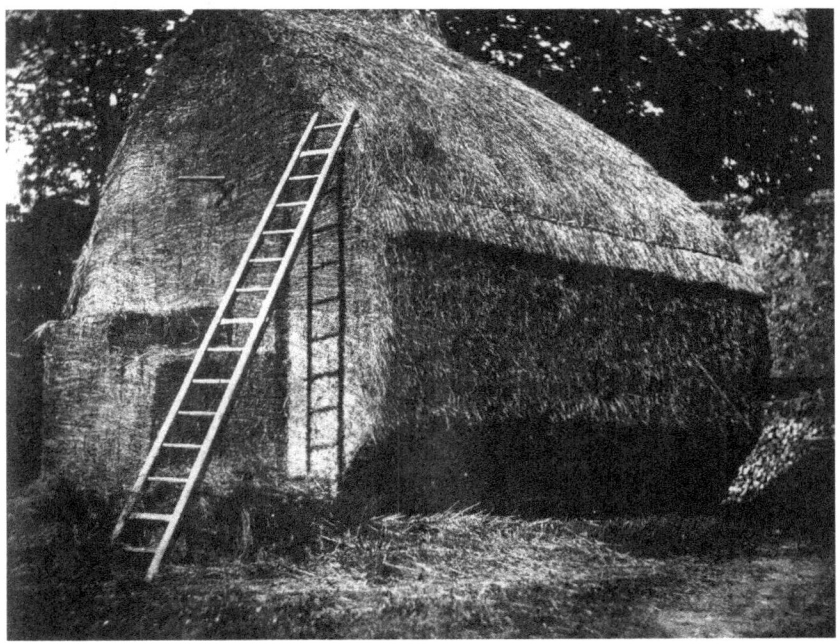

1:2 William Henry Fox Talbot, "Haystack," from *The Pencil of Nature*, Plate X. Salted paper print. Rare Book Division, Department of Rare Books and Special Collections, Princeton University Library.

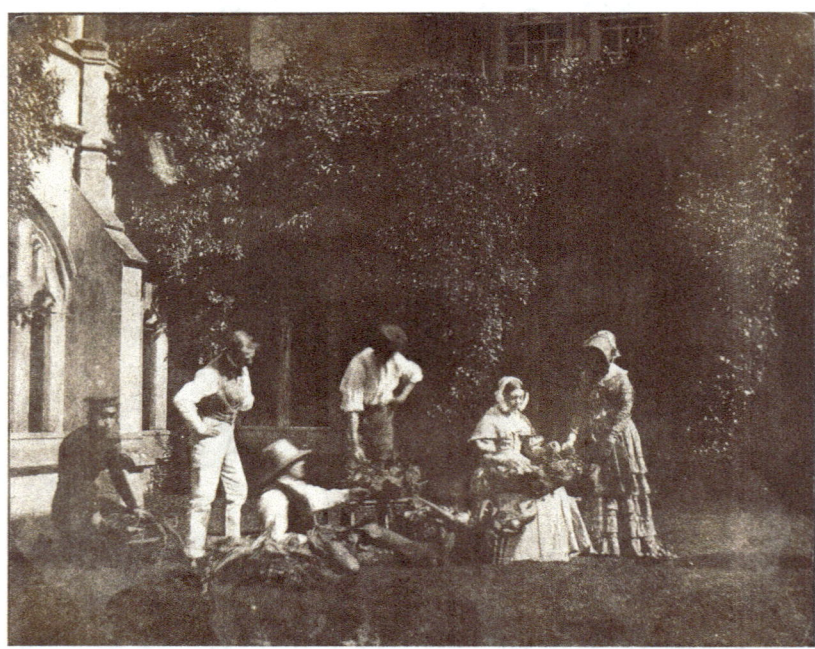

1:3 William Henry Fox Talbot (attributed to), "The Fruit Sellers." 1844. Salted paper print. Metropolitan Museum of Art. Gilman Collection, Purchase, Harriette and Noel Levine Gift, 2005, Accession Number 2005.100.607. © Metropolitan Museum.

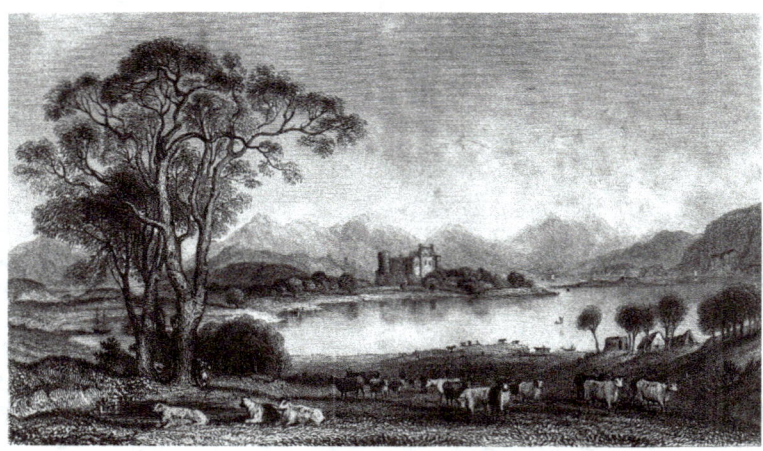

1:4 David Octavius Hill, "Dunstaffnage," from *The Poetical Works of the Ettrick Shepherd. With an autobiography; and illustrative engravings, chiefly from original drawings by D.O. Hill. R.S.A*, vol. 3 (Glasgow, Edinburgh and London: Blackie and Son, [1838]). Frontispiece. Princeton University Library.

Introduction 11

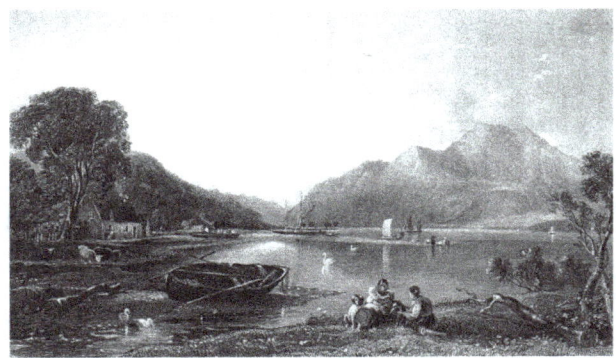

1:5 D.O. Hill, "Loch Lomond," from *The Land of Burns. A Series of Landscapes and Portraits Illustrative of the Life and Writings of the Scottish Poet. The landscapes made expressly for the work by D.O. Hill, Esq., R.S.A*, vol. 2 (Glasgow: Blackie and Son, 1840), facing p. 45. Princeton University Library.

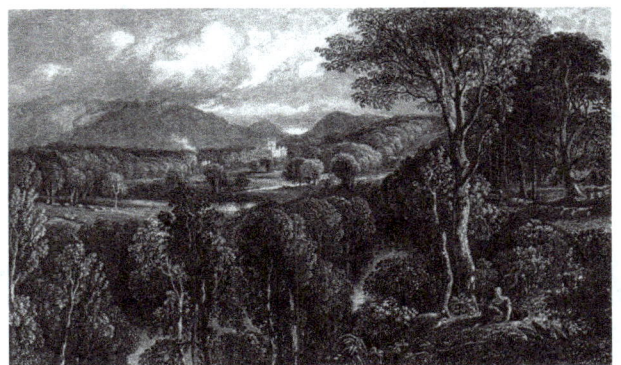

1:6 D.O Hill, "Scene on the Girvan," from *The Land of Burns*, vol. 1, facing p. 66. Princeton University Library.

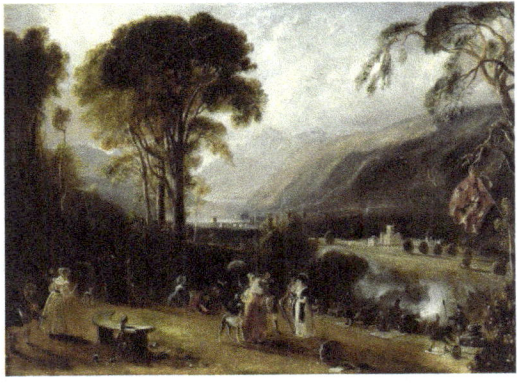

1:7 D.O. Hill, "Feu de joie-Taymouth Castle." 1835. Oil on panel. Courtesy of Perth Museum & Art Gallery, Perth & Kinross Council.

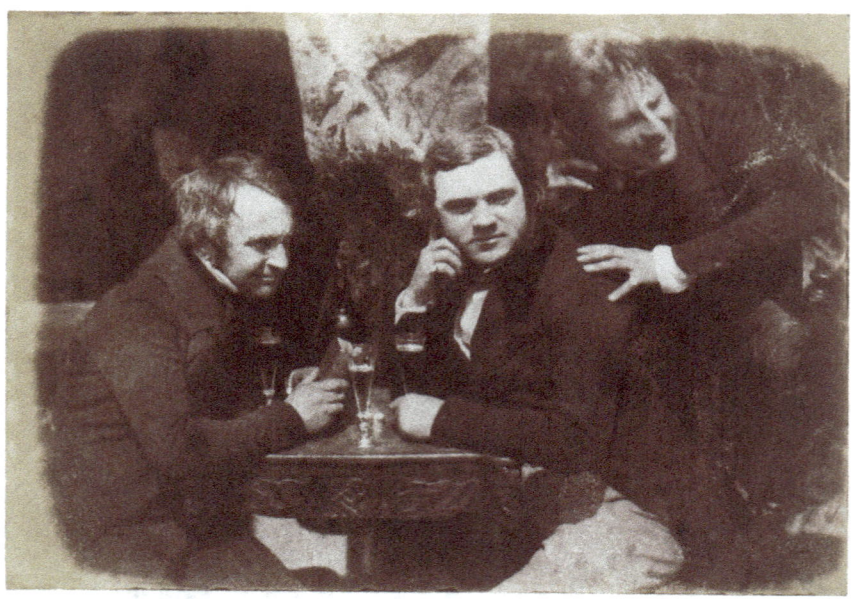

1:8 D.O. Hill and Robert Adamson, "Edinburgh Ale: James Ballantine, Dr. George William Bell and David Octavius Hill." ca.1844. Salted paper print. Wikimedia.

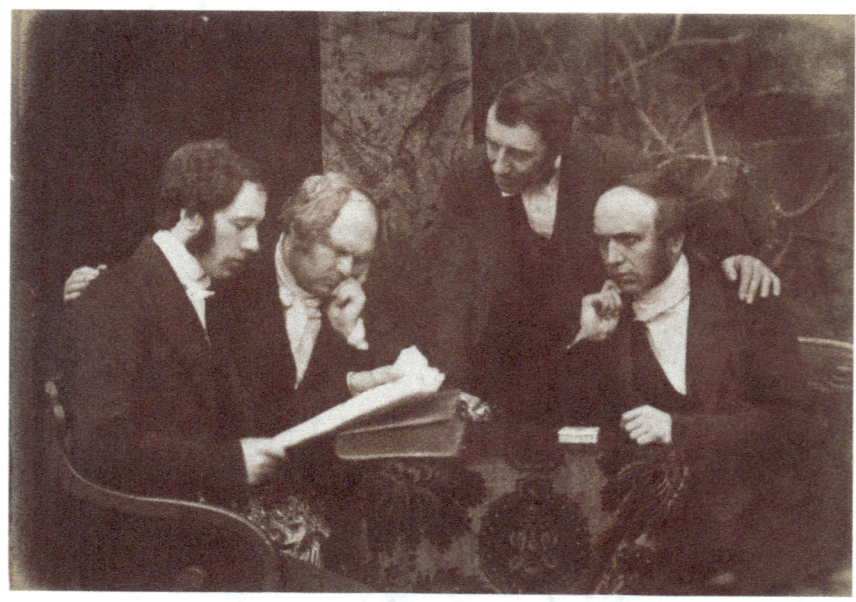

1:9 Hill and Adamson, "Presbytery of Dumbarton." 1843-1847. Salted paper print. Metropolitan Museum of Art. Gift of Mrs. Pirie MacDonald and Mr. and Mrs. Everett Tutchings, 1943, Accession Number 43.10.49. ©Metropolitan Museum.

Introduction 13

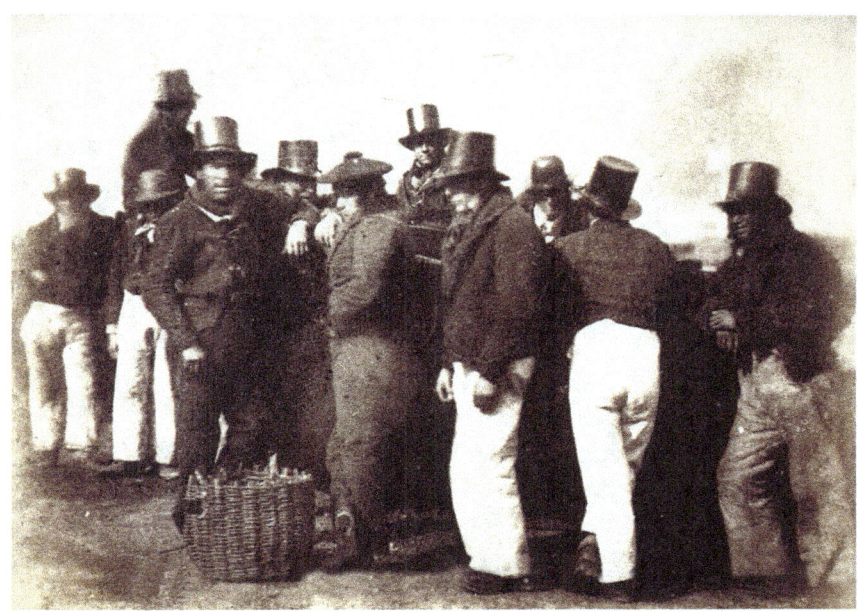

1:10 Hill and Adamson, "Newhaven Fishermen." 1845. Salted paper print. Metropolitan Museum of Art. Harris Brisbane Dick Fund, 1937, Accession Number: 37.98.1.78. ©Metropolitan Museum.

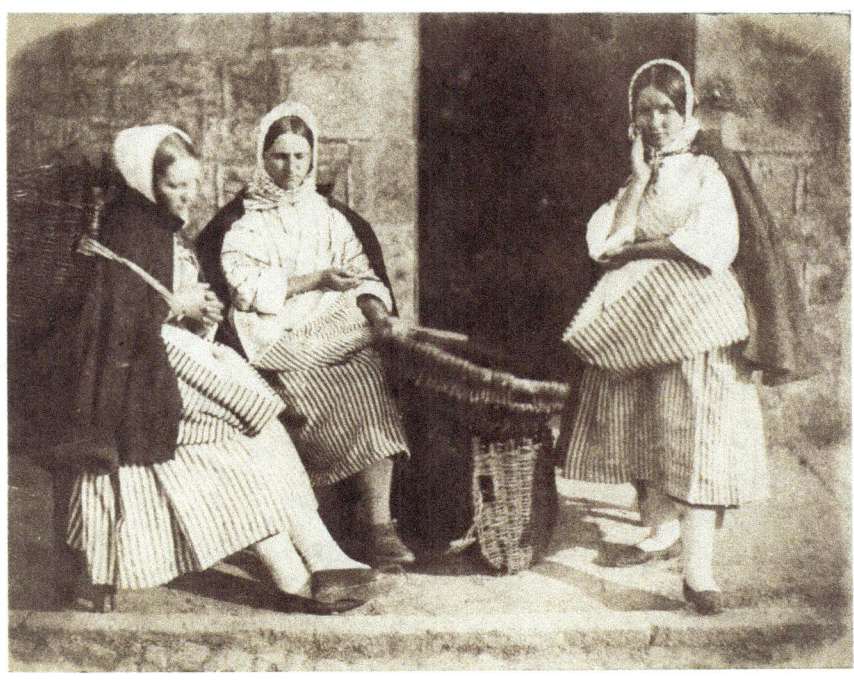

1:11 Hill and Adamson, "Newhaven Fisher Girls." 1843-1847. Salted paper print. Wikimedia.

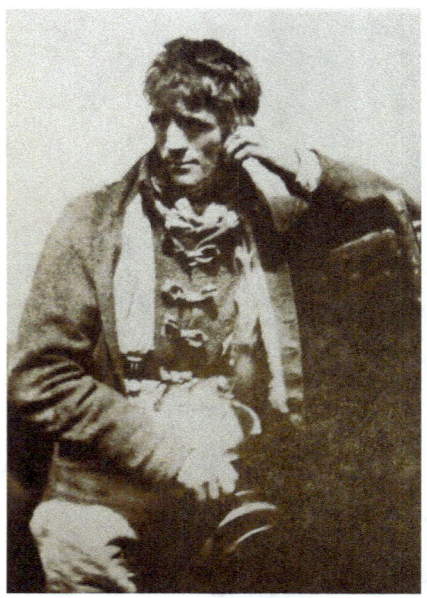

1:12 Hill and Adamson, "A Newhaven Pilot." Ca.1845. Salted paper print. Wikimedia.

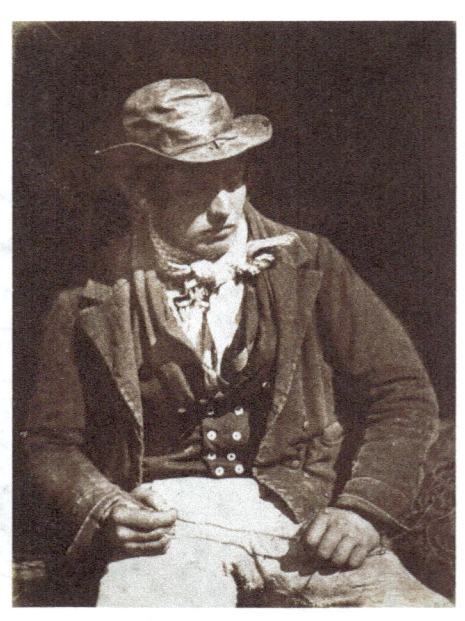

1:13 Hill and Adamson, "Willie Liston: Redding the Line." 1845. Salted paper print. Wikimedia.

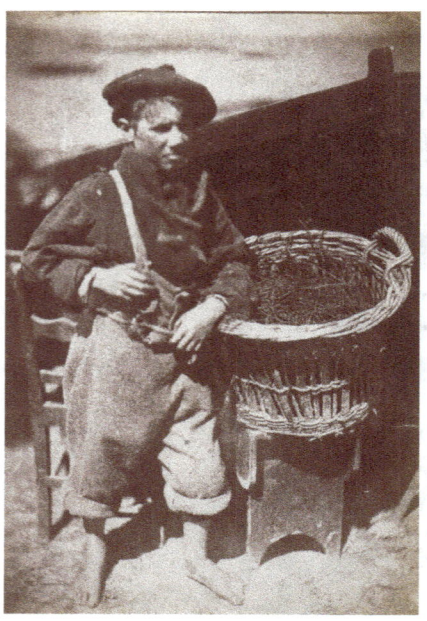

1:14 Hill and Adamson, "His Faither's Breeks." 1844. Salted paper print. Wikimedia.

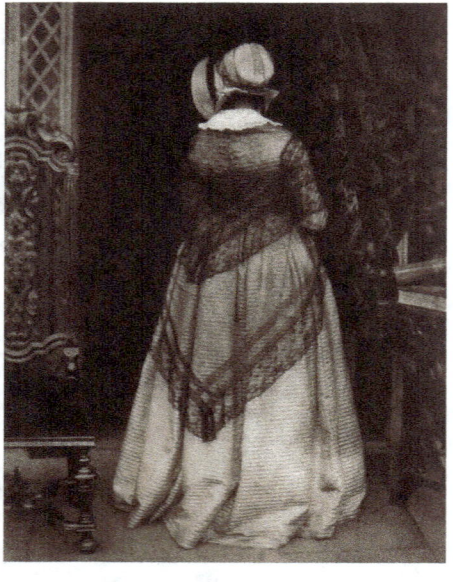

1:15 Hill and Adamson, "Lady Ruthven." Ca.1845. Salted paper print. Metropolitan Museum of Art. The Rubel Collection, Purchase, Manfred Heiting and Lila Acheson Wallace Gifts, 1997, Accession Number 1997.382.18. ©Metropolitan Museum.

Introduction 15

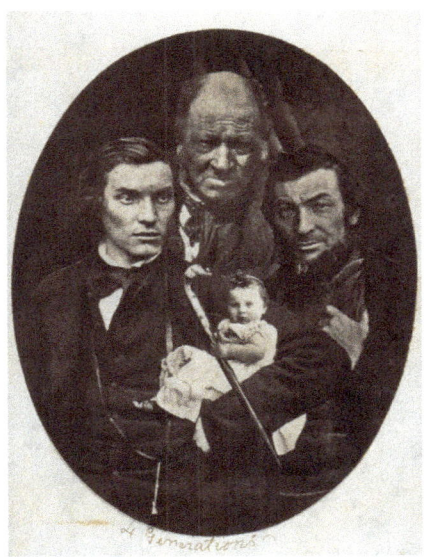

1:16 Thomas Rodger, "Four Generations of Rodger." 1856. Collage of four photographic portraits. St. Andrews University Photographic Collection, ALB-49-56. Courtesy of St. Andrews University Library.

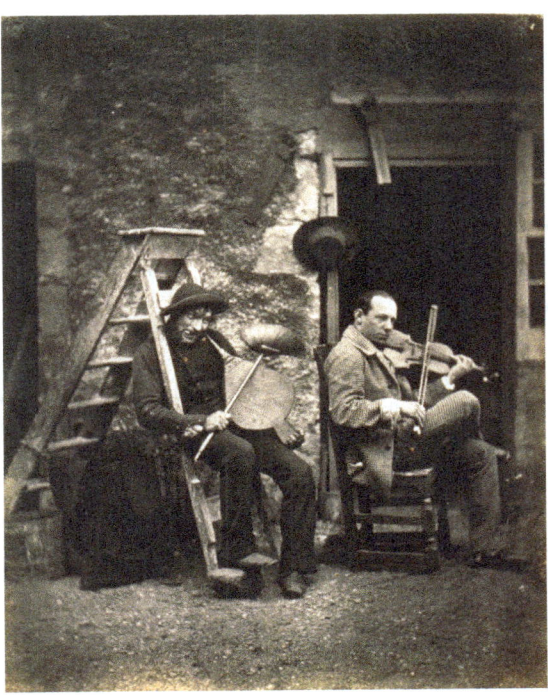

1:17 Thomas Rodger, "Thomas Rodger senior playing the bellows with Hungarian violinist Eduard Remeny." In album. St. Andrews University Photographic Collection, ALB-49-12. Courtesy of St. Andrews University Library.

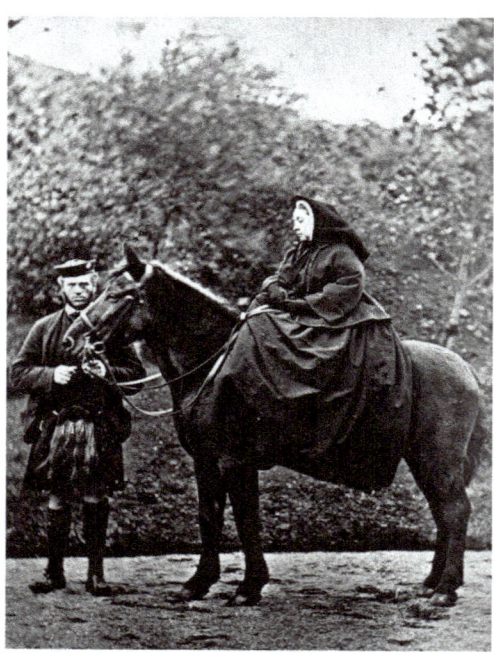

1:18 George Washington Wilson, "Queen Victoria on 'Fyvie' with John Brown." 1863. Carte-de-visite. Wikimedia.

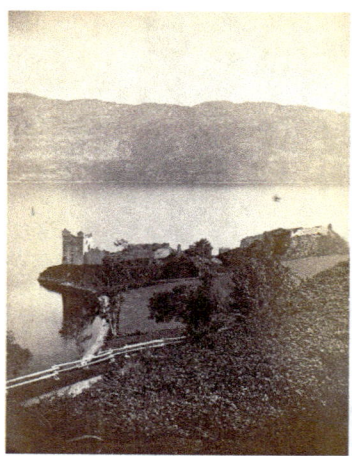

1:19 George Washington Wilson, "Castle Urquhart." 1867. Albumen print. *Photographs of English and Scottish Scenery* (Aberdeen: Printed by John Duffus, 1866-1868). British Library.

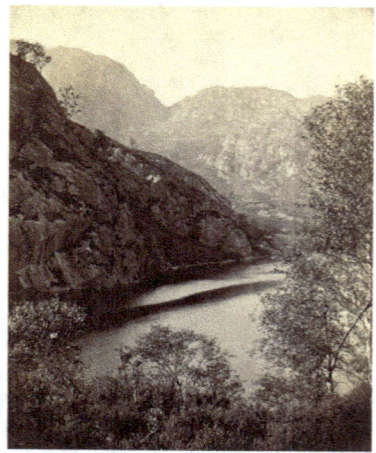

1:20 George Washington Wilson, "Pass of Beal Ach Nam Bo." 1868. Albumen print. *Photographs of English and Scottish Scenery*. British Library.

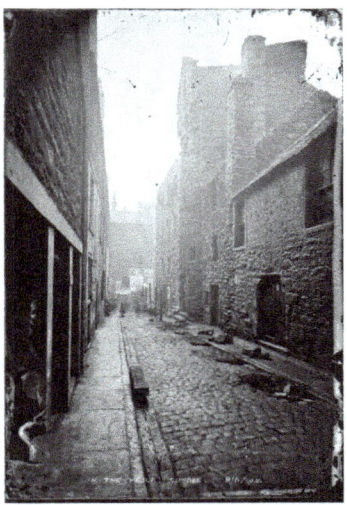

1:21 James Valentine, "In the Vault, Dundee." 1878. Gelatin dry plate negative. St. Andrews University Photographic Collection, JV-916A. Courtesy of St. Andrews University Library.

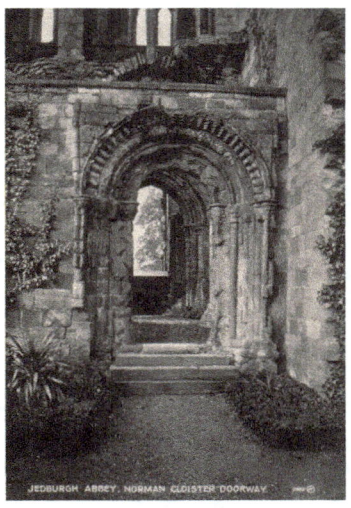

1:22 James Valentine, "Jedburgh Abbey, Norman doorway." 1878. Sepiatype (Vandyke Print). St. Andrews University Photographic Collection, JV-366. Courtesy of St. Andrews University Library.

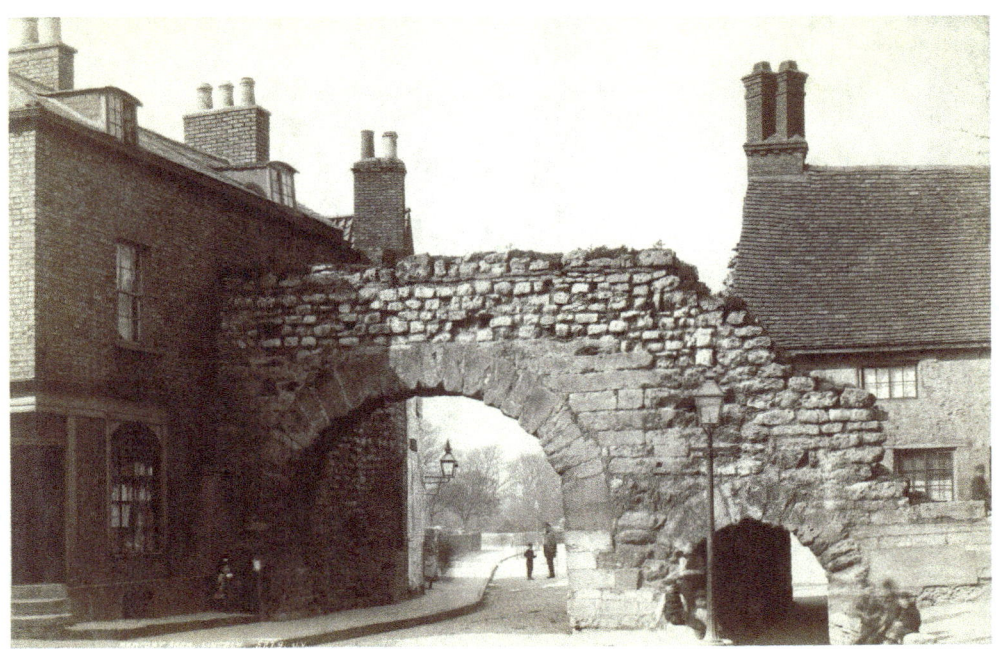

1:23 James Valentine, "Newport Arch, Lincoln." 1865-1880. Albumen print. Wikimedia.

18   Thomas Annan of Glasgow

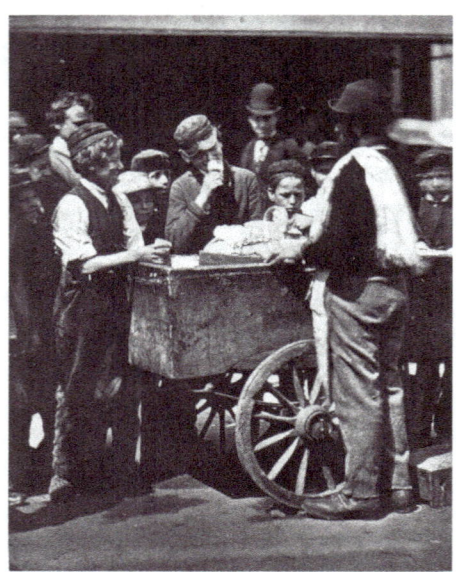

1:24   John Thomson, "Halfpenny Ices," from J. Thomson, F.R.G.S. and Adolph Smith, *Street Life in London* (London: Samson Low, Marston, Searle, & Rivington, 1877). Woodburytype. The London School of Economics and Political Science Digital Library, CC BY-NC-SA.

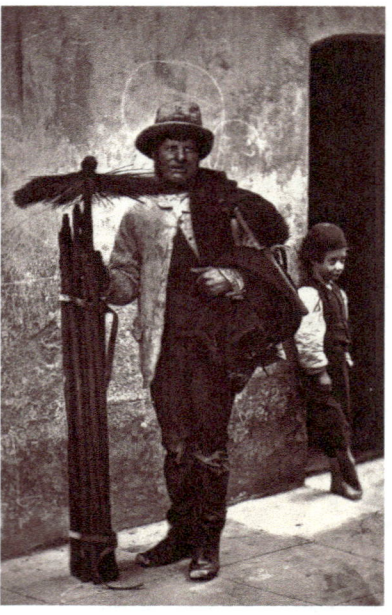

1:25   John Thomson, "The Temperance Sweep," from *Street Life in London*. Woodburytype. The London School of Economics and Political Science Digital Library, CC BY-NC-SA.

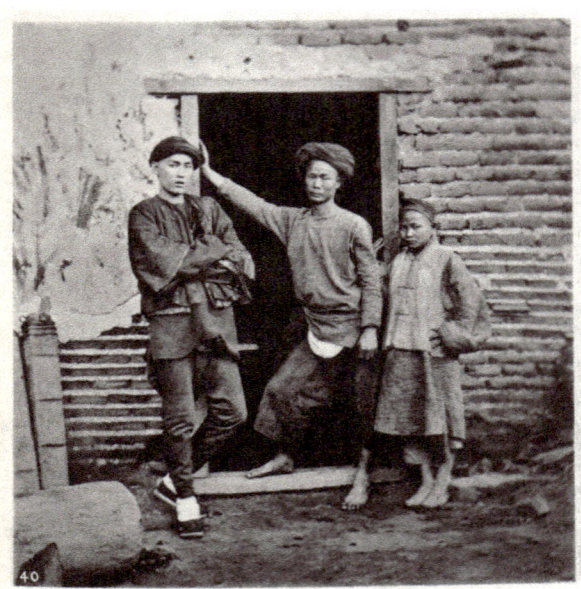

1:26   John Thomson, "Amoy Boys," from *Illustrations of China and its People*, vol. 2 (London: Samson Low, Marston, Low, and Searle, 1873), Plate XIV. Woodburytype. MIT Visualizing Cultures, CC BY-NC-SA.

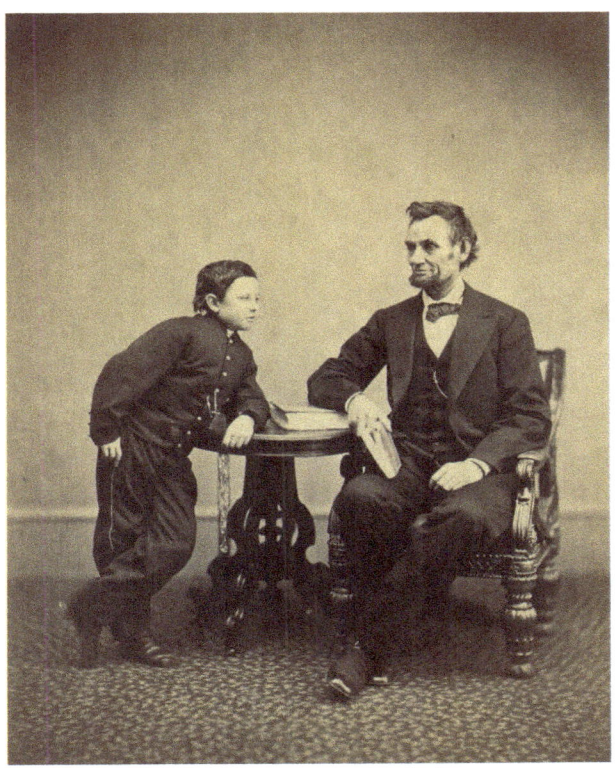

1:27 Alexander Gardner, "Abraham Lincoln and His Second Son Thomas (Tad)." Albumen print. Wikimedia.

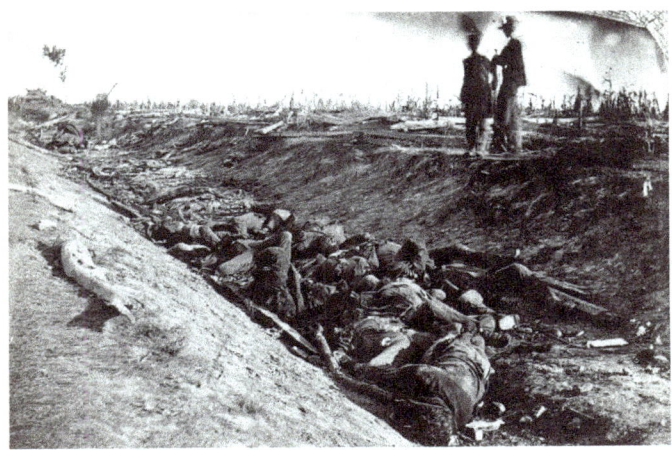

1:28 Alexander Gardner, "Ditch at Antietam." 1862. Albumen print. Library of Congress, LC-DIG-cwpb-01088.

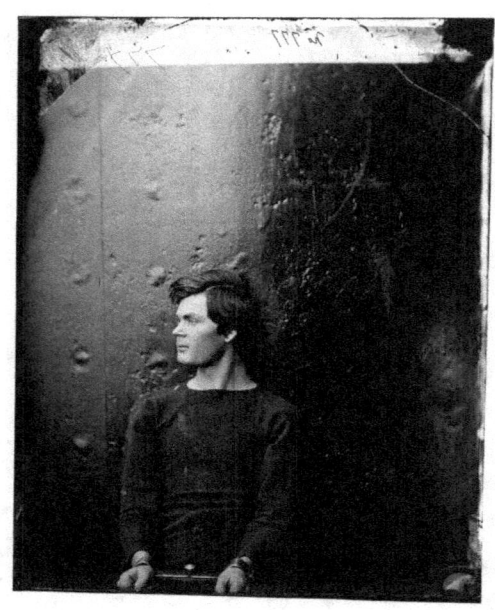

1:29 Alexander Gardner, "Washington Navy Yard, District of Columbia. Lewis Payne, in sweater, seated and manacled." 1865. Albumen print. Library of Congress, LC-DIG-cwpb-04212.

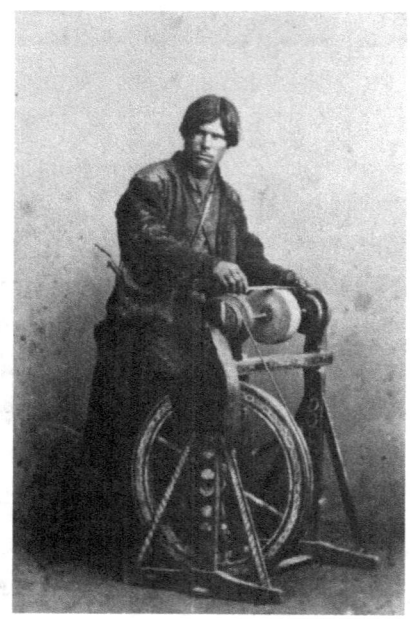

1:30 William Carrick, "Knife Grinder." Russia, 1870. Albumen print. Wikimedia.

Introduction 21

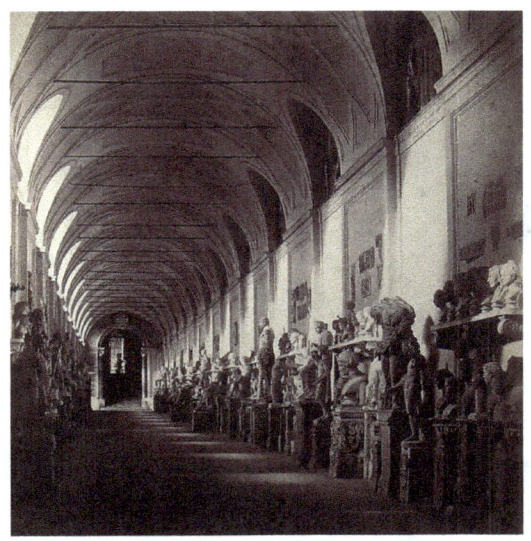

1:31 Robert Macpherson, "Museo Chiaramonti, Vatican." 1872. Albumen print. Wikimedia.

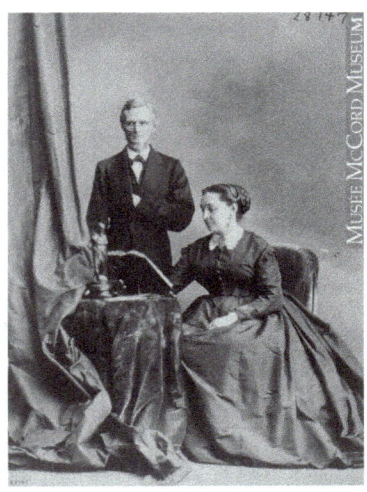

1:32 William Notman, "Jefferson Davis and Mrs Davis." 1867. Albumen print. McCord Museum, Montreal, QC. ©McCord Museum, I-28147.1. CC BY-NC-ND.

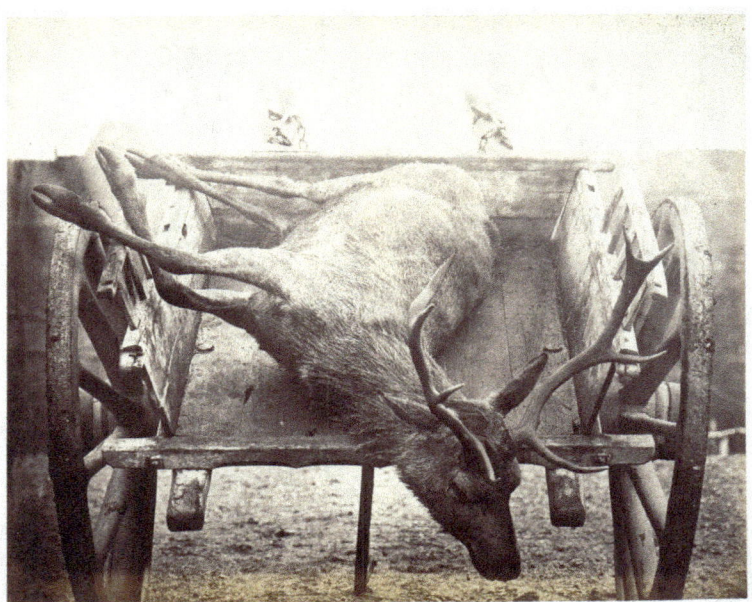

1:33 Horatio Ross, "Stag in Cart." 1858. Albumen print. Metropolitan Museum. Gilman Collection, Museum Purchase, 2005, Accession Number 2005.100.16. ©Metropolitan Museum.

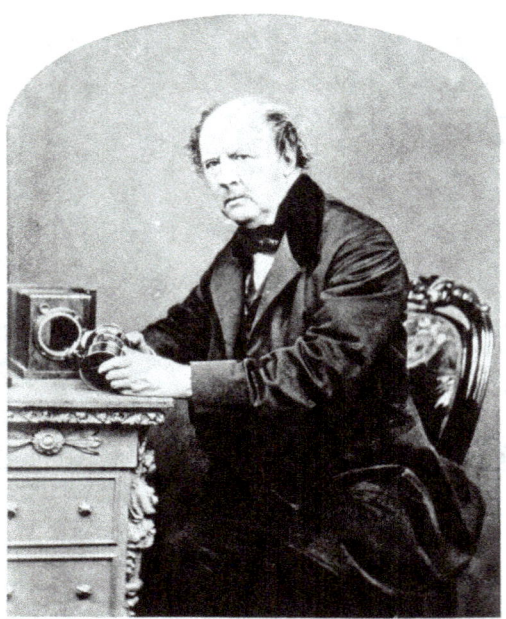

1:34 John Moffat, "William Henry Fox Talbot." 1864. Albumen print. Wikimedia.

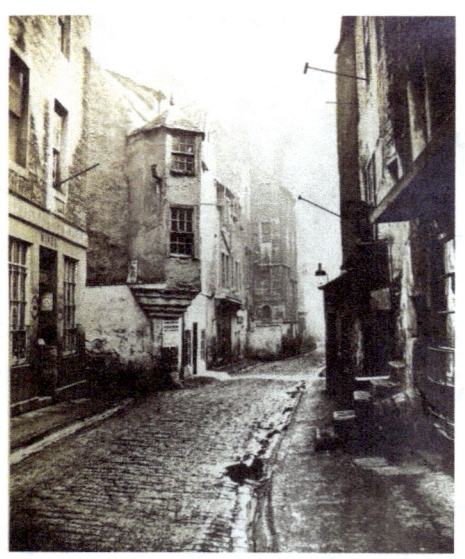

1:35 Archibald Burns, "Cardinal Beaton's House, Cowgate, Edinburgh," from *Picturesque "bits" from old Edinburgh: a series of photographs, with descriptive and historical notes by Thomas Henderson* (Edinburgh: Edmonston and Douglas, 1868). Albumen print. Graphic Arts Collection, Department of Rare Books and Special Collections, Princeton University Library.

Introduction 23

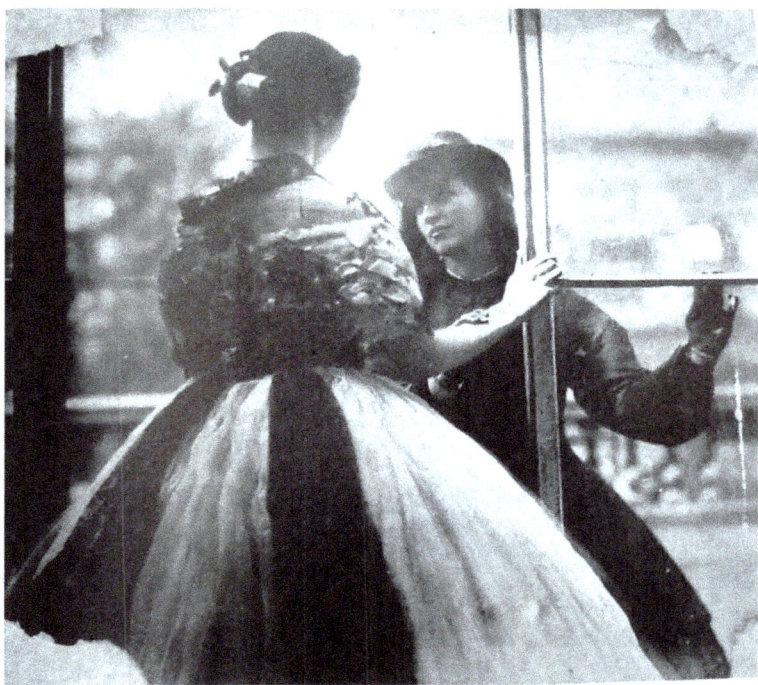

1:36 Clementina Fleeming, Lady Hawarden, "Studies from Life; Isabella Grace and Clementina Maude, 5 Princes Gardens." 1863. Albumen print from wet collodion on glass negative. Given by Lady Clementina Tottenham. Victoria and Albert Museum, London, PH267. ©Victoria and Albert Museum.

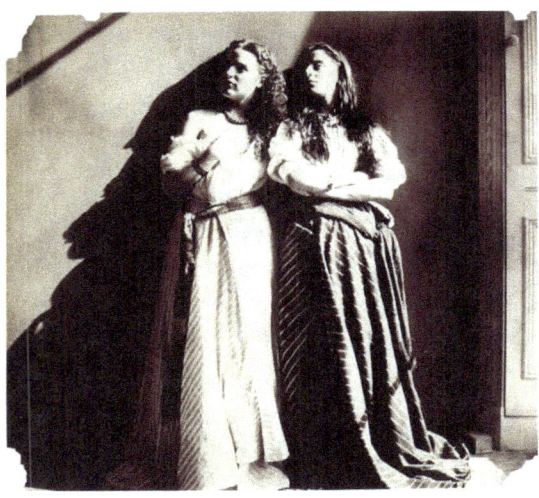

1:37 Clementina Fleeming, Lady Hawarden, Untitled (Clementina and Isabella Grace). 1863-1864. Albumen print. Given by Lady Clementina Tottenham, Victoria and Albert Museum, London, PH266-1947. ©Victoria and Albert Museum.

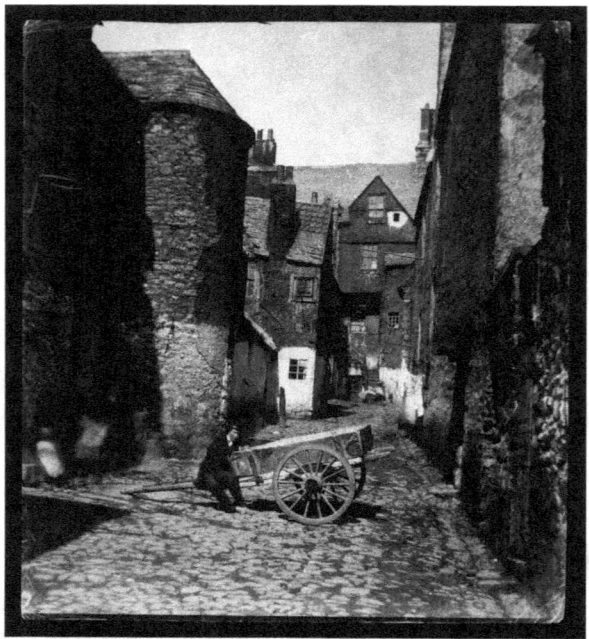

1:38 Thomas Keith, "Unidentified Close" (probably Reid's Close). 1854-56. Paper negative. City of Edinburgh Council — Libraries. By kind permission of the City of Edinburgh Council.

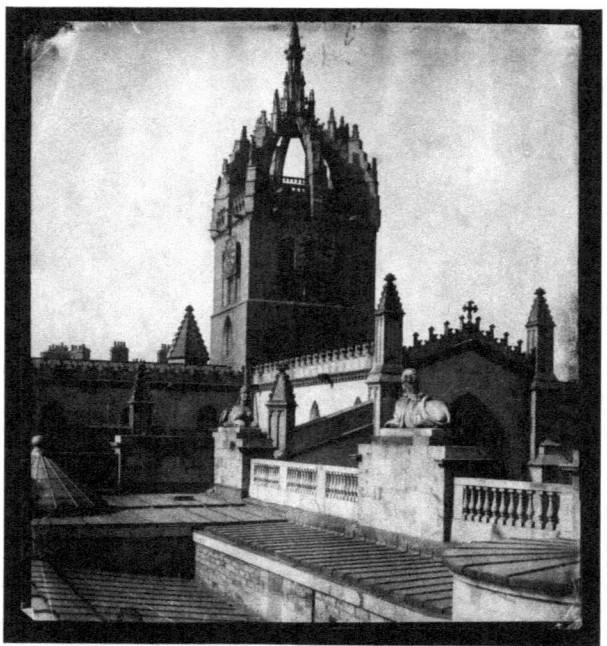

1:39 Thomas Keith, "Tower of St Giles from Parliament House, Edinburgh." Paper negative. City of Edinburgh Council — Libraries. By kind permission of the City of Edinburgh Council.

2. Paintings

In the early stages of photography, when the new technique was still widely viewed as an aid to art and science, rather than as capable of producing art of its own, the use of the camera to provide reproductions of paintings, as well as to help the contemporary painter by bringing his work to the attention of a new art purchasing public, was both common and well-regarded. Special medals were awarded at international exhibitions for outstanding work in the photographic reproduction of paintings and some photographers who specialized in that branch of photography, such as the now poorly remembered Robert Jefferson Bingham, enjoyed international renown. When it first appeared in 1858, Bingham's *Oeuvre de Paul Delaroche* was widely hailed as a "monumental" achievement.[19] "Producing images of works of art," one historian of photography has observed, "had struck W.H.F. Talbot as one of the most valuable applications of photography and had been pursued with enthusiasm by both professionals and amateurs from the outset."[20] In his first report, in 1854, J.C. Robinson, the curator of the new South Kensington Museum (founded in 1852, it was the ancestor of the Victoria and Albert Museum) declared that "the photographic art is calculated to be of extraordinary utility in extending the influence of collections such as this. Perhaps the most valuable characteristic of this extraordinary process being the perfect accuracy with which objects of art can be copied, the absolute identity in every point of detail thus received being just that which is literally unobtainable by the draughtsman, whose individuality or personal mannerism is always more or less impressed upon his work."[21] In the same vein, the art critic Théophile Thoré-Bürger (1807-1869) declared in the Preface to an album of 1862 featuring forty photographic illustrations by the Belgian photographer Edmond Fierlants of paintings in the Antwerp Museum that

> when an engraving is weak, it is without value as a translation [of a painting]. If it is good, instead of reminding us of the original, it makes us admire

the talent of the engraver-translator. [. . .] Every engraving is inevitably an interpretation and even, to some degree, a new creation. In order to obtain a faithful image of a painting we would have to have recourse to a mirror. That is where photography comes in! [. . .] Photographic reproduction of old masters is certainly by no means easy, and few photographers have succeeded at it so far. But when a good print is achieved, no engraving can match it or provide as thorough an impression of the model.[22]

The new public museums, from the start, commissioned and collected photographs of works of art. Charles Marville, for instance, the mid-nineteenth-century French photographer known chiefly today for his Paris street scenes, was regularly commissioned by the French government to photograph paintings and other works of art in the Louvre and at other locations. Roger Fenton was employed by the British Museum in 1854 to photograph objects in its collection. And in far-off Melbourne, Australia, where there were as yet few original works of art, the Trustees of the Public Library, Museum and National Gallery of Victoria arranged for the photographing of works of art in European private and public collections.[23]

Annan enjoyed a high reputation as a photographer of paintings. In fact, many considered that was where his main strength lay. "The excellence of his work, more especially in the reproduction of paintings [obtained] for him wide and most honourable distinction," according to his obituary notice in the *British Journal of Photography* in 1887. "Cultured and with great natural taste for art, he loved the society of artists, and was never so happy as when endeavouring to faithfully translate some masterpiece into monochrome through the medium of his camera."[24]

In 1862, not long after opening his studio, he received a commission from the Glasgow Art Union to photograph three paintings by J.E. Millais, the well-known portraitist James Sant, and the Scottish artist Noel Paton. These were to take the place of the engravings normally distributed at the Art Union's annual show to members who had paid their dues of one guinea.[25] On seeing Annan's work, Millais reportedly declared that he "did not think such fine photographs could be taken from pictures," while Paton acknowledged that "assuredly a photograph may be so managed as to convey with a fidelity attained by but few engravings, the more subtle, valuable, and least easily reproduced qualities of a work of art."[26] The policy adopted by the Art Union was so successful that it was taken up again the following year when the Union commissioned five drawings by Paton on an abolitionist theme and then employed Annan to photograph them with the intention of having the photographs serve as its annual prize to members (Figs. 2:1-2).

Naturally, the new policy was warmly endorsed by the *British Journal of Photography*, which laid out its advantages in a front page editorial on Annan's photographs in the issue of 2 November 1863:

> The Directors of the Glasgow Art Union have made arrangements for distributing amongst the subscribers a series of photographic reproductions of five original drawings, executed expressly for the purpose by Mr. J. Noel Paton R.S.A. [Royal Scottish Academy], entitled *Bond and Free*. As this is the second year in which the usual presentation engraving has been superseded by photographic reproductions, we presume that the experiment made last year has proved successful. [. . .] The advantages appear to us so palpably in favour of such a proceeding that we are only surprised it had not been earlier attempted. Amongst the advantages we may enumerate a few. In the first place, the artist's work is brought, as it were, face to face with his public, without the intervention of any interpretation made by another hand; because the photograph, if faithfully executed, is an attested *facsimile*—touch for touch and shade for shade—of the original work, and so far both artists and public are gainers. Secondly, as the cost of engraving a plate is very great, unless the number of subscribers be in proportion, it could not be well executed, and moreover the numerous impressions produced (supposing them all to be of equal intrinsic value) makes them so common that the value of each one suffers depreciation. Now both of these objections are obviated by enlisting photography as the reproduction agent; for, if the number of subscribers were to be very large, there would be no necessity for distributing a copy of the same work to all, though there would be no difficulty of so doing if thought desirable, and indeed a choice could be offered with great convenience. Moreover, the offer of a choice would most likely conduce to an increase in the number of subscribers.

The article concluded on praise for Annan and a brief description of the interesting technique employed by the photographer in what was clearly a close collaboration with the artist:

> In the present instance, as in the previous one, the work of reproduction has been placed in the able hands of Mr. Thomas Annan, of Glasgow; and it is therefore almost superfluous for us to add that it has been most thoroughly and conscientiously performed. The course of operation has been, we are informed, as follows:—The original sketches were made in sepia, by Mr. Noel Paton. From these photographic copies were taken by Mr. Annan, enlarged to double the original size. These enlarged copies were then touched and finished

by Mr. Paton; and from them, negatives reduced to the size of the original drawings were produced by Mr. Annan, from which the proofs for circulation have been printed. The size of each picture is about 9 inches by 7 inches.[27]

The Glasgow Art Union photographs were exhibited in Edinburgh and at the Photographic Society's 1863 show in London. It is quite likely that they were seen by David Octavius Hill, who had unsuccessfully endeavored to have photographs replace the engravings similarly distributed to the annual dues-paying members of the Edinburgh-based Association for the Promotion of the Fine Arts in Scotland, and that Hill was so favorably impressed by them, as well as by other photographs of paintings by Annan, that he decided to approach the latter about undertaking what was to be one of the most difficult photographic commissions of Annan's career.

In 1843, Hill had resolved to commemorate the first General Assembly of the new Free Church of Scotland, which had been constituted by dissidents from the established Church of Scotland, and with which he personally sympathized, in a large historical painting. In preparation for this work, he and Adamson took many photographs of individuals and groups that he planned to represent in it; indeed, Hill's canvas is often considered the first work of art ever to have been painted with the help of photographic images, even if, ironically, the photographs are still admired while the painting, finally completed 22 years later, is not.[28] It turned out to be a work rather uncharacteristic of Hill, whose landscape paintings sometimes seem to show the influence of Turner (Fig. 2:3)—a massive canvas eleven feet four inches long and well over four feet high, with an equally long title blazoned along the bottom in letters over an inch high: "The First General Assembly of the Free Church of Scotland. Signing the Act of Separation and Deed of Demission at Tanfield, Edinburgh. May 1843."

Even though the original Deed of Demission had been signed by 155 ministers, Hill depicted 457 individuals who subsequently signed or were associated with the event, including even some—Thomas Annan among them—who had not been present, but who Hill thought should or could have been. While this inclusiveness was almost certainly intended to convey both the popular character of the establishment of the Free Church and its historical significance, it made for a singularly unwieldy number of figures crammed into a limited space, despite the unusual proportions of the canvas (Fig. 2:4).

Even paintings of very large groups of people—David's "Tennis Court Oath" (1790) and "Coronation of Napoleon and Josephine" (1805-1807); Sir George Hayter's "Trial of Queen Caroline in the House of Lords, 1820" (1823), with 188 figures, or his grand (roughly 18 x 11 feet) "House of Commons, 1833" (1833-1843) packed with 320 figures, including well-known politicians such as Gladstone, Melbourne, Robert Peel, and the Duke of Wellington; fellow-Scot David Scott's large (6 x 9 feet) and busy "Queen Elizabeth Viewing the Performance of The Merry Wives of Windsor at the Globe" (1840); or William Powell Frith's (7 x 10 feet) "Marriage of H.R.H. the Prince of Wales with Princess Alexandra of Denmark" (1865)—had avoided such overcrowding and retained a greater sense of space and composition (Figs. 2:5-6).

However, this may well have been due not only to the even greater dimensions of most of those works but to the hierarchical arrangement of the figures in nearly all such large group paintings, whereas Hill obviously wanted to render visible the popular and democratic character of the Free Church movement. As a writer in the *Greenock Daily Telegraph* for 15 June 1867 noted:

> Much did we fear that Mr. Hill would find his praiseworthy attempt a disappointment and failure. What with the old wooden shed and then the total absence of drapery and the want of colour [. . .], we were inclined to compassionate his case; and while admiring his resolution, we found ourselves questioning his prudence and judgment. We confess, now we have looked upon the picture, our fears are groundless. It is more than a success, it is a triumph. A more remarkable work of the kind does not exist. Each head in the gathering is a portrait. The most obscure country brethren receive justice as ample as the most distinguished of leaders. [. . .] The artist whom we esteemed before for his beautiful reproductions of many choice landscapes of his native country, has now made good his title to a yet higher regard in proving himself so susceptible to the moral beauty of the most heroic event which has shed a lustre on Scotland in our days and generation.[29]

While Hill's painting bears some resemblance to the large group photographs that had come into favor, such as George Washington Wilson's 1857 composite photograph of Aberdeen worthies (Fig. 2:7), there is little doubt that the artist's essential aim was to find an adequate representation of what to him was a major event in the history of the Scottish people, comparable to the Declaration of Independence in the history of America.

It is not impossible that he was aware of John Trumbull's even more massive (12 x 18 feet) painting of that event, which had been commissioned in 1817 and which also represents, though in a far more traditional way, a fairly large number of individuals around a central signing ceremony (Fig. 2:8).

At the same time, it has been speculated, less generously, that one of Hill's motives for including so many figures in his canvas might have been his desire to sell photographic copies of it and therefore to include in the work as many potential purchasers as possible.[30] He certainly did his best to win subscriptions for the photographic reproductions by exhibiting the painting in many cities in England as well as Scotland.

Assured by another Edinburgh photographer, William Donaldson Clark, that he "could be in no better hands than [Annan's] both for the beauty and permanence of [his] work," Hill approached Annan, who, as it happens, was also a Free Kirker, in 1865 with a view to producing significant numbers of photographs of the painting in three different sizes: 24 x 9 inches, selling for a guinea and a half (about £160 or $245 in today's currency, according to some calculations); 32 x 14 inches, selling for four guineas (about £360 or $555); and 48 x 21¼ inches, selling for eight guineas (approximately £720 or $1,110). He and his wife personally brought the painting to Annan's premises in Hamilton, staying overnight with the family. As one historian of photography has put it, "For Thomas Annan to photograph in 1866 a painting eleven feet long and to produce in the brand new process of carbon a permanent print of it four feet long, represented a dazzling technical feat."[31] At first Annan had thought of borrowing a camera devised by John Kibble, a local Glasgow inventor, engineer and photographer, but in the end he ordered a specially designed "large Photographic Camera of the latest and most perfect construction" from the famous London lens and camera maker John Henry Dallmeyer.[32]

Annan continued throughout his life to find occasion to exercise and develop his skill as a photographer of paintings. He habitually photographed paintings in the picture galleries of the many country houses whose owners hired him to make a visual record of their property.[33] In 1867-68, the Arts Council of Glasgow once again called on Annan, asking him to photograph four paintings illustrating the story of Mary, Queen of Scots by the popular Scottish artist Robert Herdman (1829-1888) for distribution to the members of the Council in the form of an album containing a short poem on Mary by Henry Glassford Bell, a distinguished local lawyer and the author of a *Life of Mary Queen of Scots* (Edinburgh: Constable, 1828).[34] Around the same time, Annan's firm itself brought out an album of 43 photographs of the controversial stained glass windows that had been commissioned for Glasgow Cathedral from the *Königliche Glasmalerei-Anstalt* in Munich, to the dismay of many donors and politicians, as well as the local stained glass makers, who felt the windows should have been ordered from British artists instead (*Painted Windows of Glasgow Cathedral*, 1867).[35]

In 1868 the Town Council of Glasgow organised an exhibition of portraits "of deceased persons," as the catalogue Preface put it, "who have been connected with Glasgow—with its University and other public institutions, with its Municipality, manufactures, and trades, as well as those who have been distinguished at home or abroad." The exhibition was held not far from the Annan studio in a gallery in Sauchiehall Street, which had been known (and is again known now) as the McLellan Gallery after its founder, a local patron of the arts and town councillor, and which the city had acquired, after his death, to serve as a municipal gallery. Annan was charged with providing photographs for the handsome catalogue of paintings in the show, one of the relatively rare surviving copies of which is in Princeton University's Graphic Arts Collection (*Catalogue of Portraits on Loan in the New Galleries of Art, Corporation Buildings, Sauchiehall Street* [Glasgow: William Munro, 1868]). It contains 120 small photographs, usually approximately 2½ by 3½ inches, of portraits by Raeburn, Sir Thomas Lawrence, Johan Zoffany and many less well-known artists, chiefly of the Scottish School.

A few years later, Annan's reputation as a photographer of artworks led to his being commissioned to provide photographs of a number of paintings by the President of the Royal Scottish Academy, George Harvey, for a volume of *Selections from the Works of Sir George Harvey P.R.S.A., described by A.L. Simpson* (Edinburgh: Andrew Elliott, ca.1870); he was simultaneously engaged to photograph over thirty lively and sometimes witty drawings of Scottish advocates (i.e. members of the Faculty of Advocates, the Scottish bar) at the time of Sir Walter Scott by one of their number, Robert Scott Moncrieff, for a publication entitled *The Scottish Bar Fifty Years Ago: Sketches of Scott and his Contemporaries with Biographical Notices by G*[eorge] *B*[urnett] (Edinburgh: Andrew Eliot, 1871). In the words of the Preface to that work, "The task of photographing the portraits"—which their creator had kept discreetly private and which his family released to the public only after his death—"has been entrusted to Mr. Annan of Glasgow, who has reproduced them with wonderful success." The following year saw the publication of Alexander Fraser's *Scottish Landscape. The Works of Horatio McCulloch R.S.A., photographed by T. Annan. With a Sketch of his Life by Alexander Fraser, R.S.A.* (Edinburgh: Andrew Elliot, 1872). Annan provided photographs of twenty paintings by the then popular and highly regarded Scottish landscape painter for this book, along with a photographic portrait of the painter himself. As late as 1887, the last year of Annan's life, 32 photographs of works by Sir Henry Raeburn, the great Scottish portrait painter of the eighteenth and early nineteenth centuries, were used to illustrate *Portraits by Sir Henry Raeburn, with Biographical Sketches* (Edinburgh: Andrew Elliot, 1887).[36]

Annan's willingness to devote much of his time and expertise to "faithfully translating" the "masterpieces" of admired painters may perhaps be accounted not insignificant evidence of a disinclination to take sides in the contemporary debate between defenders of the traditionalist view of photography—as subservient to material reality, a valued handmaid of the arts and sciences—and advocates of photography as an art in its own right, equivalent to painting or drawing. One cannot, of course, rule out commercial considerations. As Annan's well respected photographs of paintings were a valuable source of income, he can only have read with pleasure the editorial in the *British Journal of Photography*, quoted above, commending the Directors of the Glasgow Art Union for having substituted his photographs of Noel Paton's work for the usual engravings as the Art Union's annual award to dues-paying members. Nevertheless, he may well have responded no less positively to the suggestion, in the same editorial, that the Directors should consider offering original photographs as awards, rather than photographs of paintings, and that his own "artistic" landscapes were eminently suitable for that purpose.

> In distributing photographic reproductions, the Directors of the Glasgow Art Union are doing much for the graphic, but very little for the photographic, art. It would be a great thing if they could be induced another year to distribute one specimen, at least, of art-photography—such as Mr. Annan could readily produce for them—to each subscriber, in addition to as many photographic copies as their funds would allow. [. . .] Mr. Annan, if he has any influence with the Directors, should not miss the opportunity of placing before them some of his own artistic landscape productions.

Paintings 33

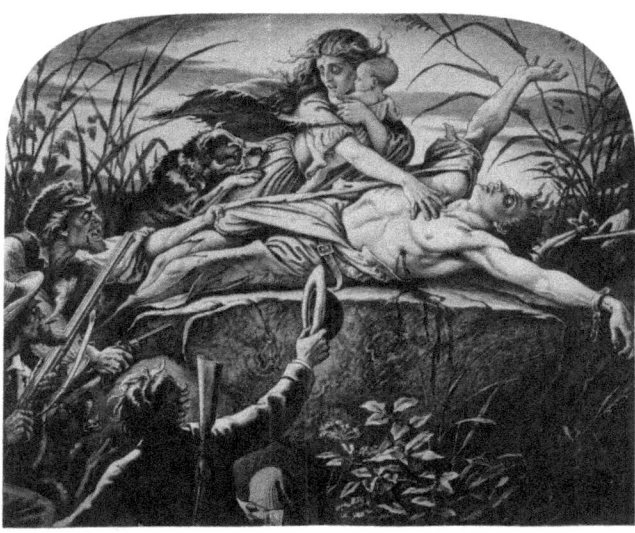

2:1 Joseph Noël Paton, "The Capture or The Slave Hunt," from *Bond and Free: Five sketches illustrative of slavery by J. Noël Paton; photographed by Thomas Annan* (Glasgow: Maclure and MacDonald, 1863), Plate 3. Reproduced in Alfred T. Story, "Sir Noël Paton: His Life and Work," *The Art Journal* (1895), 97-128 (p. 98). Marquand Library, Princeton University.

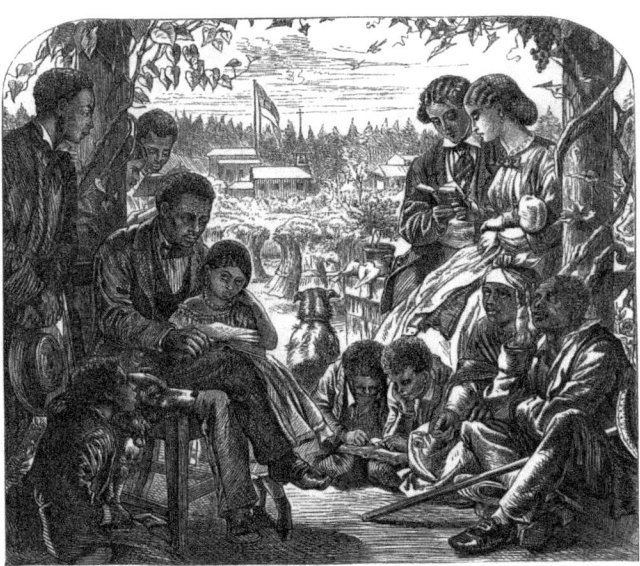

2:2 Joseph Noël Paton, "Freedom," from *Bond and Free*, Plate 5. Reproduced in *Sunday Magazine* (1 June 1865, pp. 672-76). Princeton Theological Seminary Library.

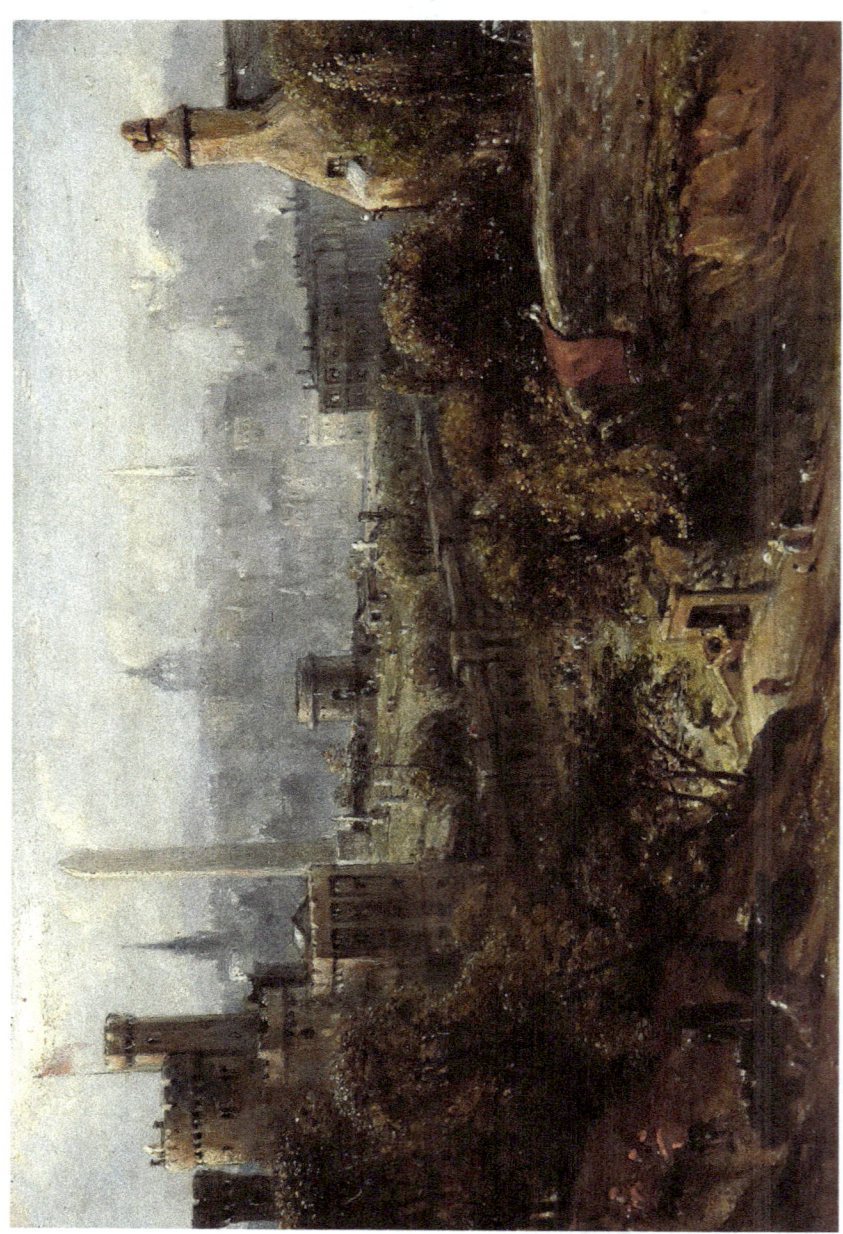

2:3 David Octavius Hill, "In Memoriam: The Calton." 1862. Oil on panel. City Art Centre: Edinburgh Museums and Galleries. By kind permission of Edinburgh Museums and Galleries.

Paintings 35

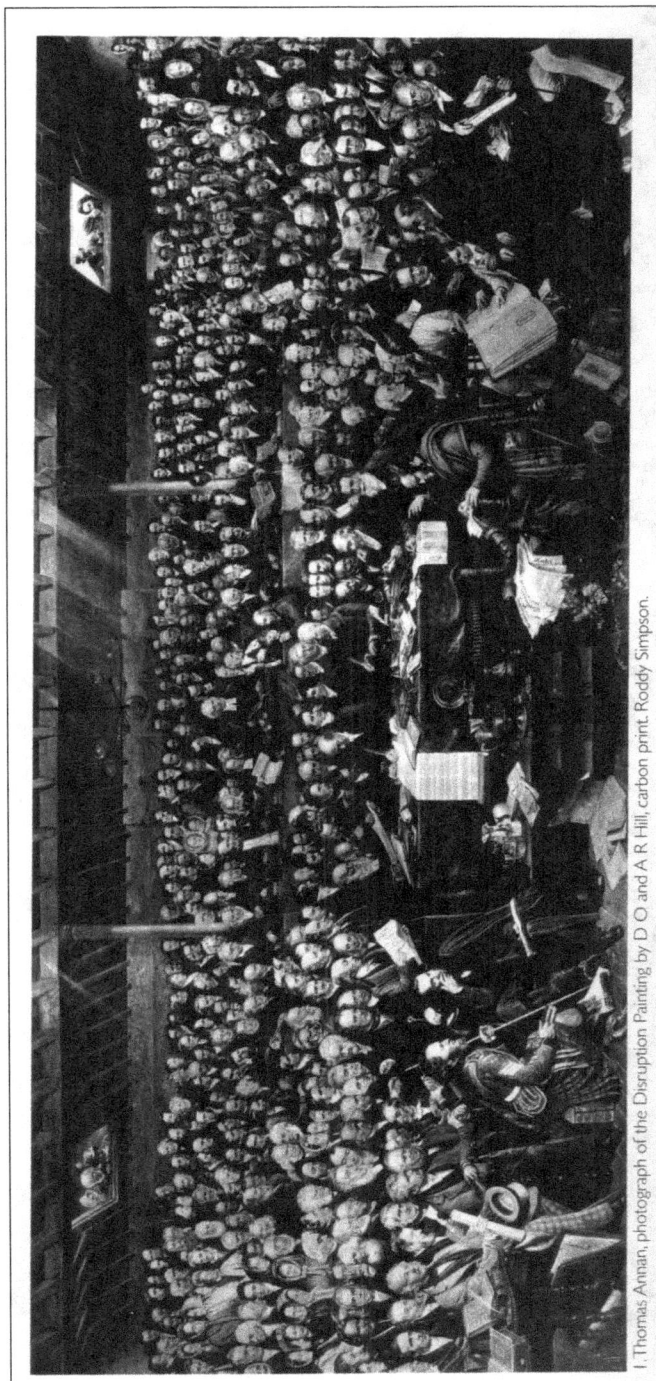

2.4 Thomas Annan, Photograph of D. O. Hill's "Disruption" painting ("First General Assembly of the Free Church of Scotland. Signing the Act of Separation and Deed of Demission at Tanfield, Edinburgh, May 1843"). 1868. Carbon print. By kind permission of the photograph's owner, Roddy Simpson.

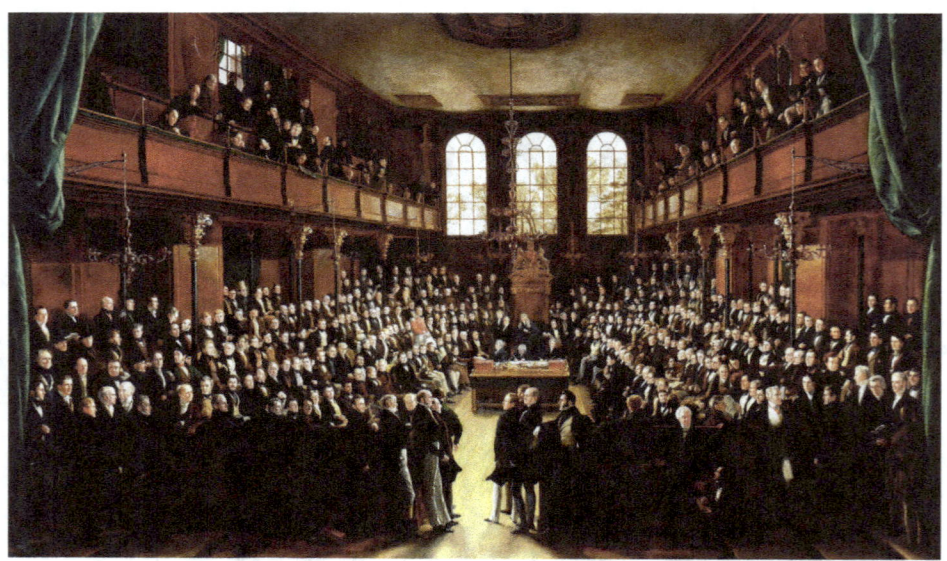

2:5 Sir George Hayter, "The House of Commons, 1833." 1833-1843. Oil on canvas. ©National Portrait Gallery, London, Asset no. 54. By kind permission of the National Portrait Gallery.

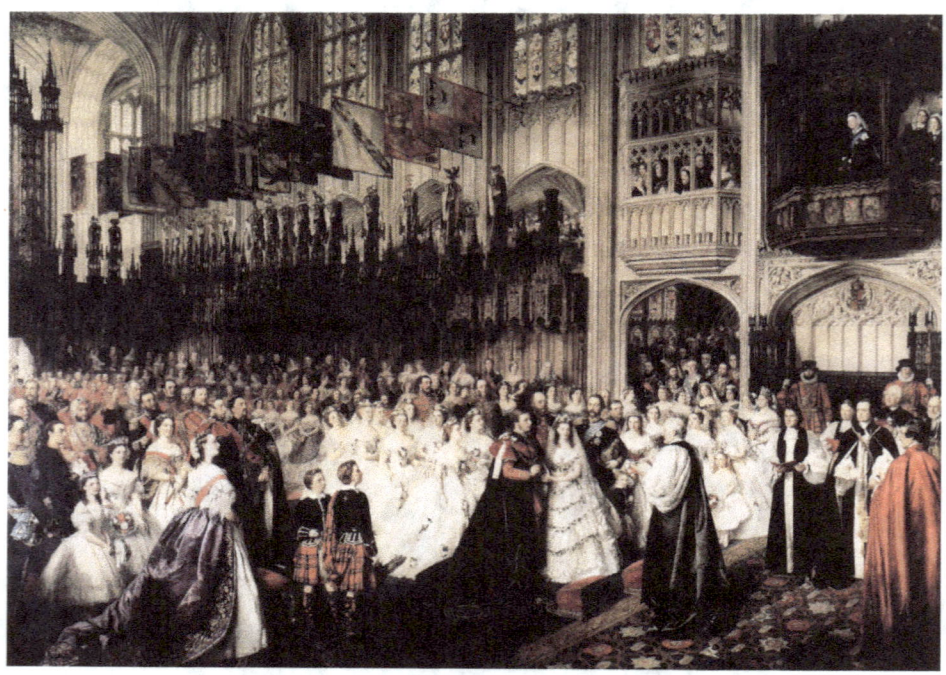

2:6 William Powell Frith, "The Marriage of H.R.H. the Prince of Wales with Princess Alexandra of Denmark, St. George's Chapel, Windsor, 10 March, 1863." Oil on canvas. 1865. Wikimedia.

Paintings 37

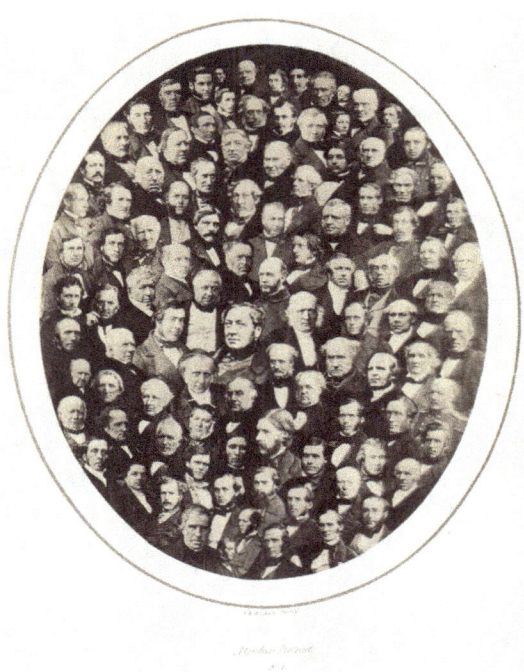

2:7 George Washington Wilson, "Aberdeen Portraits No. 1." 1857. Albumen silver print. Metropolitan Museum. The Horace W. Goldsmith Foundation Fund, through Joyce and Robert Menschel, 2011, Accession Number 2011.424. ©Metropolitan Museum.

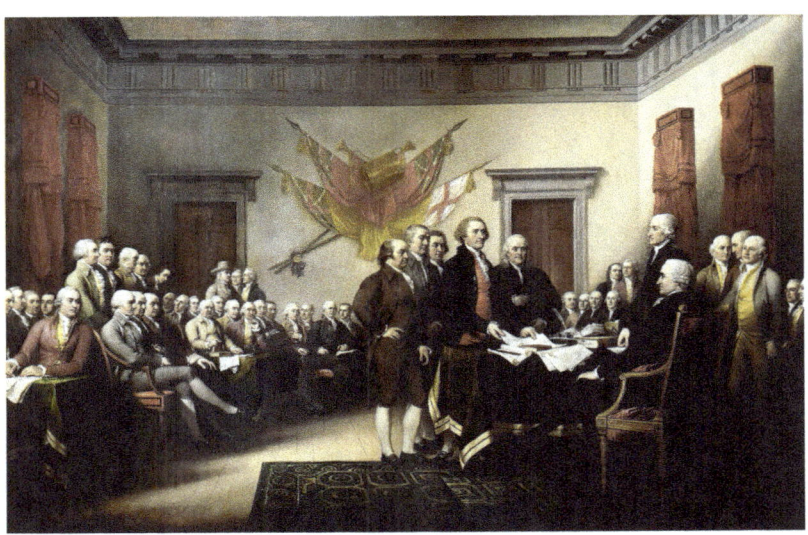

2:8 John Trumbull, "The Declaration of Independence." 1818. Oil on canvas. Installed in Rotunda of U.S. Capitol, Washington, D.C., 1826. Architect of the Capitol.

3. Portraits

By the late eighteenth and early nineteenth centuries, having a portrait made of oneself or one's family members was not the exclusive privilege of wealthy aristocrats and "great men," as is evident from the list of painted portraits in the previously mentioned *Catalogue of Portraits on Loan in the New Galleries of Art, Corporation Buildings, Sauchiehall Street*. In many small European cities and towns a local artist might make a living by painting portraits, often miniatures, of local people. These were not cheap, of course, and the clientele was still relatively restricted. The camera put portraiture within reach of a wider, rapidly-expanding middle class, especially after the introduction of the carte-de-visite format in 1854 and the cabinet format in 1866. Even if Lady Eastlake's description, in 1857, of the immense popularity of photography is exaggerated, it probably had some basis in reality.

> Who can number the legions of petty dabblers, who display their trays of specimens along every great thoroughfare in London, executing for our lowest servants, for one shilling, that which no money could have commanded for the Rothschild bride of twenty years ago? Not that photographers flock especially to the metropolis; they are wanted everywhere and found everywhere. The large provincial cities abound with the sun's votaries, the smallest town is not without them. [. . .] Where not half a generation ago the existence of such a vocation was not dreamt of, tens of thousands [. . .] are now following a new business, practising a new pleasure, speaking a new language.[37]

The Annan firm certainly benefited from this development, and it produced many small, relatively inexpensive carte-de-visite portraits of fairly obscure individuals. More substantial portraits in the cabinet or larger formats were also made of eminent persons, such as the popular painter Horatio McCulloch and the already celebrated missionary and explorer David Livingstone, who happened to be Thomas Annan's next-door neighbor in Hamilton and with whose family the Annans were on friendly terms (Figs. 3:1-2).

In general, however, as was often the case with Annan, a considerable body of work was due to commissions from public bodies. Thus *Memorials of the Old College of Glasgow*, commissioned by the University and published in 1871 by the Annan company and James MacLehose (then, and until the early twentieth century, publisher to the University), contains, along with many large (approximately 9¼ x 7¼ inches) mounted albumen prints illustrative of the soon-to-be-demolished old college buildings in the High Street, similarly mounted portraits (approximately 8¼ x 6¼ inches) of the Principal and 25 of the professors (Figs. 3:3-4).

Likewise, the extensive collection of Annan's photographs at Glasgow's Mitchell Library includes over fifty portraits of ministers, mostly from the fairly liberal United Presbyterian Church. These were also published in album form in 1875.[38] While well-arranged and interestingly-lighted, there does not appear to be anything exceptional about these portraits. They do seem livelier than the elegant but restrained portraits being made around the same time by John Fergus in the little Ayrshire town of Largs (Figs. 3:5-6). The poses and expressions are varied and the viewer has the sense of an individual personality. Annan's portraits probably owe something to his familiarity with the work of Raeburn (Fig. 3:7).[39]

It is fitting that they are used to illustrate many modern Wikipedia articles (e.g. those on David Livingstone, the explorer; the theologians John Caird and Thomas Barclay; Caird's younger brother Edward Caird, an influential idealist philosopher and expositor of Hegel; William Tennent Gairdner, professor of medicine and sanitarian; the botanist Alexander Dickson; the mathematician Hugh Blackburn; the poet, philosopher and historian John Veitch; the chemist Thomas Anderson). Still, on the whole, they conform, as they had to, to the typical image of the learned doctor and savant. The Livingstone and McCulloch portraits are stronger and more expressive, but still fairly conventional.

Though clearly influenced by the example of Hill and Adamson, Annan's portraiture almost never demonstrates the liveliness, humor, whimsy and imaginative presentation (pose, lighting, grouping, etc.) that often characterize not only the work of Hill and Adamson, but also that of John Adamson (the older brother and teacher of the now better-known Robert) and Thomas Rodger, another of John Adamson's protégés at St. Andrews (Figs. 3:8-12).[40]

As Helmut Gernsheim put it in his classic *History of Photography*, Thomas Annan's "fine portraits" are "simple and straightforward."[41] The best of them are comparable with many portraits from the same years by the far more celebrated Nadar, but Annan rarely rises to the peaks reached by Nadar in his finest work—for example, in the portraits of Baudelaire, Corot, Gustave Doré, Alexandre Dumas, *père* or George Sand.

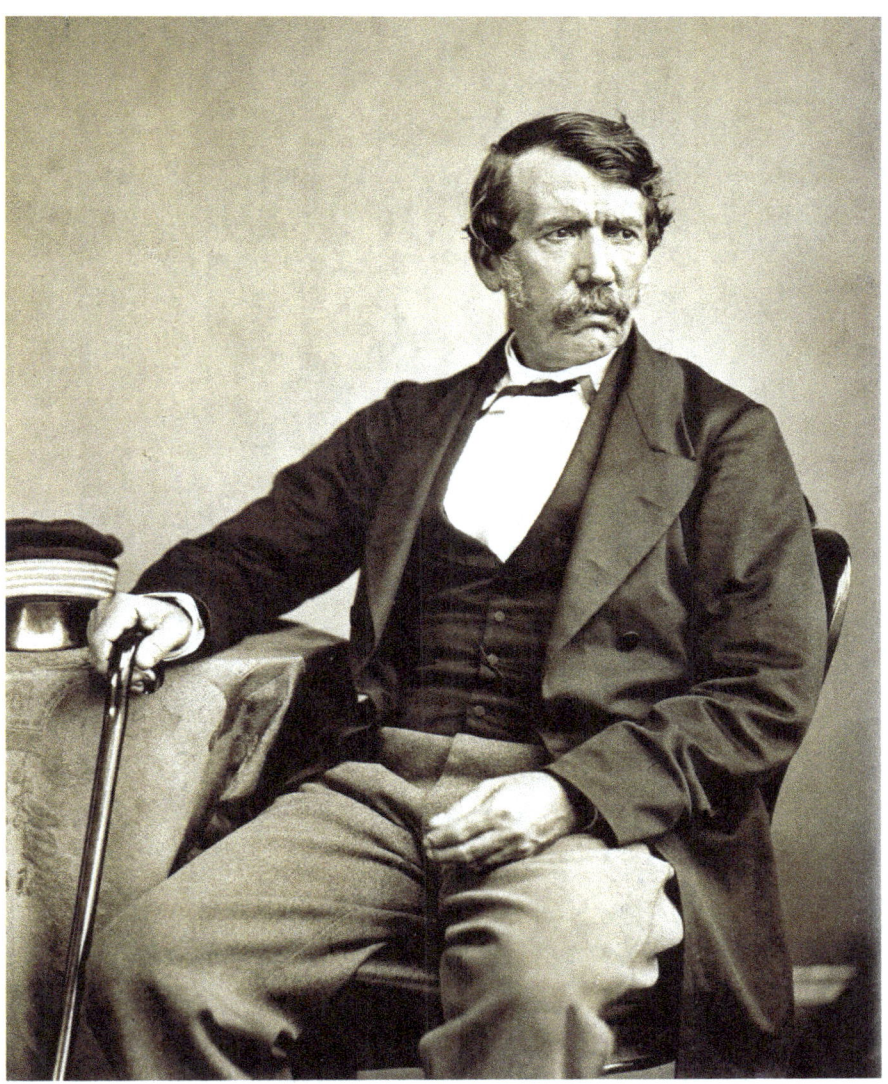
3:1 Thomas Annan, Portrait of David Livingstone. 1864. Carbon print. Wikimedia.

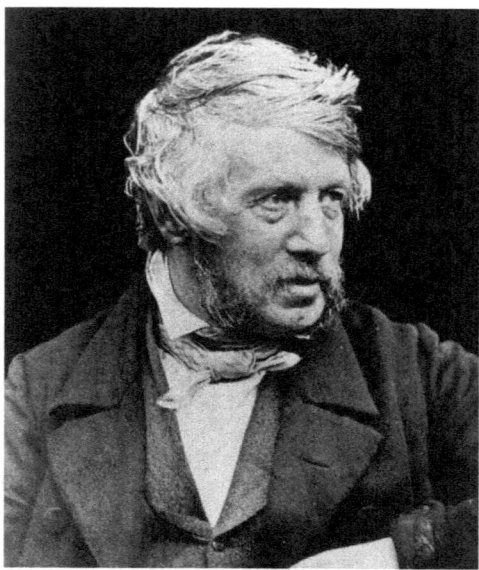

3:2 Thomas Annan, Portrait of Horatio McCulloch, from Alexander Fraser, *Scottish Landscape: The Works of Horatio McCulloch, R.S.A.* (Edinburgh: Andrew Eliot, 1872). Frontispiece. Carbon print. British Library.

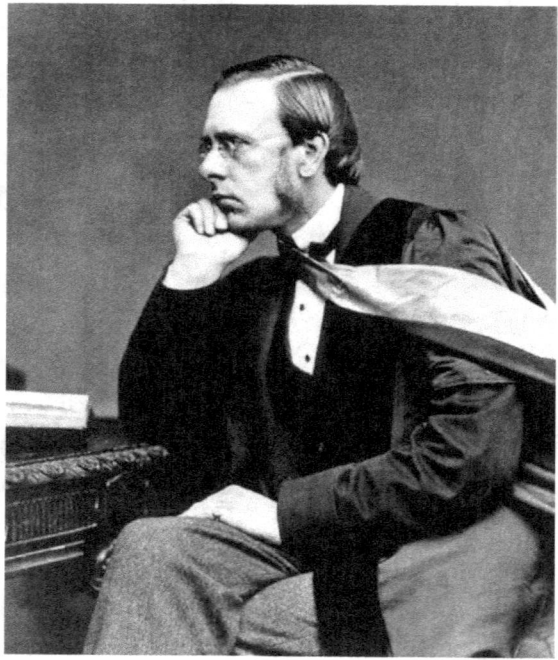

3:3 Thomas Annan, Portrait of William T. Gairdner, Professor of the Practice of Medicine, from *Memorials of the Old College of Glasgow* (Glasgow: Thomas Annan; James MacLehose, 1871), Plate XVI. Albumen print. Courtesy of University of Glasgow Library, Department of Special Collections.

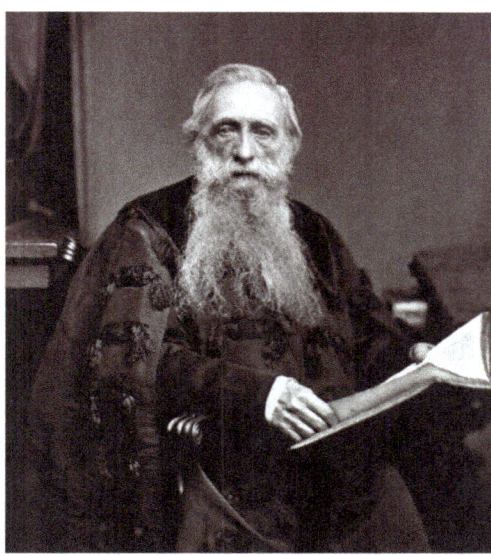

3:4 Thomas Annan, Portrait of Thomas Barclay, Principal of Glasgow University 1858-1873, from *Memorials of the Old College of Glasgow*. Unnumbered plate. Albumen print. Courtesy of University of Glasgow Library, Department of Special Collections.

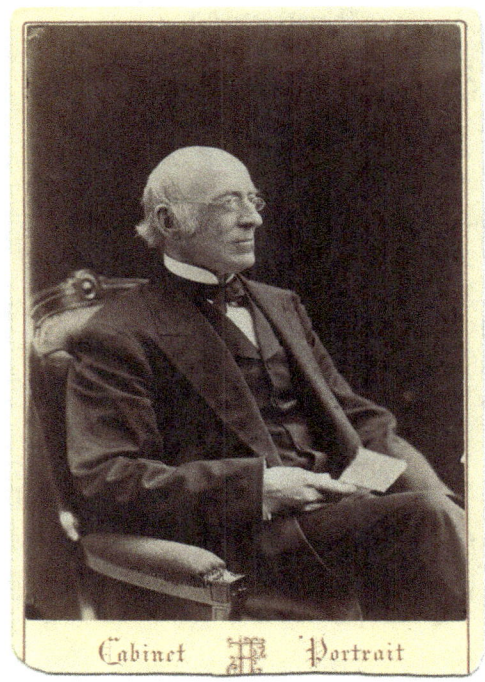

3:5 John Fergus of Largs, William Lloyd Garrison (American abolitionist). Albumen cabinet card. 1870s. National Portrait Gallery, London. Asset Number x28191. ©National Portrait Gallery. By kind permission of the National Portrait Gallery.

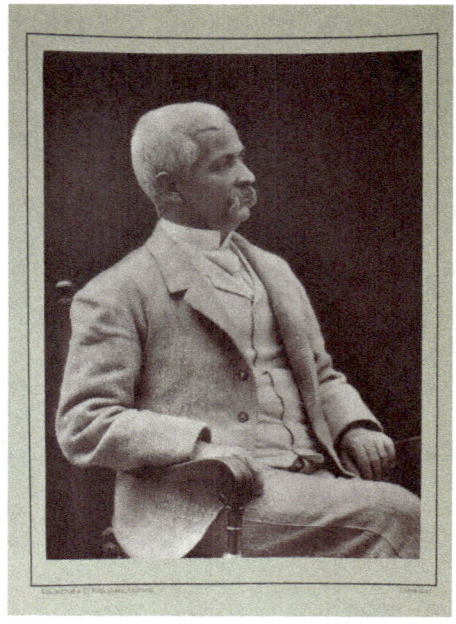

3:6 John Fergus of Largs, carte-de-visite portrait of Henry Morton Stanley (Explorer). Carbon print published by Eglington & Co., 1890. National Portrait Gallery, London, Asset Number Ax5497. ©National Portrait Gallery. By kind permission of the National Portrait Gallery.

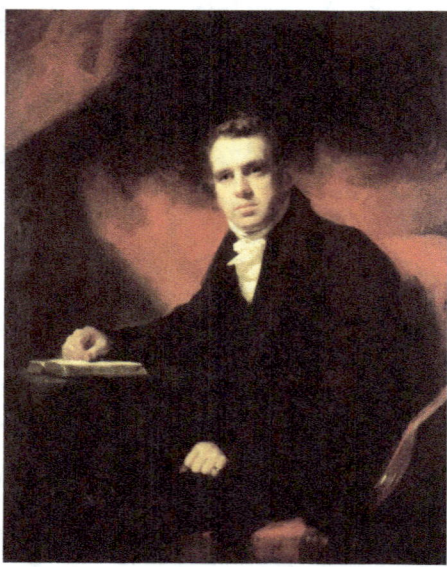

3:7 Sir Henry Raeburn, "Francis Horner." 1812. Oil on canvas. National Portrait Gallery, London, Asset Number 485. ©National Portrait Gallery, London. By kind permission of the National Portrait Gallery.

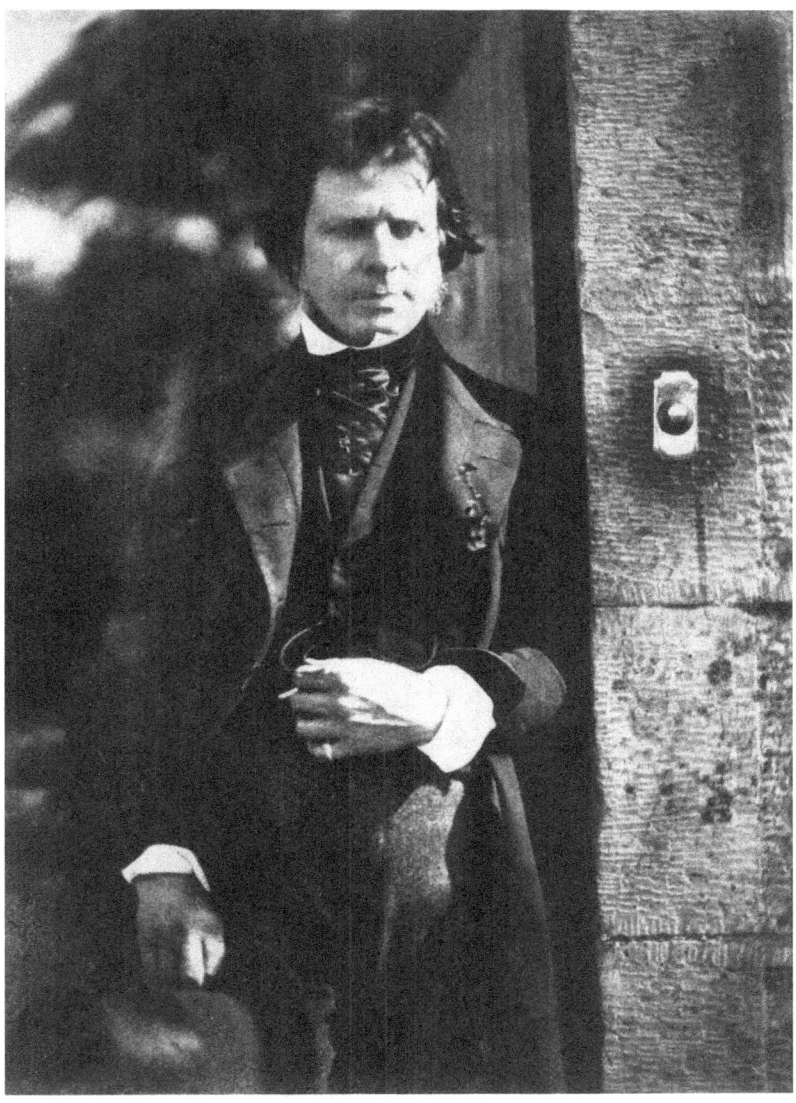

3:8 D.O. Hill and Robert Adamson, Portrait of D.O. Hill. 1843-47. Salted paper print. Wikipedia.

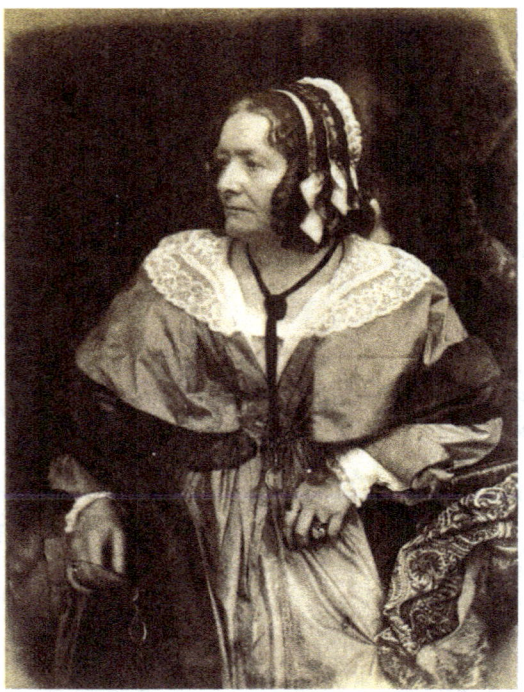

3:9 D.O. Hill and Robert Adamson, Portrait of Mrs. Anna Brownell Jameson. 1844. Salted paper print. Wikimedia.

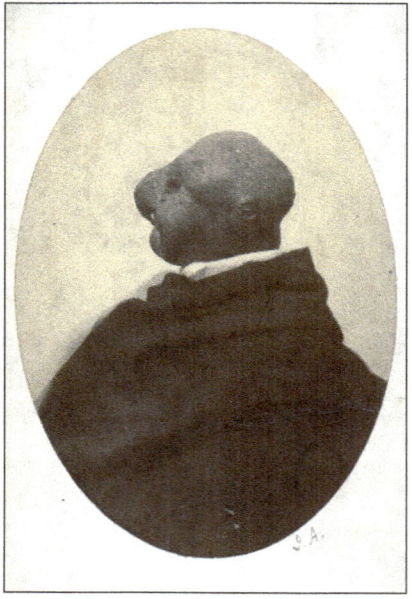

3:10 Dr. John Adamson, "Potato Head." 1855. Salted paper print. St. Andrews University Photographic Collection, ALB-6-158. Courtesy of St. Andrews University Library.

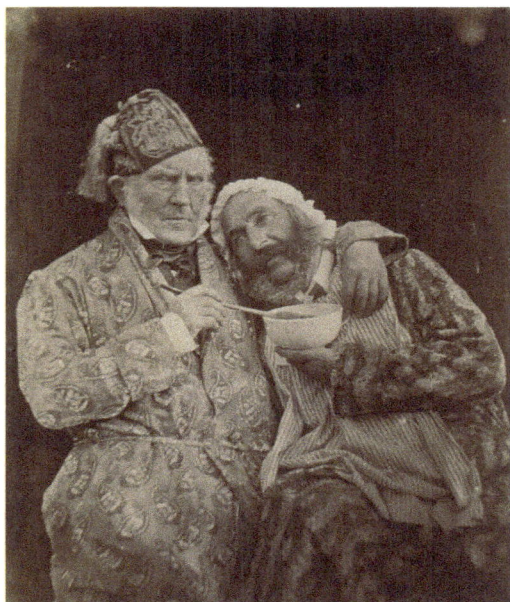

3:11 Dr. John Adamson, "The Sick Baby" (Professor Hugh Lyon Playfair and Professor William Macdonald). 1855. Salted paper print. St. Andrews University Photographic Collection, ALB-6-131-1. Courtesy of St. Andrews University Library.

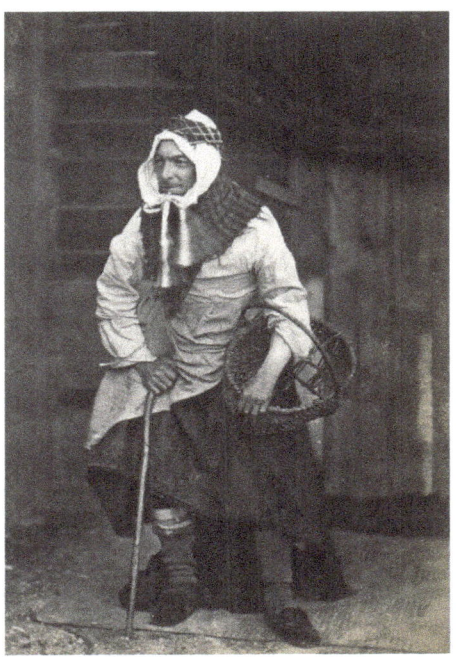

3:12 Thomas Rodger, Portrait of Thomas Rodger Senior in Fishwives' Costume. 1860. In album. St. Andrews University Photographic Collection, ALB-49-11. Courtesy of St. Andrews University Library.

4. Landscapes

Like portraiture, landscape was a major genre of painting and was similarly adopted by the earliest photographers. As Ray McKenzie, a contemporary scholar at the Glasgow School of Art, notes:

> Since the publication, in 1845, of William Henry Fox Talbot's *Sun Pictures in Scotland*, landscape has been one of the most abiding obsessions in the Scottish photographic tradition. Aspects of the country's physical appearance have proved a source of endless fascination both for indigenous photographers, as well as for those who, following Talbot, have come to Scotland for no other reason than to photograph it. [...] There is scarcely a single early Scottish photographer of any note who did not at some point engage with landscape as a subject.

McKenzie draws attention to the role of the poems and novels of Scott in promoting landscape photography in Scotland. Thus Talbot's *Sun Pictures in Scotland*, even though it makes no direct reference to Scott's literary texts, "was conceived primarily as a tribute to Scott's literary achievement," while George Washington Wilson's *Photographs of English and Scottish Scenery: Trossachs and Loch Katrine. 12 Views* (1868) actually incorporates extensive quotations from *The Lady of the Lake*, Scott's narrative poem of 1810, the action of which unfolds in and around Loch Katrine and to which the lake owed its celebrity.[42]

Thomas Annan probably had ample practice with landscape when working for the engraver and publisher Joseph Swan. He may have had occasion to examine the Scott-inspired *Vues pittoresques de l'Écosse*, consisting of about fifty views of Scottish scenes engraved by the Frenchman François-Alexandre Pernot, with texts based on the writings of Scott by Amédée Pichot, a prolific author of books about the British Isles and British men of letters (Paris, 1826 and Brussels, 1827) (Fig. 4:1).

http://dx.doi.org/10.11647/OBP.0057.04

He was almost certainly familiar with the books featuring Scottish scenes put out by both Swan[43] and Blackie, the well-known Glasgow publisher who illustrated several of his publications of Scottish scenes and Scottish writers, such as Burns and James Hogg, with engravings of landscape paintings by David Octavius Hill (Figs. 1:4-6; 4:2-3).[44]

Annan must have known the relatively inexpensive (twopenny) engravings of Glasgow buildings and city scenes published in 1843 by David Allan and William Ferguson, another local firm of lithographers and engravers, and reproduced in James Pagan's popular *Sketch of the History of Glasgow* (Glasgow: Robert Stuart, 1847) (Fig. 4:4).

A commercial handlist with details of Annan's photographic stock for 1859 included approximately 75 titles of landscapes and topographical works available in various print sizes and also in the then-popular stereo format.[45] Landscapes were also prominent among the works he selected for display at photographic exhibitions.

Annan produced landscape (and cityscape) photographs throughout his career, notably, in the 1860s, for the quarto edition of John Eaton Reid's *History of the County of Bute and families connected therewith* (Glasgow: T. Murray, 1864), to which he contributed eight mounted albumen prints of 7 x 4¾ inches; for two volumes put out by the Glasgow publisher Andrew Duthie, *Photographs of the Clyde* (1867) and *Photographs of Glasgow* (1868, with text by Rev. A.G. Forbes); and for Duthie's 1865 edition of *Days at the Coast*, a local bestseller by the popular Glasgow writer Hugh MacDonald, to which Annan contributed twelve plates (Figs. 4:5-10, 4:12).[46] He also supplied landscape illustrations for an 1866 edition of Scott's *Marmion* (London: A.W. Bennett).

In addition, Annan was able to combine his skill as a photographer of artworks with his taste for landscapes, providing photographs of twenty paintings for Alexander Fraser's *Scottish Landscape: The Works of Horatio McCulloch R.S.A.* (Edinburgh: Andrew Elliot, 1872). Landscape paintings also seem to have directly influenced his landscape photographs. A photograph, in Reid's *History of the County of Bute,* of Glen Sannox on the Isle of Arran in the Firth of Clyde, for instance, appears to replicate the view painted by the popular Glasgow artist John Knox (Figs. 4:11-12).

At the Edinburgh photographic exhibition of 1861, the *British Journal of Photography* praised "Loch Ranza" (another landscape from Arran that would be used in Reid's *History*) as the best photograph in the show; in 1863, a review of the Photographic Society exhibition in London described Annan's landscapes, which included "Loch Ranza," "Ben Venue from Loch Achray,"

"Waterfall at Inversnaid," and "Aberfoyle," as of such "great photographic excellence and high artistic merit" that "from this time forth he must rank amongst our first class artists"; in 1864, a large photograph of Dumbarton Castle was awarded a silver medal as "the best landscape in Scotland" by the Photographic Society of Scotland and was lavishly praised in *The Photographic Journal* on 15 April of the following year; and in 1865, *Photographic News* noted his "deep and poetic feeling and strong appreciation of the beautiful." (Fig. 4:13) One scholar of our own time recently judged Annan "arguably the finest Scottish landscape photographer of the Victorian period." In the view of another, "Annan's landscapes, once highly regarded, should be highly regarded again."[47]

Still, whatever his artistic talent and inclination, photography was in the first instance Annan's business and his livelihood. Not surprisingly, therefore, his first major photographic album, *Views on the Line of the Loch Katrine Water Works* (1859), was the result of a commission from "the Water Committee" of the Town Council or Corporation of Glasgow. It consisted almost exclusively of images of landscapes traversed by a massive engineering project—an extensive system of dams, sluices and siphon pipes constructed at various points around the famous loch and connected to a chain of aqueducts and tunnels—that the Corporation had undertaken in order to bring fifty million gallons of fresh water daily to the city 35 miles to the south and that had taken three and a half years to complete.

Over the years, as the population of Glasgow continued to grow at a vertiginous rate and the Loch Katrine project was further expanded, this first and extraordinarily rare album of Annan's was reproduced and amplified with new photographs, in 1877 and again in 1889, as *Photographic Views of Loch Katrine, and of some of the principal works constructed for introducing the water of Loch Katrine into the city of Glasgow*. These expanded albums, still produced in extremely limited numbers, were undertaken, in the words of the 1877 Preface, "at the suggestion of the Hon. James Bain, Lord Provost [i.e. Lord Mayor], to enable the members [of the Water Committee] to better understand the nature and extent of the works which supply the City with Water, and which have cost about two millions sterling; and thereby to assist them in controlling the details of the management of so necessary an element to a population which now approaches three quarters of a million."[48]

Annan's albums also included a few Romantic images of scenes immortalized by *The Lady of the Lake*; the final photograph is of a fountain built in a Glasgow city park to commemorate the opening of the waterworks and topped by a bronze female figure of Ellen, the heroine of Scott's poetic narrative. In contrast to the albums of Talbot and Wilson, however, or the many paintings of Loch Katrine by Scottish artists, or, for that matter, the earlier Turner painting of 1832 and its often reproduced engraved versions—all of which celebrate a scene that, thanks to Scott, had become emblematic of rugged, unspoiled nature (Figs. 4:14-18)—Annan's reminders of the Romantic vision of the loch (Fig. 4:19) have the effect of highlighting the intrusion of modernity, in the form of a spectacular engineering project, into the famously primitive environment.

At a banquet given in his honor in 1860, John Frederick Bateman, the chief engineer of the project, who had experience designing and building other city water supplies, himself noted the stark contrast between, on the one hand, the scale and modernity of the project, together with the engineering skill required to execute it, and, on the other, the beauty and isolation of the countryside in which the construction had been carried out.

> My merit is that of seeing my way more clearly through the rugged country that guards the peaceful bosom of Loch Katrine from the too familiar approach of man, and in determining at once what I believe to be the best and only practicable method by which the water could have been conveyed. It is impossible to convey to those who have not personally inspected it, an impression of the intricacy of the wild and beautiful district through which the Aqueduct passes for the first ten or eleven miles after leaving Loch Katrine. [...] The country consists of successive ridges of the most obdurate rock, separated by deep, wild valleys, in which it was very difficult, in the first instance, to find a way. There were no roads, no houses, no building materials, nothing which would ordinarily be considered essential to the successful completion of a great engineering work for the conveyance of water; but it was a consideration of the geological character of the material which gave all the romantic wildness to the district, which at once determined me to adopt that particular mode of construction that has been carried out.[49]

Annan's photographs communicate vividly the striking juxtaposition of untamed nature and modern planning for an urban community (Figs. 4:20-21).

In this respect, Ray McKenzie has observed, *Views on the Line of the Loch Katrine Water Works*, "as a landscape debut by a still comparatively inexperienced photographer is a work of great maturity and assurance" and "one of the key landscape statements of the period."[50] Whereas the countryside was generally viewed by the well-to-do of the nineteenth century as a healthy refuge from the more and more densely-populated, polluted and disease-ridden cities, Annan's landscapes illustrated how a major work of modern engineering placed the pristine purity of a remote and wild countryside, extolled in Romantic literature, at the service of a huge, ever-growing urban population. In the words of the address by the Secretary to the Waterworks Commissioners at the official opening by Queen Victoria on October 14, 1859, the Loch Katrine Waterworks was "a great public work—alike important to the social and domestic comfort and enjoyment of the numerous inhabitants of the city of Glasgow, whose interests are entrusted to our management, as of incalculable benefit to many branches of manufacturing and commercial industry in the city and neighbourhood."[51]

Annan's images also highlight the civic character of the enterprise, the role played in initiating and sustaining it by Glasgow's elected officials and by the members of the Water Committee, representing the wards of the ceaselessly expanding city. In several photographs, the "water commissioners" and the Lord Provost are shown as a group, sometimes in the landscape, sometimes gathered together in front of a significant engineering feature of the project, their city clothes clashing incongruously with the natural environment (Figs. 4:22-24). In the closing words of the Preface, "The book is meant to be a record of a work which, among the many large and successful enterprises of the Town Council of Glasgow, is pre-eminently the most extensive and beneficial of them all. Among the works, both ancient and modern, for the supply of water to the large cities of the world, it is acknowledged to hold a prominent place, both as regards the purity of the water, the large quantity available, and the small cost at which it is delivered to the inhabitants." It was, as the Secretary noted in his speech to the Queen, "one of the most interesting and difficult works of engineering and at the same the largest and most comprehensive scheme for the supply of water which has yet been accomplished in your Majesty's dominions." Along with Annan's photographs, it was probably chief engineer Bateman who, in an address to the town councillors, underlined most effectively the modernity of the Loch Katrine water scheme, its immense distance from the Romantic old clan world of Scott's poem—and from the numerous landscape photographs that aimed to confirm and propagate that Romantic vision of a pre-modern, pre-industrial world.

> I leave you a work which I believe will, with very slight attention, remain perfect for ages, which, for the greater part of it, is as indestructible as the hills through which it has been carried,—a truly Roman work; not executed like the colossal monuments of the East by forced labour, at the command of an arbitrary sovereign, but by the free will and contributions of a highly

civilized and enlightened city, and by the free labour of a free country. It is a work which surpasses the nine famous aqueducts which fed the city of Rome; and among the works of ornament or usefulness for which your City is now distinguished and will hereafter be famous none, I will venture to say, will be more creditable to your wisdom, more worthy of your liberality, or more beneficial in its results, than the Loch Katrine Water Works.[52]

Though George Washington Wilson's *Trossachs and Loch Katrine* appeared in a first edition seven years after the completion of the remarkable engineering project that Annan's images had memorialized and that had been widely reported in the press (handsome engravings made from Annan's photographs illustrated major articles in the *London Illustrated News* for 15 and 22 October 1859 [Figs. 4:25-26]), Wilson sedulously avoided any hint of the intrusion of modernity into the Romantic landscape defined by Scott's *Lady of the Lake* (Figs. 4:27-28). The James Valentine firm followed suit: a view of Loch Katrine in a photograph of 1878 was carefully identified as that from the watchtower of Roderick Dhu, one of the heroes of Scott's poem (Fig. 4:29).

Likewise, in Queen Victoria's journals, Scotland's remote highlands and lochs continued to stand for a refuge from modernity, an admired ancient world, which she repeatedly associated with the works of Scott and unconsciously contrasted, by means of an allusion to the weather, with the world represented by the Loch Katrine Waterworks:

> Leaving this little loch to our left, in a few minutes we came upon Loch Katrine, which was seen at its greatest beauty in the fine evening light. Most lovely! We stopped at Stronachlachar, a small inn where people stay for a night sometimes, and where they embark coming from Loch Lomond and vice versa. As the small steamer had not yet arrived, we had to wait for about a quarter of an hour.
>
> But there was no crowd, no trouble or annoyance, and during the whole of our drive nothing could be quieter or more agreeable. Hardly a creature did we meet, and we passed merely a very few pretty gentlemen's places, or very poor cottages with simple women and barefooted, long-haired lassies and children, quiet and unassuming old men and labourers.
>
> This solitude, the romance and wild loveliness of everything here, the absence of hotels and beggars, the independent simple people, who all speak Gaelic here, all make beloved Scotland the proudest, finest country in the world. [. . .] It was about ten minutes past five when we went on board the very clean little steamer *Rob Roy*—the very same we had been on under such different circumstances in 1859 on the 14th of October, in dreadful weather, thick mist and heavy rain, when my beloved husband and I opened the Glasgow Waterworks.[53]

Landscapes 55

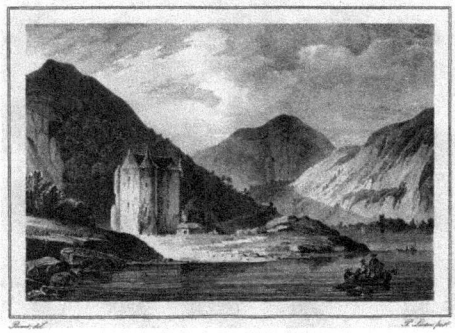

4:1 "Château de Dunderaw sur le Lac Fine," from François-Alexandre Pernot and Amédée Pichot, *Vues pittoresques de l'Écosse* (Paris: Charles Gosselin et Lami-Denozan, 1826; Brussels: A. Wahlen, A. Dewasme, 1827). Courtesy of Ancestry Images.

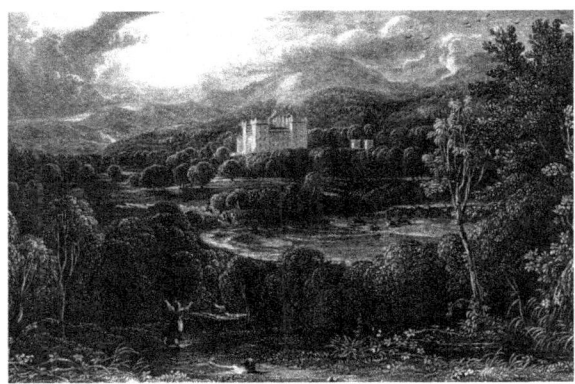

4:2 D.O. Hill, "Drumlanrig Castle," from *The Land of Burns* (Glasgow: Blackie and Son, 1840), vol. 2, facing p. 20.

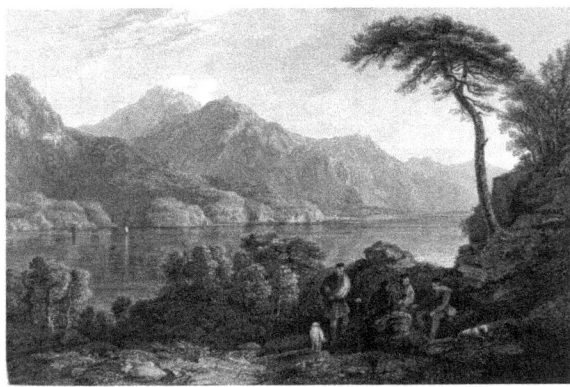

4:3 John Fleming, "Loch Maree," from *Select Views of the Lakes of Scotland: from Original Paintings by John Fleming engraved by Joseph Swan; with historical and descriptive illustrations by John M. Leighton* (Glasgow: J. Swan, [1834-1840]). Princeton University Library.

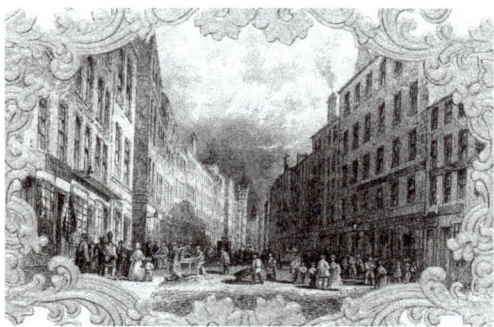

4:4 "The Saltmarket," from James Pagan, *Sketch of the History of Glasgow* (Glasgow: Robert Stuart, 1847), facing p. 161; originally plate 20 of "Illustrated Letterpaper comprising a Series of Views in Glasgow" (Glasgow: Allen and Ferguson, 1843).

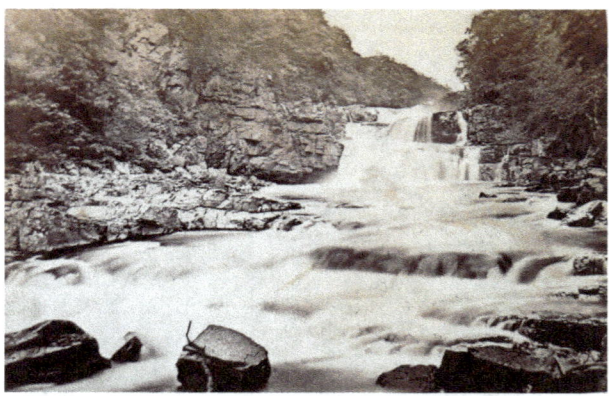

4:5 Thomas Annan, "Stonebyres Linn," from his *Photographs of the Clyde* (Glasgow: Andrew Duthie, 1867). Graphic Arts Collection, Department of Rare Books and Special Collections, Princeton University Library.

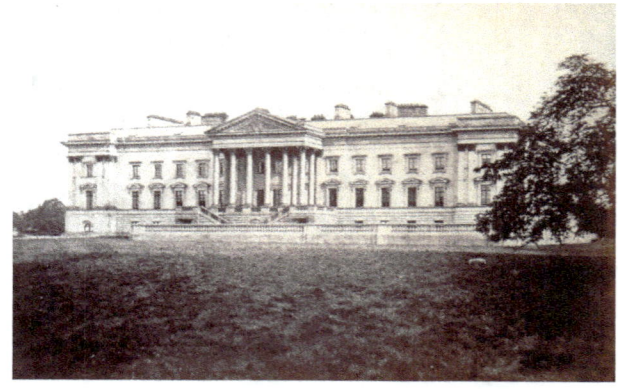

4:6 Thomas Annan, "Hamilton Palace," from his *Photographs of the Clyde*. Graphic Arts Collection, Department of Rare Books and Special Collections, Princeton University Library.

Landscapes 57

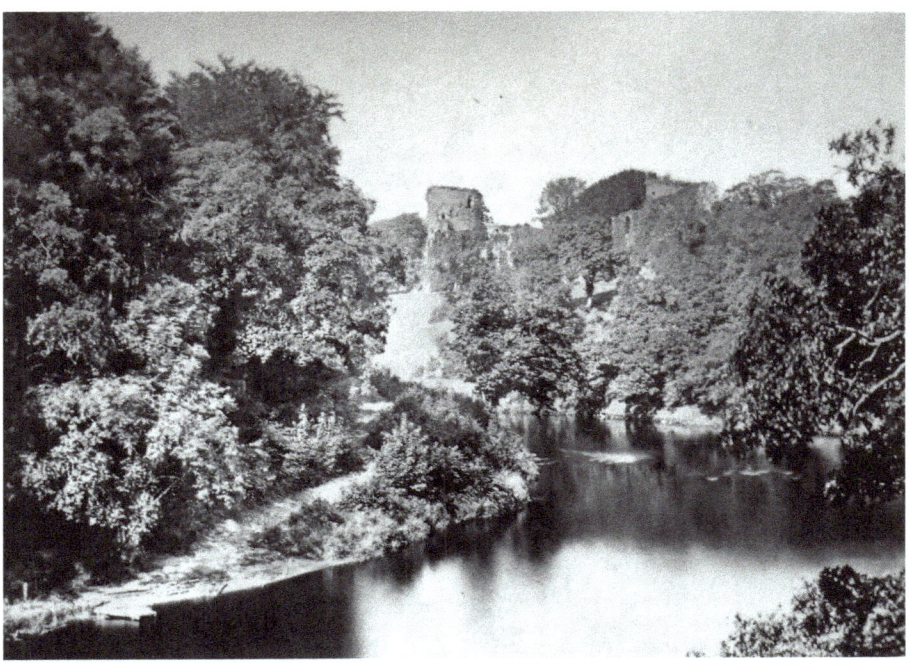

4:7 Thomas Annan, "Bothwell Castle," from his *Photographs of the Clyde*. Graphic Arts Collection, Department of Rare Books and Special Collections, Princeton University Library.

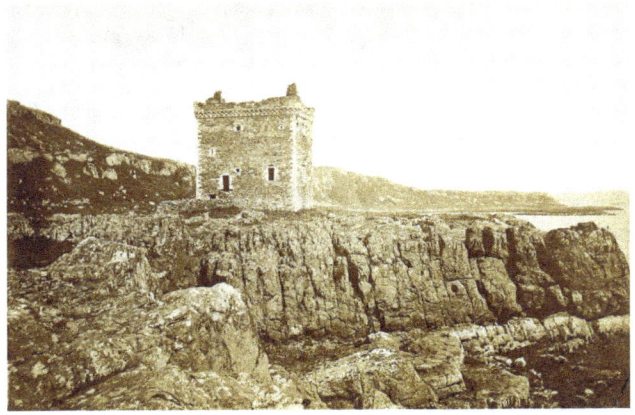

4:8 Thomas Annan, "Castle, Little Cumbray," from John Eaton Reid, *History of the County of Bute and Families connected therewith* (Glasgow: T. Murray and Son, 1864). British Library, London.

58 Thomas Annan of Glasgow

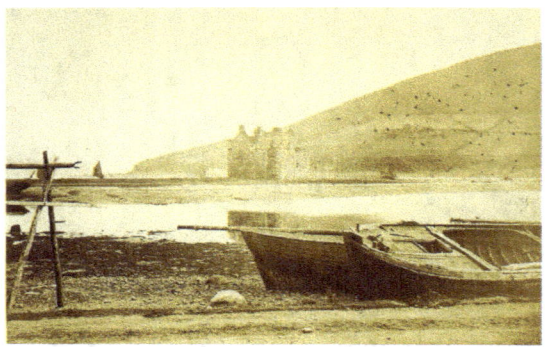

4:9 Thomas Annan, "Loch Ranza Castle," from *History of the County of Bute*. British Library, London.

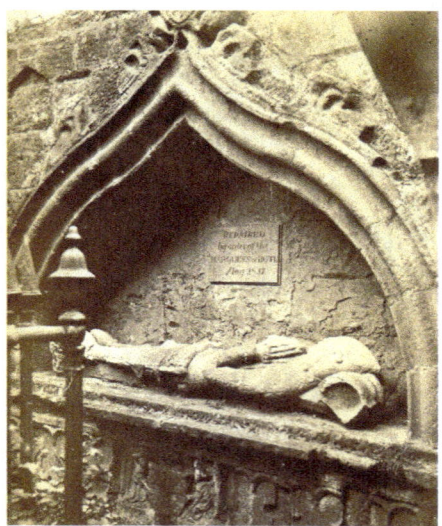

4:10 Thomas Annan, "Tomb, St. Mary's Chapel, Rothesay," from *History of the County of Bute*. British Library, London.

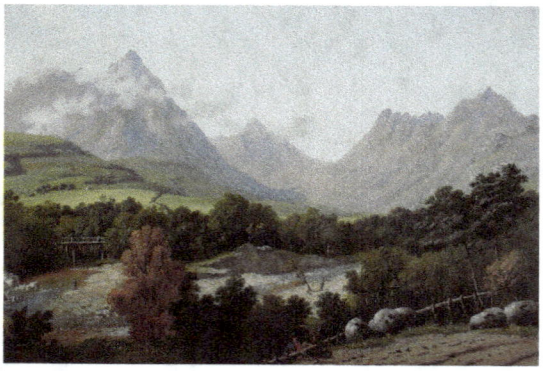

4:11 John Knox, "The Head of Glen Sannox." Oil on canvas. Wikimedia.

Landscapes 59

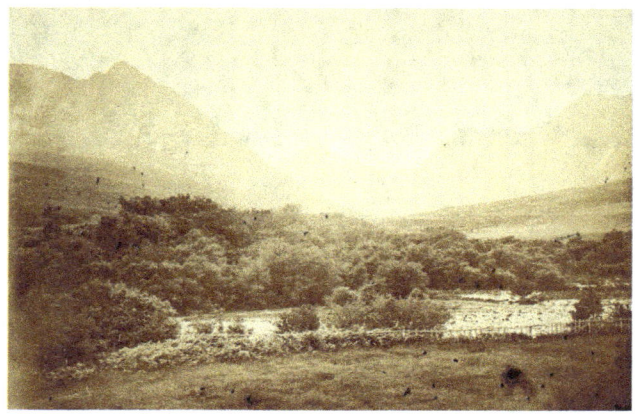

4:12 Thomas Annan, "Glen Sannox," from *History of the County of Bute*. British Library, London.

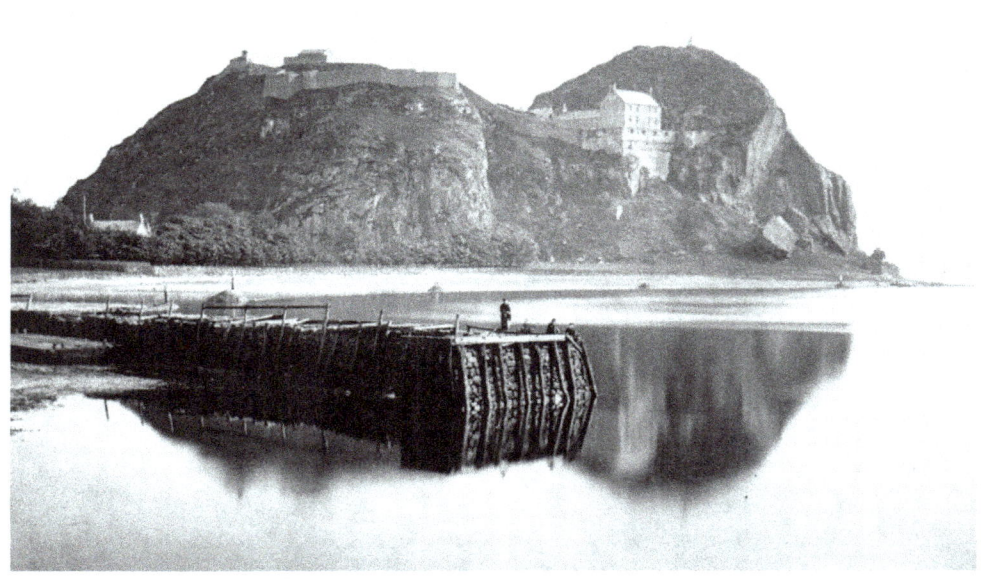

4:13 Thomas Annan, "Dumbarton Castle." Exhibited 1864. ©CSG CIC Glasgow Museums and Libraries Collection: The Mitchell Library, Special Collections.

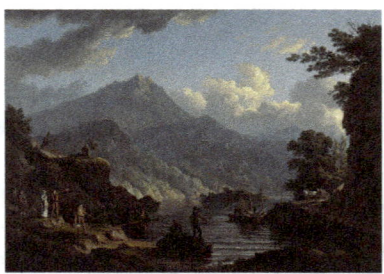

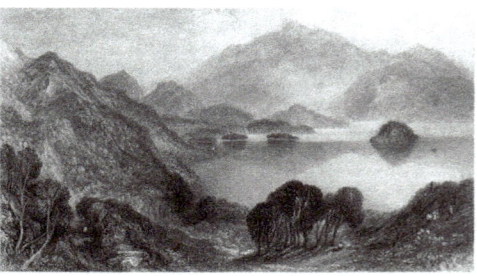

4:14 John Knox, "Landscape with tourists at Loch Katrine." Ca.1820. Oil on canvas. Wikimedia.

4:15 W. Miller, "Loch Katrine," engraving by W. Miller after the painting by J.M.W. Turner. Published in *The Poetical Works of Sir Walter Scott, Bart.* (Edinburgh: Robert Cadell & Whittaker, 1833-34). Wikimedia.

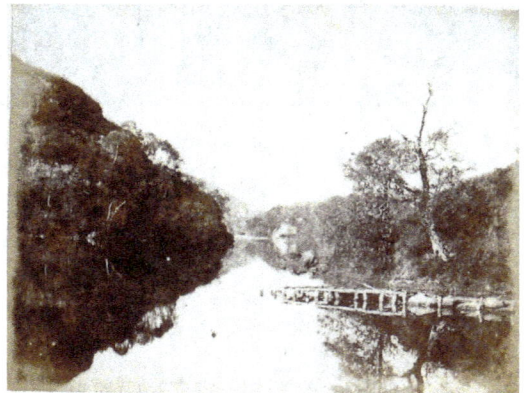

4:16 William Henry Fox Talbot, "Loch Katrine," from H. Fox Talbot, Esq., F.R.S., *Sun Pictures in Scotland* (London: [n. pub.], 1845), Plate 16. Salted paper print. Division of Rare Books, Marquand Library, Princeton University.

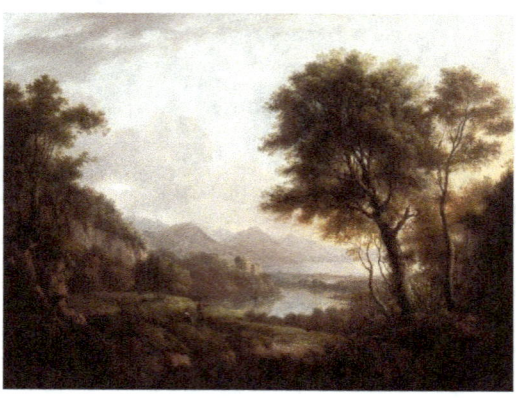

4:17 Alexander Nasmyth, "Landscape, Loch Katrine." 1862. Oil on canvas. Kelvingrove Art Gallery, Glasgow. Courtesy of Glasgow Museums Collection.

Landscapes 61

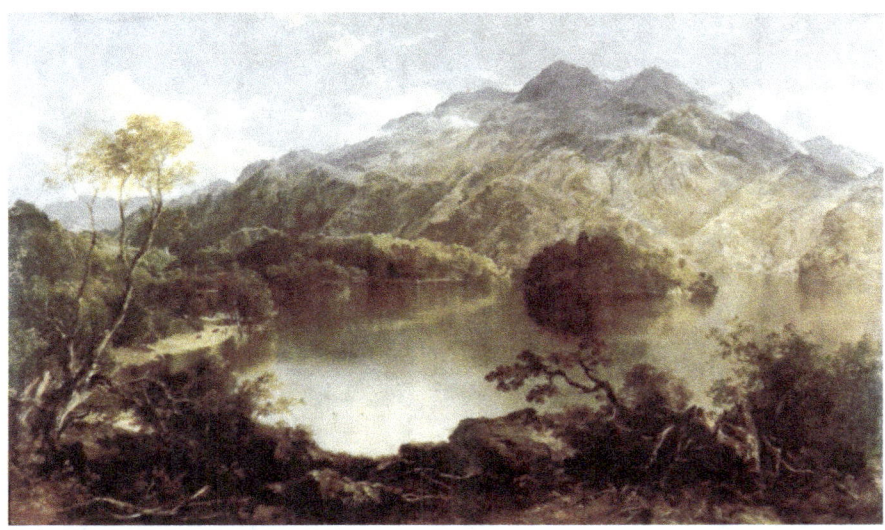

4:18 Horatio McCulloch, "Loch Katrine." 1866. Oil on canvas. Courtesy of Perth Museum & Art Gallery, Perth & Kinross Council.

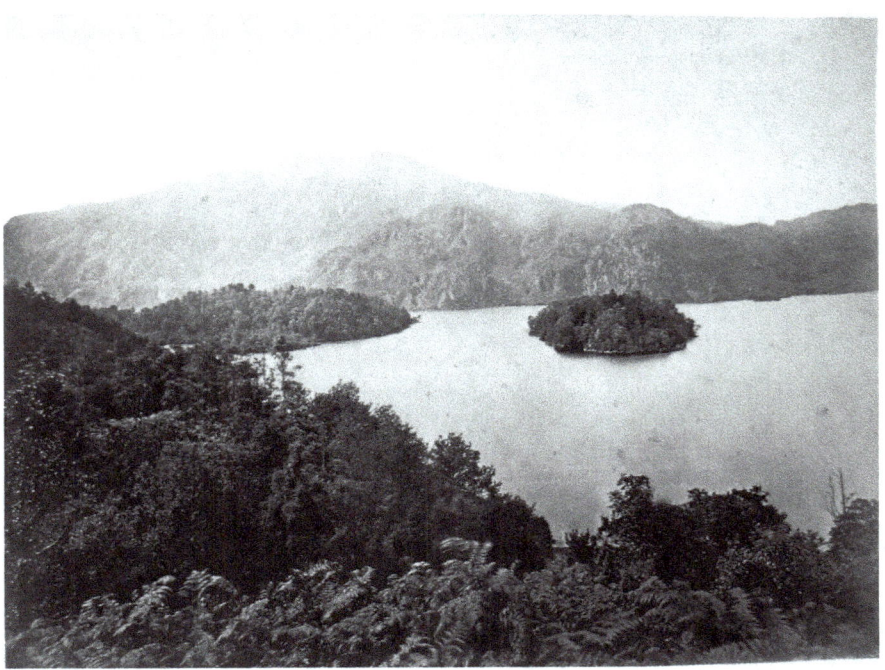

4:19 Thomas Annan, "Loch Katrine and Ellen's Isle and Ben Venue," from Glasgow Corporation Water Works. *Photographic Views of Loch Katrine, and of some of the principal works constituted for introducing the water of Loch Katrine into the city of Glasgow* (Glasgow: Printed by James C. Erskine, 1889). Albumen print. (Original photograph, 1859). Graphic Arts Collection, Department of Rare Books and Special Collections, Princeton University Library.

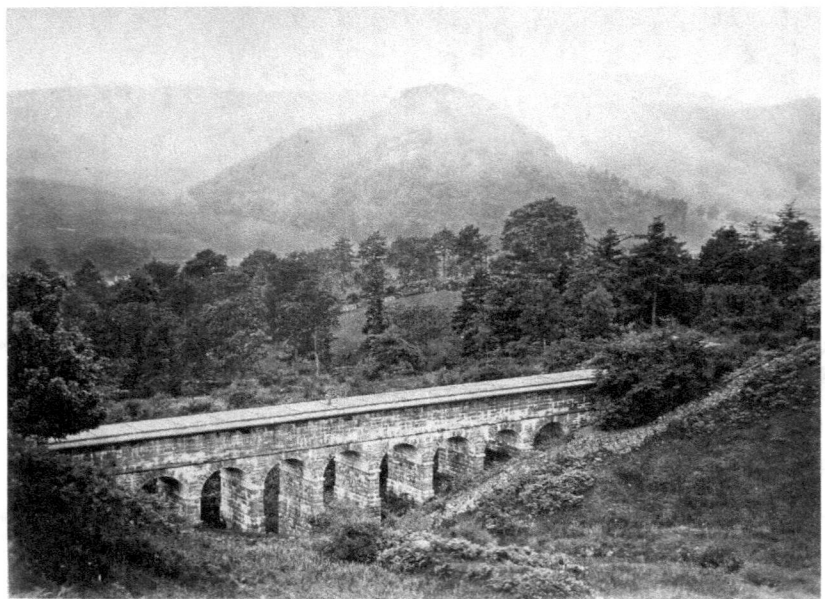

4:20 Thomas Annan, "Aqueduct Bridge near Duntreath Castle, 22 miles from Loch Katrine," from Glasgow Corporation Water Works. Albumen print. (Original photograph, 1859). Graphic Arts Collection, Department of Rare Books and Special Collections, Princeton University Library.

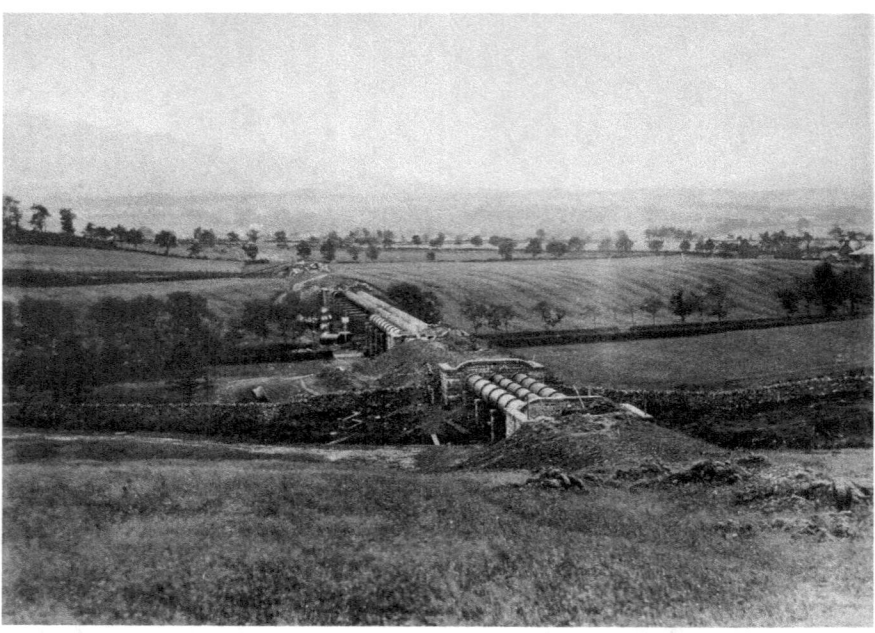

4:21 Thomas Annan, "Endrick Valley looking South," from Glasgow Corporation Water Works. Albumen print. (Original photograph, 1859). Graphic Arts Collection, Department of Rare Books and Special Collections, Princeton University Library.

Landscapes   63

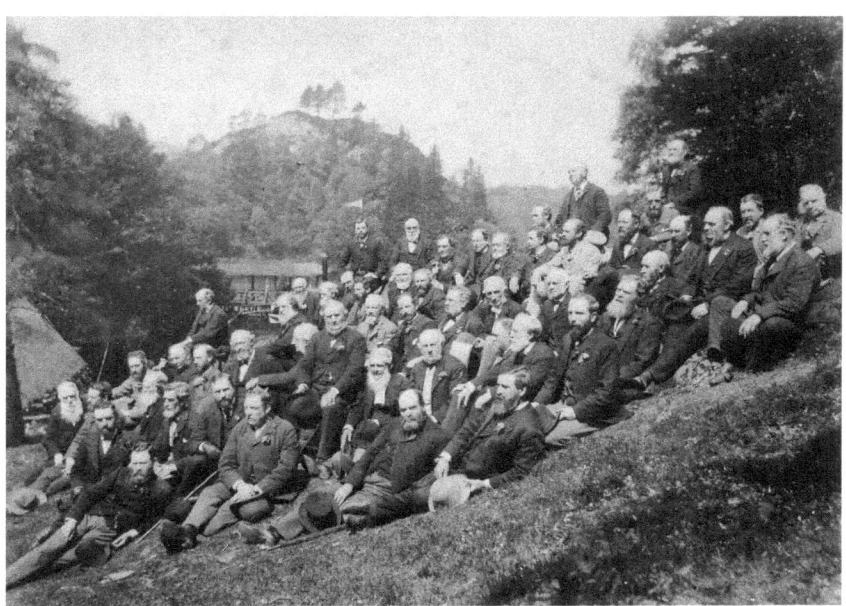

4:22 Thomas Annan, "Glasgow Corporation Water Commissioners at Loch Katrine, 1886," from Glasgow Corporation Water Works. Albumen print. Graphic Arts Collection, Department of Rare Books and Special Collections, Princeton University Library.

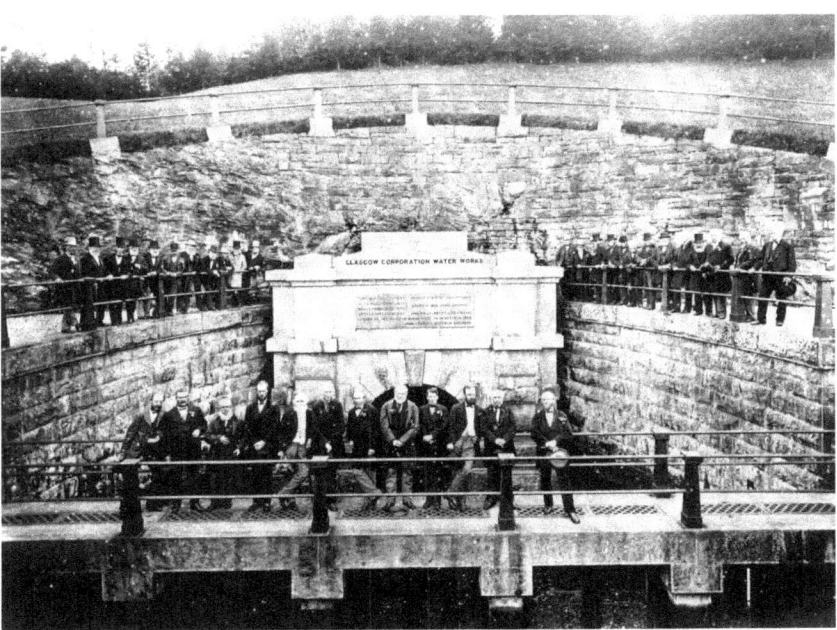

4:23 Thomas Annan, "Glasgow Water Commissioners at Loch Katrine, 1878," from Glasgow Corporation Water Works. Albumen print. Graphic Arts Collection, Department of Rare Books and Special Collections, Princeton University Library.

64 Thomas Annan of Glasgow

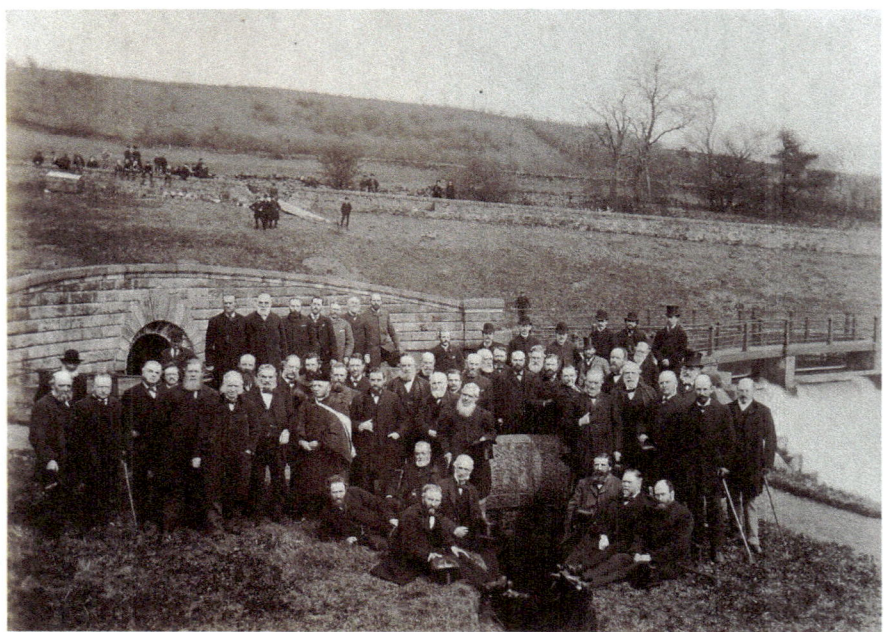

4:24 Thomas Annan, "Glasgow Water Commissioners at opening of a new aqueduct, 1886," from Glasgow Corporation Water Works. Albumen print. Graphic Arts Collection, Department of Rare Books and Special Collections, Princeton University Library.

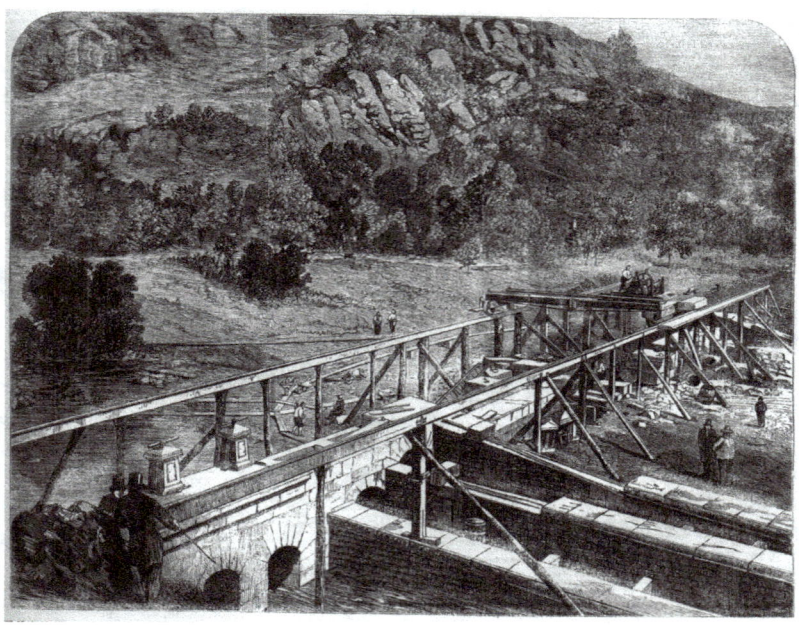

4:25 Engraving from a photograph by Annan in *Illustrated London News*, 15 October 1859. Princeton University Library.

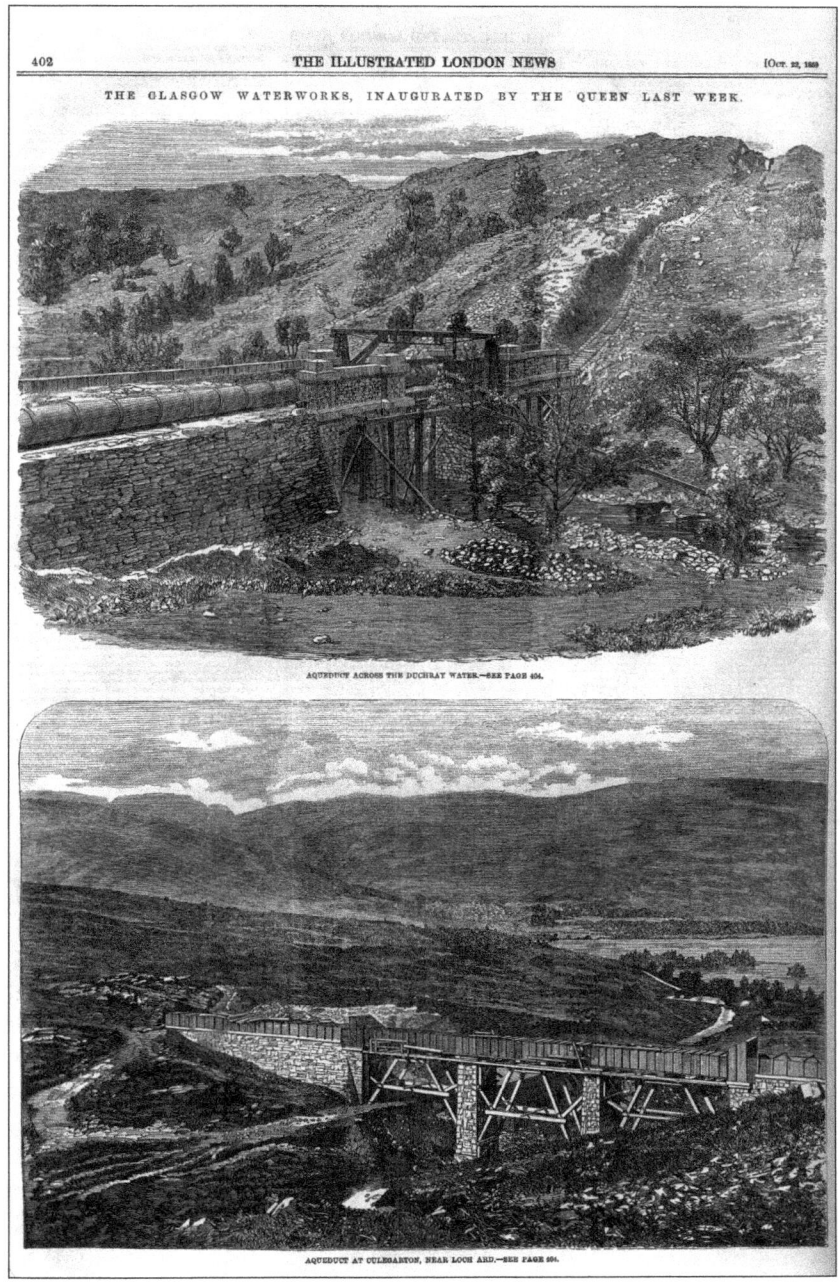

4:26 "Views of the Loch Katrine water works," *Illustrated London News*, 22 October 1859. Princeton University Library.

66 *Thomas Annan of Glasgow*

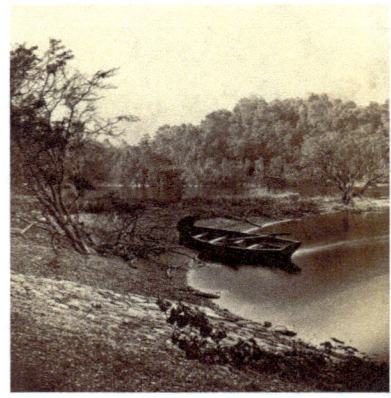

4:27 George Washington Wilson, "Loch Katrine. The Silver Strand," from *Photographs of English and Scottish Scenery*, vol. 11 (Aberdeen: Printed by John Duffus, 1865-1868). Albumen print.

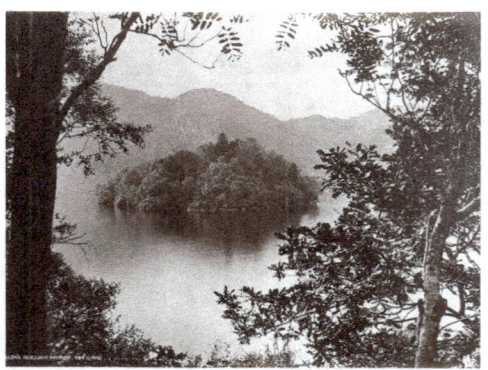

4:28 George Washington Wilson, "Ellen's Isle, Loch Katrine." 1870s. Albumen print. Smith College Art Museum, SC 1982-38-565.

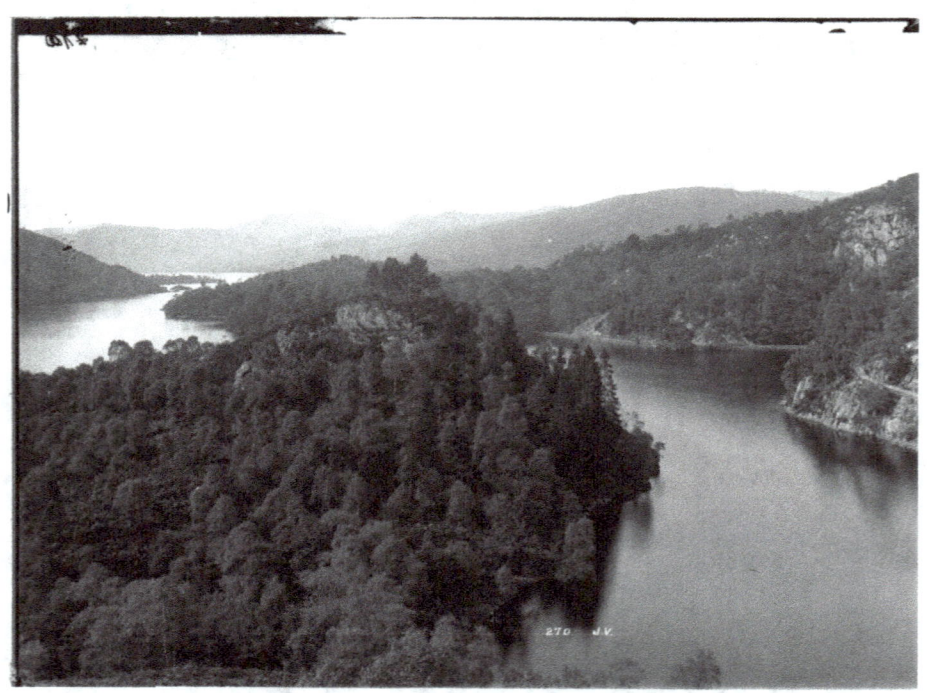

4:29 James Valentine, "Loch Katrine. Trossachs from Roderick Dhu's Watch Tower." 1878. Gelatin dry plate negative. St. Andrews University Photographic Collection, JV-270.A. Courtesy of St. Andrews University Library.

5. The Built Environment

Annan appears to have had a genuine appreciation of architecture as well as of painting. Once again, however, much of his published work resulted from commissions. Two large volumes illustrating local gentlemen's mansions—*The Old Country Houses of the Old Glasgow Gentry. One hundred photographs by Annan, of well-known places in the neighbourhood of Glasgow, with descriptive notices* (Glasgow: MacLehose, 1870, 2nd ed. 1878) and *Castles and Mansions of Ayrshire illustrated in seventy views* (Edinburgh: William Paterson, 1885)[54]—were essentially commissioned by well-to-do members of the old aristocracy and merchant class. Dismayed by the rapidity with which the city and its surroundings were being transformed and its old buildings torn down in the wake of breakneck industrialization and massive immigration, these men of an earlier age sought to preserve a visual record of a vanishing world and saw photography as an effective means of doing so. Though not highly original, the full-page mounted photographs (6¼ x 4½ inches for *The Old Country Houses*, 7½ x 5½ inches for *Castles and Mansions*) of these structures, some dating back to the Middle Ages, most of them built in the eighteenth and early decades of the nineteenth century—the heyday of Glasgow as a merchant city and center of trade in tobacco and cotton with the New World—demonstrate Annan's skill at architectural photography, his sensitivity to compositional values and to the effects of light and shade (Figs. 5:1-6).

Earning his living as a professional photographer, Annan was not in a position, whatever his personal views may have been (the most that scholars have been able to come up with is that he was "a man of liberal and Christian commitment [. . .] involved in the Church's effort to improve the lot" of the poor),[55] to pick and choose commissions. His task was to execute, as a photographer, the orders of his clients. If the texts of the two volumes can be taken as evidence, those who commissioned and subscribed to both *The*

http://dx.doi.org/10.11647/OBP.0057.05

Old Country Houses and *Castles and Mansions* must be assumed to have been unfavorably disposed to the new, fast-changing world of modern industry. Likewise, it would appear that their interest was directed more towards the history and genealogy of the landlords and their social role than towards the buildings themselves. The chief subscribers to both volumes seem to have been either the owners of the properties illustrated or their family members and friends.[56] Thus only 120 copies of the first edition and 225 copies of the second edition of *The Old Country Houses* were printed. The editors—two keen local antiquarians, John Guthrie Smith (1834-1894) and John Oswald Mitchell (1826-1904) in the case of *The Old Country Houses*; the antiquarian and historian Alexander Hastie Millar (1847-1927) in the case of *Castles and Mansions*—offer virtually no comment on the architecture itself in the fairly extensive texts accompanying Annan's photographs, other than an occasional short descriptive passage or the mention of a date or an architect's name. Moreover, the primary interest, not only of the editors but of readers as well, is indicated by handwritten corrections to the editors' texts that were made by an early reader of the Princeton University Library copy of *Castles and Mansions*: they chiefly concern family histories. Even though, as noted, the texts of these relatively rare volumes have little direct bearing on the photographs themselves, they throw light on Annan's clientele and help us to understand the social and historical context in which he worked. I shall therefore quote from them freely.

The author of a 1905 memoir on John Oswald Mitchell, one of the editors of *The Old Country Houses*, observed of Mitchell's historical essays that "a constitutionalist might have noted other things, might have dwelt on the growth of civic rights, the rivalry of the merchants and the crafts, the broadening of self-government, and the resulting evolution of the modern municipality." Mitchell, however, "chose otherwise. His interests were frankly not democratic, and he turned with a glow to the old dons who had—'what some of their successors would give,' he thought, 'a good part of their riches for'—a distinct position of aristocracy, and who enjoyed its first condition, an unquestioned social supremacy. Those old merchants, in great part a hereditary caste," the writer concluded, "were the centre of his world."[57]

While moderate in tone, rather than harshly critical, the texts of *The Old Country Houses* express great consternation at the social transformation of Glasgow. The disappearance of distinguished properties in and around the city, as it expanded into previously outlying suburbs, is seen as the physical manifestation of the decline of the social caste associated with those properties. The well-written Introduction to the first edition opens on an elegiac note: "We get nothing for nothing in this world, and our wonderful present prosperity costs us, among more valuable things, many an interesting monument of the past in Glasgow and round Glasgow."[58] The volume is then presented explicitly as "a memorial of the old Burgher Aristocracy who built or owned so many of these hundred houses" and of the values that that class represented. To be sure, it was a "ruling class."

> They or their nominees were Provosts and Deans of Guild and Bailies. They controlled the election of that quarter of a Member that Glasgow then sent to Parliament. They worked the patronage of the place. Even the Banks were in their hands. And, however their fortunes might look now-a-days, wealth is a relative term, and they were certainly the wealthiest people, rather, the only wealthy people, of their day.

But "money," it is asserted, "used not to be the power, even in pure trading communities, that it has since become, and mere money would not have given them their position." Rather it was the temperament and the moral qualities fostered by the possession of stable wealth that won social distinction for the old merchant gentry. "To be a rich merchant was some warrant then for good breeding. This delicate plant, which may be found indigenous in the poorest soil, can be cultivated, but it cannot be forced: and it does not thrive, on either side of the Atlantic, beside a rapid growth of fortune." Modern conditions, however, are unfavorable to the stable or slow-growing fortunes of the old merchant class.

> Now-a-days, when the capable man can so readily get at both information and connection and capital, the best built business can only be kept up by a succession of talent and application not common in rich families. But, in old times, if a position was worse to win, it was the easier to hold, and a good business was almost as good as an entailed estate. And so it was that the Merchant Rank was in great part a hereditary caste, and its members were of good birth, *if* to come of a line of merchants be to be well-born. All experience shows that this quality of good birth passes current for more than its worth in communities much more democratic than Old Glasgow. But it is worth something. Hereditary opulence does, in the main, soften manners, and the sense of his conspicuous position ought to do good service both in encouraging and in restraining the bearer of a well-known name.

Now, however, "Glasgow looks almost as new as Chicago"; it is virtually forgotten that its "luxuriant growth hides an ancient stem"; and the attachment to the city of the old gentry of merchants and local lairds has been replaced by the wider ambitions of a new class of free-wheeling entrepreneurs and social climbers, to whom the city is no more than the place where their businesses are located and their fortunes made.

> Whatever [the] faults of the old gentry, absenteeism was not one. If Glasgow chanced not to have been their birth-place, it certainly was their home. Even when they came to own their country house, it would be within an easy distance of the Cross, and the town house would be still kept on. They were proud of Glasgow, of its ancient name, and its modern growth, of the High Kirk and the College, the Greens, and the Trongate with its stately Arcades. They were ready to serve the town as Provost, or Dean of Guild, or Bailie. They could be counted on at all times and in all companies to stand up for its rights and its dignities. They knew every body, and every body knew them. [...] They sent their boys to the Grammar School and the College, and brought up their girls at home.
>
> Now-a-days, our leading merchant has too often ceased to be a citizen. Glasgow is the place where he has his office, and which is always wanting subscriptions from him. But he lives as far from it as he can. He cultivates other society. Outside of his own business the circle of his acquaintance here is gradually narrowing. He would no more mix in municipal matters than Lord Westminster would join the Pimlico Paving Board. If he has himself the misfortune to "speak Glasgow," his sons and his daughters shall escape that unmelodious shibboleth, and they come back from their English schools strangers, knowing nothing and caring nothing about Glasgow or Glasgow folk, and rather ashamed of having anything to do with the big smoky town. [...] They read Burns or Scott, if at all, with a glossary. And they have no idea of the difference between a Free Kirker and a U.P. [United Presbyterian], or any other of those puzzling Scotch sects.

The Introduction to the 1878 edition reinforces the conservative message of 1870. The pace of change has not diminished: "Glasgow has seen great changes since this book was published eight years ago. A man who had lived here all his life till then might to-day be set down in many parts of the city without having an idea where he was." While the few remaining buildings of note in the center of the city are probably now preserved from destruction,

> we can feel no such assurance as to any of the ancient buildings of the outskirts. The advancing town tramples down without pity whatever bars its way. Of the hundred old houses whose likeness and story this book perpetuates, ten are already gone: others, with every shrub and tree cut away, stand like victims bared for the axe: and we know not how many more are doomed.

In the body of the second (1878) edition, the editors note the disappearance or degradation of several mansions in the eight years since the publication of the first edition.[59] New ones, they concede, will arise in their stead and some of these may well be grander than those they replace. Still, "with the old houses we shall root out many an old association that clustered round them." The theme of the alienation accompanying the passage from old to new patterns of trade and industry is then developed again with emphasis on the dangerous social and political consequences of this development.

> The old, it must always be remembered, were in the main the near-hand summer lodgings of men whose home was in Glasgow. The modern are in the main the homes, miles away, of men whom summer scatters still further a-field. The difference is immense socially, and therefore politically: for habit and sentiment are stronger forces in politics than law and reason. That unwritten law of deference to rank that underlay our old code rested itself on the old social conditions. Those whom people here used to own as their natural leaders were kent [known] folk, who made no pretence to count them their equals, but who shared their feelings, opinions and prejudices: who spent their lives within hearing of the Tolbooth chimes: who found in Glasgow, kirk and market, the centre of their interests in business and out of business. Every year the notables of our day grow more of strangers in the place that they live by: spend fewer hours in its smoke and din: outside their own little circle are more and more unknown even by face: till it has come to this, that a man may be in the foremost rank on 'Change, may by all who know him be looked up to, and recognized as exceptionally fitted by talent, knowledge and force of character for the highest post in the citizens' gift, and may yet be to the bulk of these so unknown that his candidature is resented as the intrusion of a stranger. The class that used to have the power, those who stand first commercially and socially, are drifting away from their fellow-citizens, and power is ebbing away from them: for the people will not follow leaders whom they do not see and know.

The editors make it clear that they consider this development, which, they emphasize, is taking place not just in Glasgow but in all the major cities of the land, to be socially and politically dangerous.

> Some of us take all this lightly: does not the penny of income tax nowadays yield two millions? why croak? Some would even hail with delight the downfall of whatever opposeth or exalteth itself against the Gospel of Equality: if Aristocracy, burgher or territorial, be dying, let it die and let us dance on its grave!

From the editors' conservative perspective, however, such insouciance reflects a grave misunderstanding:

> The commonwealth stood solid and firm when its courses were bonded by mutual acquaintanceship and consideration, common habits and feeling and sympathies. For this kindly cement there is no substitute. Without it, the ancient and imposing edifice opposes to the shock of revolution nothing but the dead weight of its loose parts.

Thomas Annan's photographs of the old country houses of the old Glasgow gentry thus constituted the visual component of a eulogy of old money as opposed to new, and of the old ruling class of Glasgow—the merchants of the pre-industrial city, who, it is claimed, had been part and parcel of their community—as opposed to enterprising and hustling *nouveaux riches* with little or no attachment to the community in which their fortunes are made. Appropriately, the images in the book convey a sense of order and stability. Annan brought all his technical skill as a photographer of paintings to bear on the still, silent, stone witnesses to a vanished society.

According to the author of several scholarly articles on Annan, the photographer worked in producing these images within the parameters of the Picturesque movement in painting and photography, "showing the subject in such a way as would be esthetically pleasing by virtue of form, line and texture." Specifically, "he selected viewpoints which either revealed the mansion at the apex of the carriage-way which led to the front door or which showed the parkland in which the house was situated. He positioned the camera at a discreet distance from his subject, looking up at it rather than down, an indication of respect."[60] This judgment appears all the more persuasive as Annan himself—as we shall see in the next chapter—once declared his "constant aim" to have been to make his "Photographs like Pictures" (i.e. paintings). The dominant impression made on the viewer by Annan's photographs of country houses seems to me, nevertheless, to be one of sobriety and restraint. Of the "two distinct approaches to photographing architectural subjects" identified by the authors of a recent book on the topic—a traditional commitment to "documentary veracity" and "an impressionistic, romantic tradition [. . .] fascinated by atmosphere over detail" and best represented by the work of the Pictorialist school of Edward Steichen and Alfred Stieglitz—Annan appears to me to adhere still to the first.[61]

In contrast to the albums of *Views on the Line of the Loch Katrine Water Works*, which recorded and quietly celebrated a monumental achievement of modern engineering and the foresight and judgment of a modern municipal council, the albums on the country houses in and around Glasgow and in nearby Ayrshire recorded and quietly celebrated the values of tradition and stability symbolized by the often quite modest but tasteful houses of the old gentry. Annan was evidently willing to place his professional expertise at the service of a variety of groups and interests. He was, after all, in business as a professional photographer. It is not surprising therefore that among the numerous photographs in the Annan collections at the Mitchell Library in Glasgow, there are many of properties that do not figure in the two printed volumes of country houses. Presumably they were commissioned by individual owners.

In general, Annan's skill as a photographer was so appreciated that he was often asked to use his camera to record and memorialize visible elements of the environment that, for one reason or another, were fated to disappear. Since the 1840s there had been a sense that the old College of Glasgow (founded in 1451 and the fourth oldest university in the English-speaking world) would have to relocate. The old buildings on the High Street could no longer accommodate either the growing number of students crowding the classrooms or the growing number of subjects being taught. In addition, the fabric itself was in poor condition, and the old part of the city in which the college was located had become a slum. An official report of 1858 described how

> the localities [. . .] around the College have been filled up by a dense mass of the lowest class of the labouring population, with a considerable admixture of much more unsuitable neighbours, and a large proportion of chemical and other nuisance-creating manufactories of the city. [. . .] The College is, in consequence, surrounded with an atmosphere impregnated with the effluvia arising from the filth occasioned by such a population in a town of which the sewerage is far from being in a satisfactory condition, and with the fumes and vapours of the aforesaid chemical and other manufactories.

No situation, it was asserted, could be "less favourable to the bodily and mental well-being of the youth attending a University or less suitable for conducting the business of a public seminary of instruction."[62] Attempts were made—in 1846 and again in 1853—to arrange for the University to relocate; finally, in 1865, a new site for it was identified and the funds to finance its construction found. Demolition of the old buildings was inevitable, for there was no question of using taxpayer money to preserve these when it was urgently needed to help finance the new buildings. Besides, part of the funds facilitating the move came from the purchase by the City of Glasgow Union Railway Company of the land on which the old College had stood. By 1870, the move to the new site in the city's modern, recently-developed West End had been completed.

It was in this context of imminent demolition that, around 1860-1864, Annan began to photograph the buildings of the old College of Glasgow.

This resulted in an album of thirteen albumen prints, *Photographs of Glasgow College* (1866), which was probably commissioned by the College itself—the University arms with the motto *Via, Veritas, Vita* are cut into the leather binding—and of which one of the rare copies is in Princeton University Library's Graphic Arts Collection, and a little later in the publication by MacLehose of *Memorials of the Old College of Glasgow* (1871). This substantial volume consisted of fifteen mounted albumen prints of exterior and a few interior views of the college, each measuring approximately 9¼ x 7¼ inches, together with 26 similarly mounted, slightly smaller (8 ¼ x 6¼) portraits of the professors who, according to the Preface, "formed the Senate at the time of the removal to the New Buildings"; the work also included extensive textual material on the history of the University and of its various faculties.[63]

Annan's images still constitute an invaluable record of the seventeenth- and eighteenth-century fabric of the old College before demolition. The pictures are taken from interesting angles, emphasizing archways, the relation of the buildings to their surrounding spaces, and architectural details. Figures in some of them enliven the scene while also providing a sense of scale (Figs. 5:7-13).

The professors' portraits, while always respectful and consequently fairly conventional, are executed with attention to good lighting effects and, as noted earlier, do suggest individual character (Figs. 5:14 and 3:3-4).

There is an elegiac quality to both the two country house publications and the album devoted to the old College of Glasgow—an almost inevitable feature of photographs dedicated to familiar sites that are about to disappear or are under threat of demolition and of which the photographer hopes to preserve a permanent image. Both Charles Marville's photographs of Paris streets in the 1860s and—even more strongly—the later Paris street scenes of Eugène Atget exhibit this quality, as does the work of the photographers who gave their services to the Society for Photographing Relics of Old London, founded in 1875 (Figs. 5:15-18).

All were motivated by a desire to record for the ages old, familiar sites and traditional ways of life threatened by new, fast-changing times—by time itself. Annan's photographs of the old country houses and the old College have a matter-of-factness, however, an objectivity that precludes sentimentality. Most of the "old country houses," moreover, were not *very* old; they dated from the end of the eighteenth century or the early years of the nineteenth, the heyday of the city's merchant class, which, while lamenting its displacement by brash new industrialists, saw itself as community-minded and committed to civic improvement. Annan himself, as the Loch Katrine album demonstrates, was by no means averse to the new. Of the twelve *Photographs of Glasgow*, in the album put out by Duthie in 1868, six depict the old city and an equal number the new Glasgow, with its regularly laid out streets and squares, that was arising as the center of the city moved westwards from its crumbling former location: the rebuilt, Telford-designed Glasgow Bridge and the harbor; George Square, the site of impressive monuments to modern heroes (James Watt, Sir Walter Scott, Sir John Moore, Robert Peel, Carlo Marochetti's equestrian Queen Victoria and Prince Albert); the Royal Exchange, with its equestrian statue of Wellington, also by Marochetti; Buchanan Street, once "fields," then "villas and gardens," according to the author of the texts accompanying the photographs, and "now, distinguished by its fine shops and warehouses, [. . .] the most fashionable promenade in the city," with "600 omnibuses passing the foot [of it] daily"; the elegant Park Circus on the edge of West End Park (or Kelvingrove Park, as it was also called), which had been created in 1852 from plans by Sir Joseph Paxton, the designer of the pioneering cast-iron and plate-glass Crystal Palace at the 1851 Great Exhibition; a model of the new University under construction on the land of the demolished Gilmorehill House (built in 1802 by one of the city's West Indies merchants and photographed by Annan as it was being demolished) (Figs. 5:19-25).[64]

The verses adorning the title page of the 1868 album convey the Glasgow merchant class's sense of itself as not only a guardian of threatened traditions but a force for progress and justice in the years of Thomas Annan's activity as a photographer:

> For Christian merchants we make our plea,
> The pulse of the business world are we;
> With tenants and servants at our command,
> And spending ever with liberal hand.
> Yet e'en by us how much has been won
> For the cause of right. See what we have done!
> And say, in view of facts like these,
> Do we only live to take our ease?

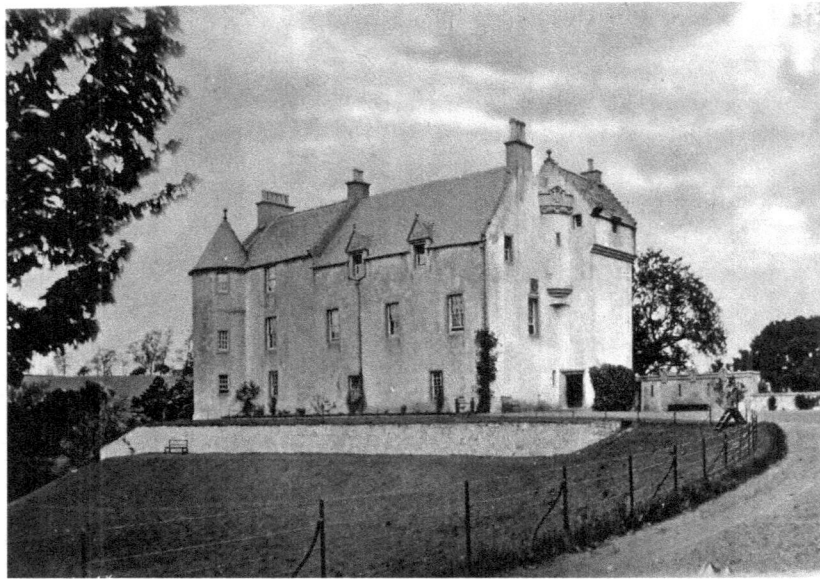

5:1 Thomas Annan, "Bedlay," from *The Old Country Houses of the Old Glasgow Gentry*, 2nd enlarged edition (Glasgow: James MacLehose, 1878). Carbon print. (The photographs in the first edition of 1870 are albumen prints.) Graphic Arts Collection, Department of Rare Books and Special Collections, Princeton University Library.

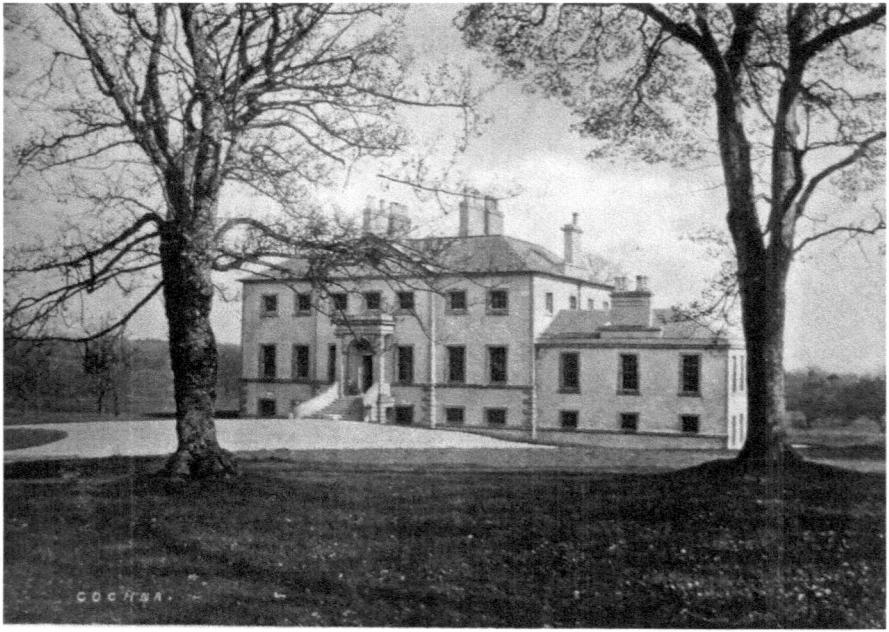

5:2 Thomas Annan, "Cochna," from *The Old Country Houses*. Carbon print. Graphic Arts Collection, Department of Rare Books and Special Collections, Princeton University Library.

The Built Environment   77

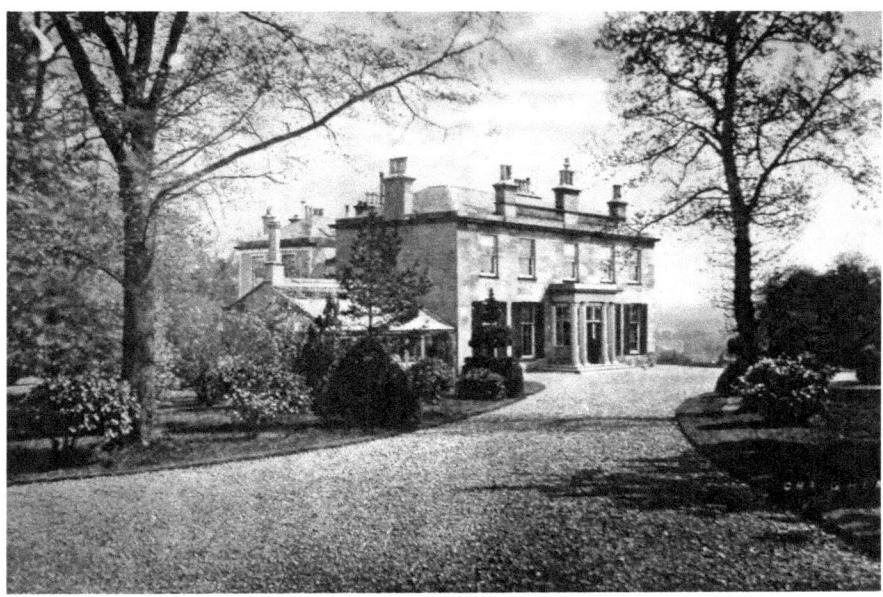

5:3 Thomas Annan, "Craighead," from *The Old Country Houses*. Carbon print. Graphic Arts Collection, Department of Rare Books and Special Collections, Princeton University Library.

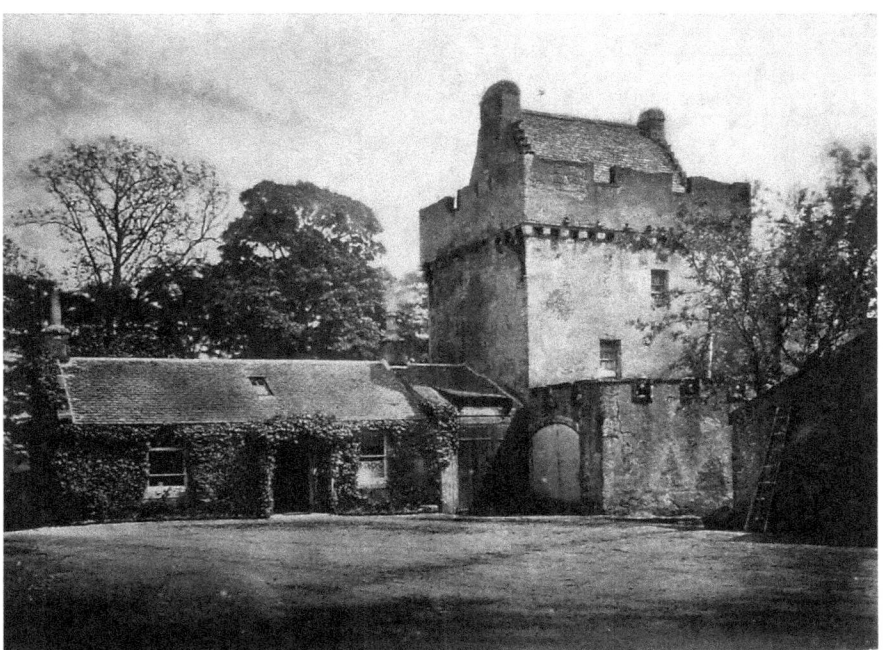

5:4 Thomas Annan, "Hunterston Castle, West Kilbride," from *Castles and Mansions of Ayrshire, illustrated in seventy views* (Edinburgh: W. Paterson, 1885). Albumen print. Graphic Arts Collection, Department of Rare Books and Special Collections, Princeton University Library.

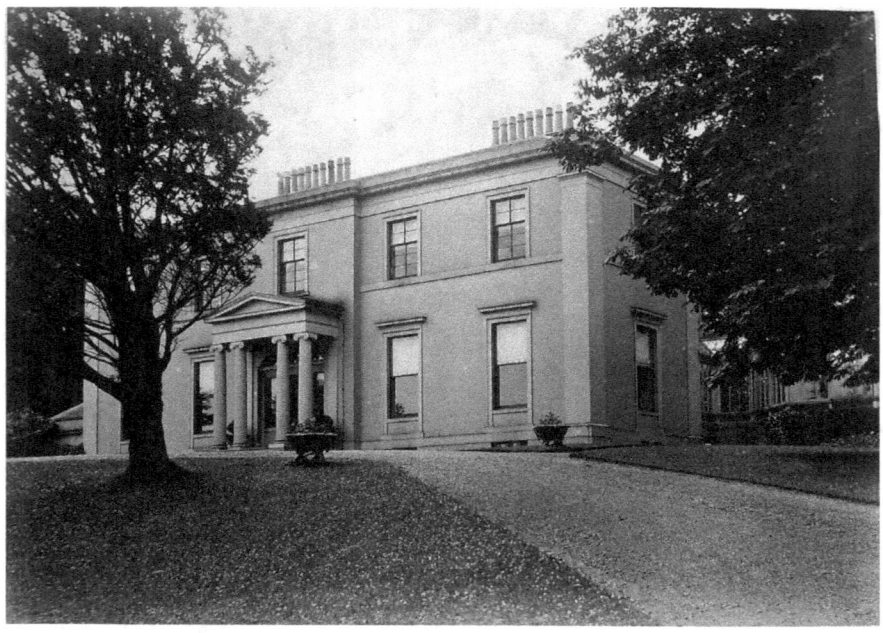

5:5 Thomas Annan, "Mount Charles," from *Castles and Mansions*. Albumen print. Graphic Arts Collection, Department of Rare Books and Special Collections, Princeton University Library.

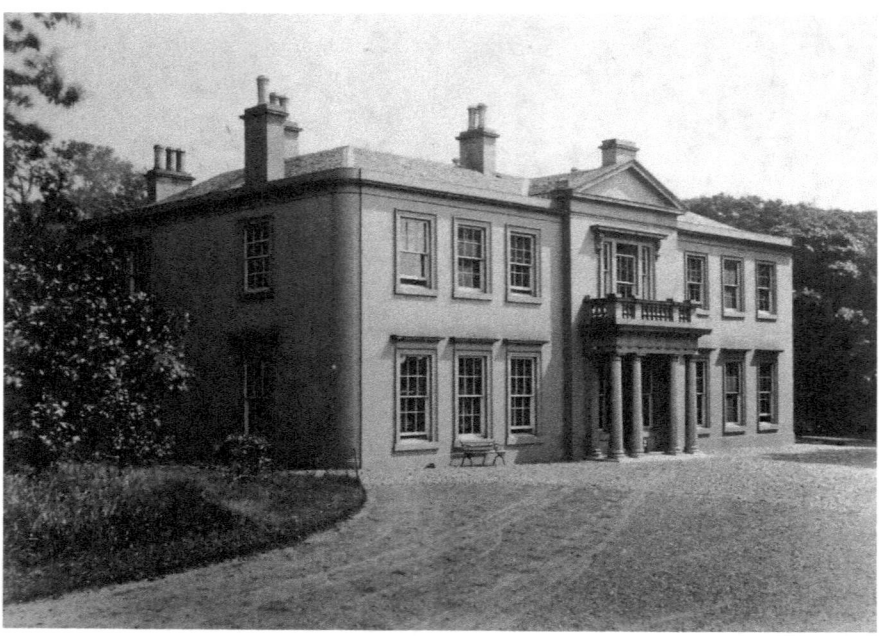

5:6 Thomas Annan, "Ardeer," from *Castles and Mansions*. Albumen print. Graphic Arts Collection, Department of Rare Books and Special Collections, Princeton University Library.

The Built Environment 79

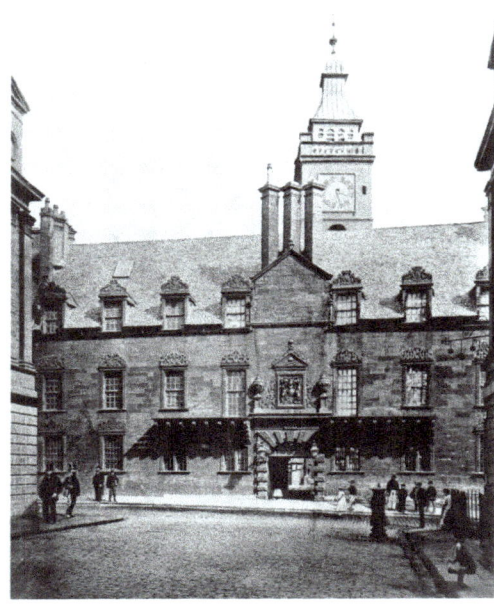

5:7 Thomas Annan, "The College from College Street," from the album *Photographs of Glasgow College* (Glasgow: T. Annan, [1866?]). Albumen print. Graphic Arts Collection, Department of Rare Books and Special Collections, Princeton University Library.

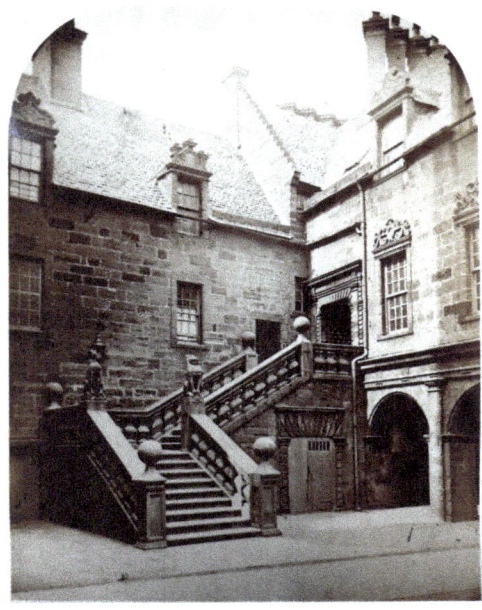

5:8 Thomas Annan, "The Outer Court with the great stair leading to the Fore-Hall," from *Photographs of Glasgow College*. Albumen print. Graphic Arts Collection, Department of Rare Books and Special Collections, Princeton University Library.

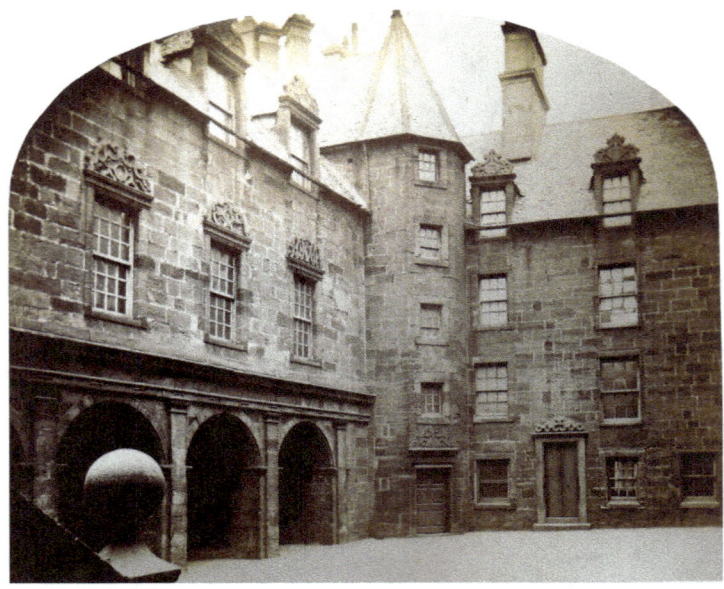

5:9 Thomas Annan, "The Outer Court from the top of the Fore-Hall stair," another view, from *Photographs of Glasgow College*. Albumen print. Graphic Arts Collection, Department of Rare Books and Special Collections, Princeton University Library.

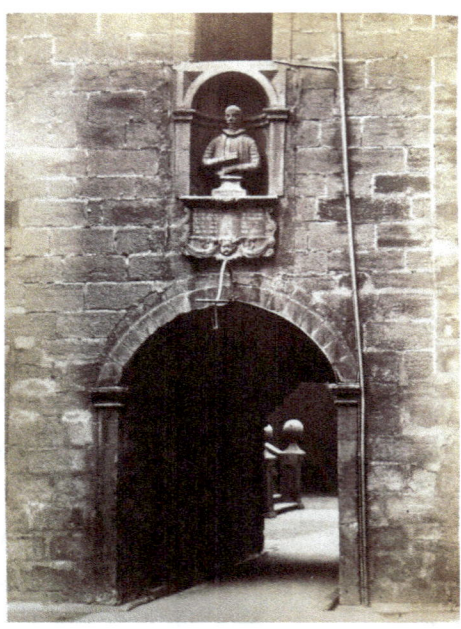

5:10 Thomas Annan, "Archway in Inner Court looking towards the Outer Court with Zachary Boyd's bust," from *Photographs of Glasgow College*. Albumen print. Graphic Arts Collection, Department of Rare Books and Special Collections, Princeton University Library.

The Built Environment 81

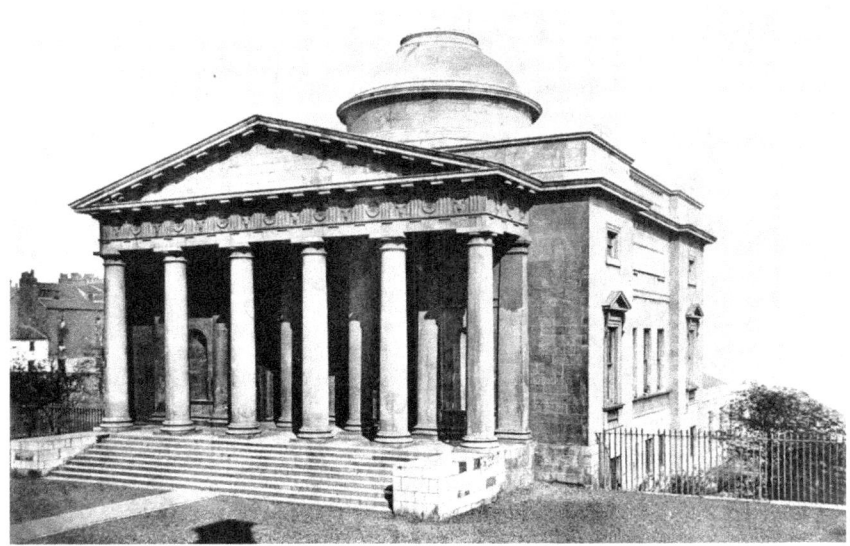

5:11 Thomas Annan, "Hunterian Museum," from *Memorials of the Old College of Glasgow* (Glasgow: Thomas Annan; James MacLehose, 1871), reproduced in *University of Glasgow Old and New, illustrated with views and portraits in photogravure* (Glasgow: T.&R. Annan & Sons; James MacLehose, 1891), Plate 16. Division of Rare Books, Marquand Library, Princeton University.

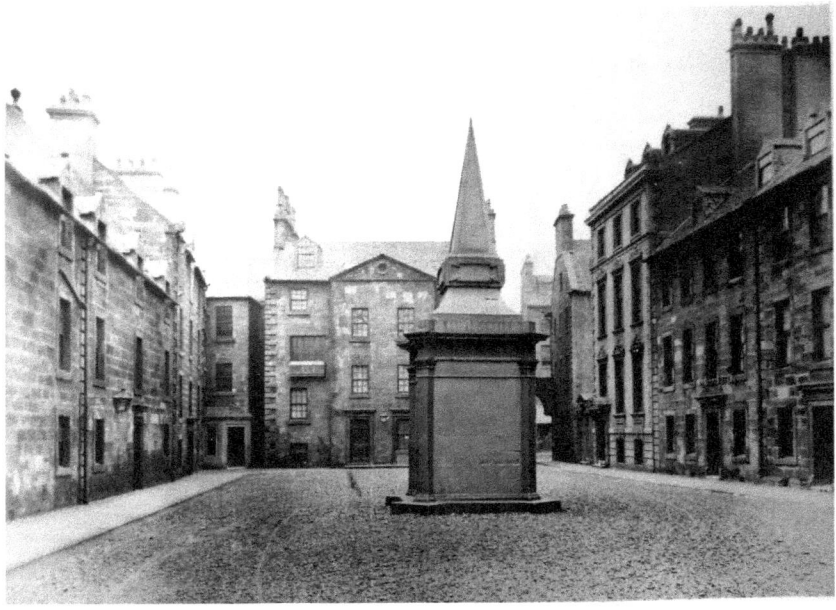

5:12 Thomas Annan. "The Professors' Court," from *Photographs of Glasgow College*. Albumen print. Graphic Arts Collection, Department of Rare Books and Special Collections, Princeton University Library.

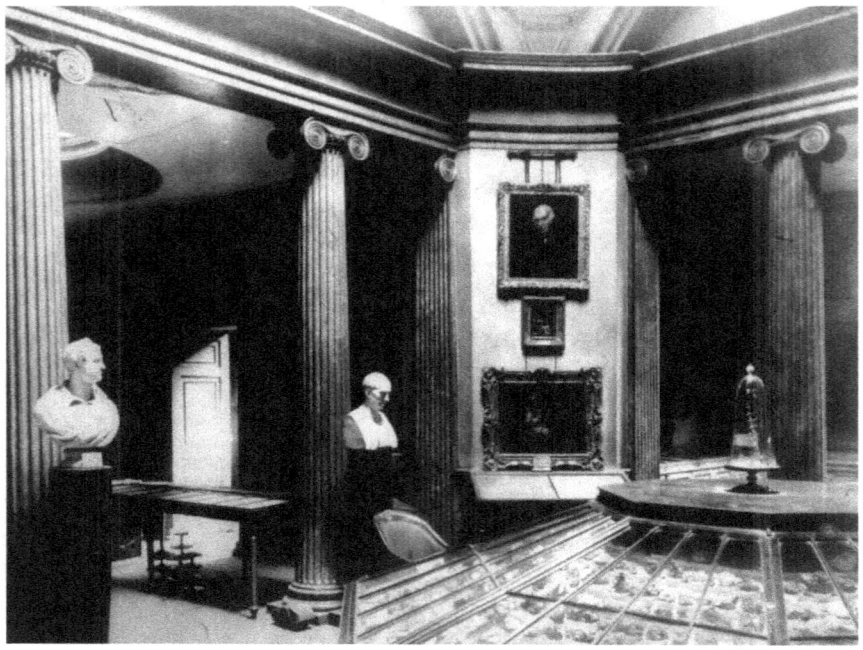

5:13 Thomas Annan, "Interior of Hunterian Museum," from *Memorials of the Old College of Glasgow*, reproduced in *University of Glasgow Old and New*, Plate 17. Division of Rare Books, Marquand Library, Princeton University.

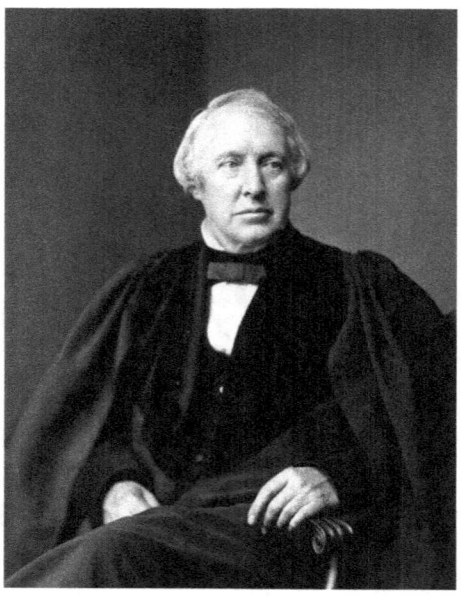

5:14 Thomas Annan, Portrait of Professor Allan Thomson, Professor of Anatomy at Glasgow from 1848 to 1877, from *Memorials of the Old College of Glasgow*. Albumen print. Courtesy of University of Glasgow Library, Department of Special Collections.

The Built Environment 83

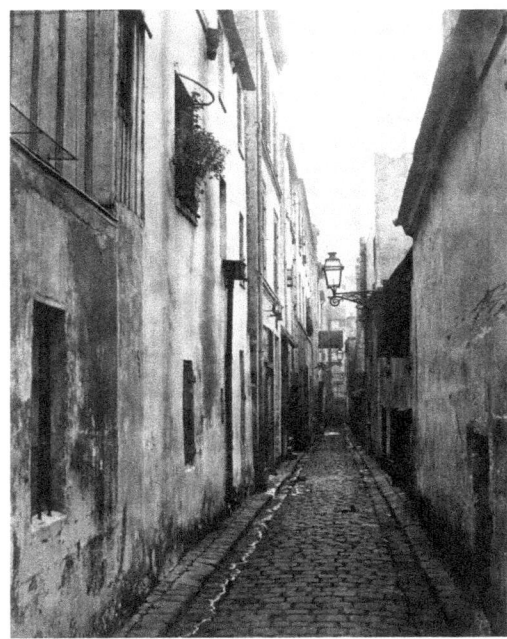

5:15 Charles Marville, "Impasse Briare." 1868. Albumen print. Wikimedia.

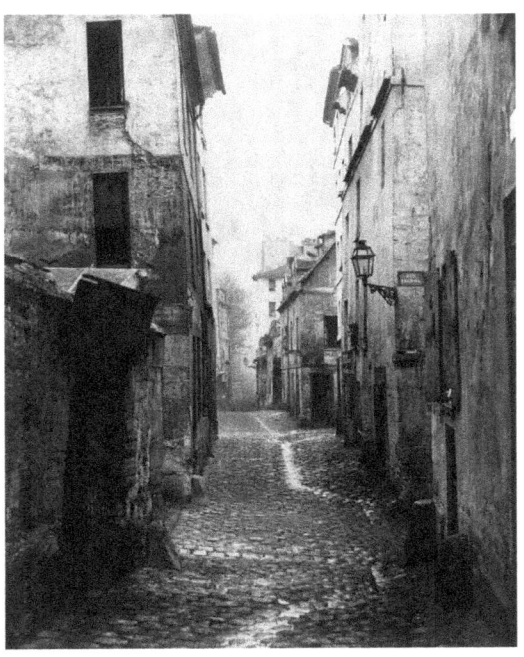

5:16 Charles Marville, "Rue Traversine (from the rue d'Arras)." Ca.1868. Albumen print. Metropolitan Museum, Gift of Howard Stein, 2010. Accession Number 2010.513.2. ©Metropolitan Museum.

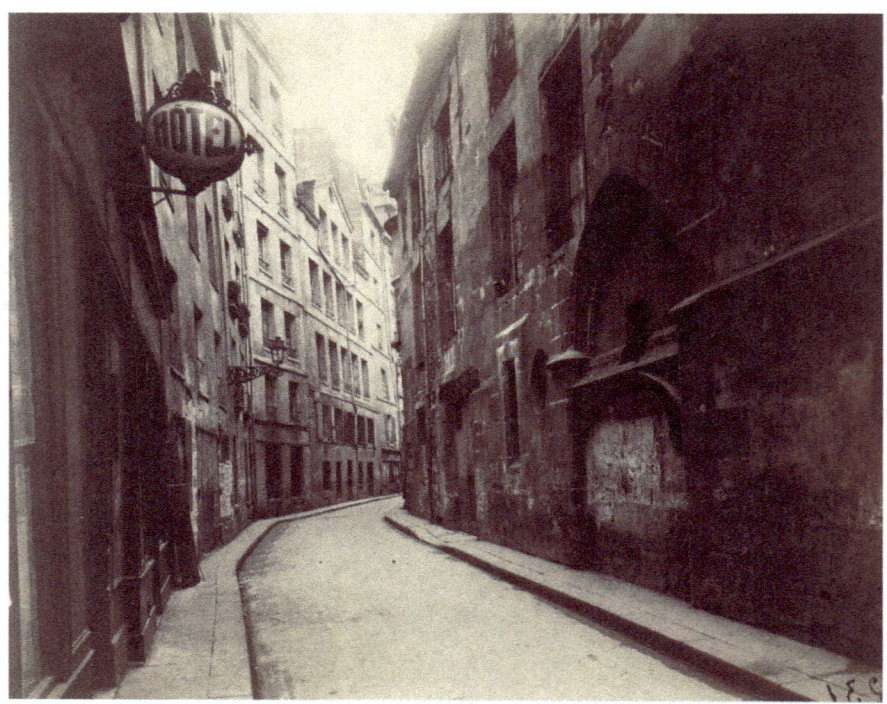

5:17 Eugène Atget, "Hôtel de Sens, rue de l'Hôtel de Ville." Early 1900s. Albumen print. Metropolitan Museum. The Rubel Collection, Gift of William Rubel, 1997. Accession Number 1997.398.2. ©Metropolitan Museum.

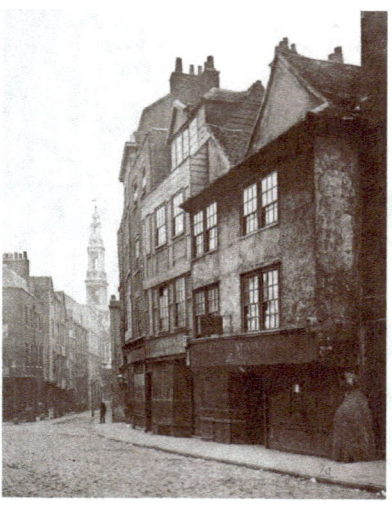

5:18 Henry Dixon, "Old Houses in Drury Lane." 1880. Albumen print. British Library, London.

The Built Environment 85

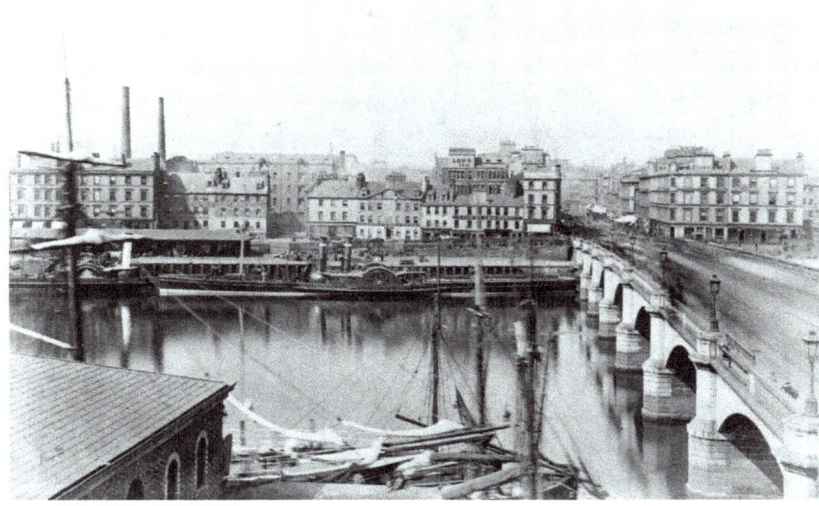

5:19 Thomas Annan, "Glasgow Bridge and Harbour," from *Photographs of Glasgow*, with descriptive letterpress by Rev. A.G. Forbes (Glasgow: Andrew Duthie, [1868]), Plate III. Albumen print. Courtesy of Fine Arts Library, Harvard University.

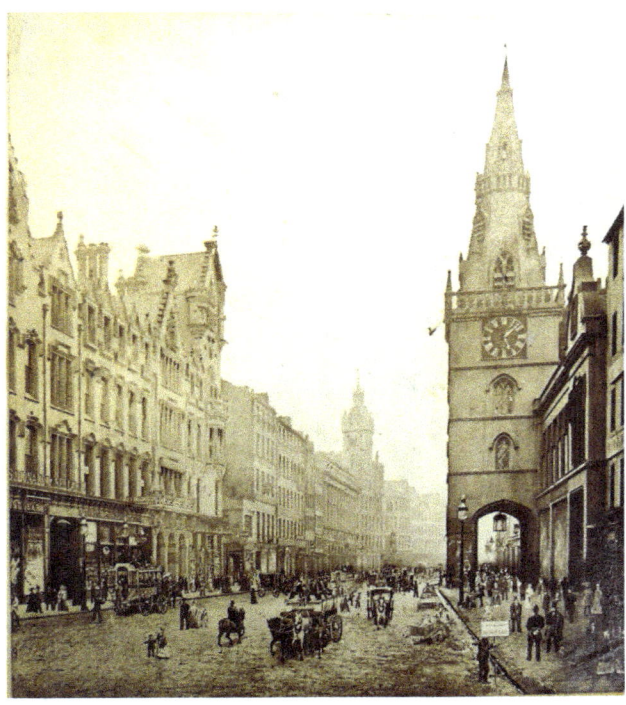

5:20 Thomas Annan, "Trongate and Cross," from *Photographs of Glasgow*, Plate IX. Albumen print. Courtesy of Fine Arts Library, Harvard University.

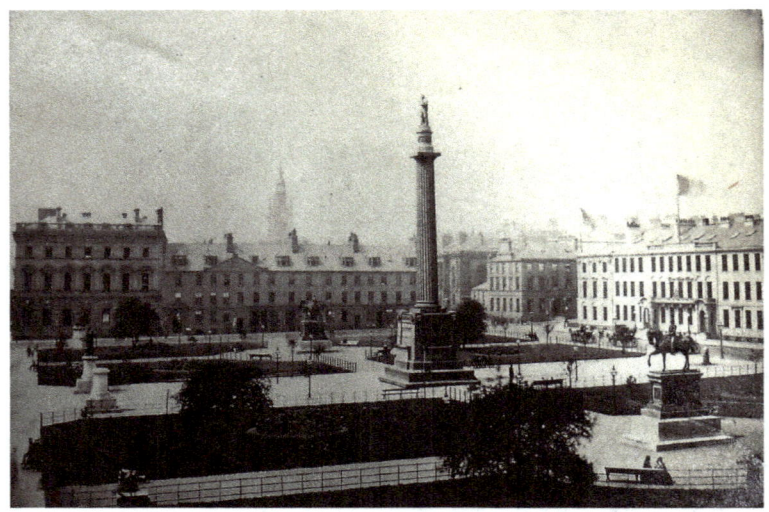

5:21 Thomas Annan, "George Square," from *Photographs of Glasgow*, Plate II. Albumen print. Courtesy of Fine Arts Library, Harvard University.

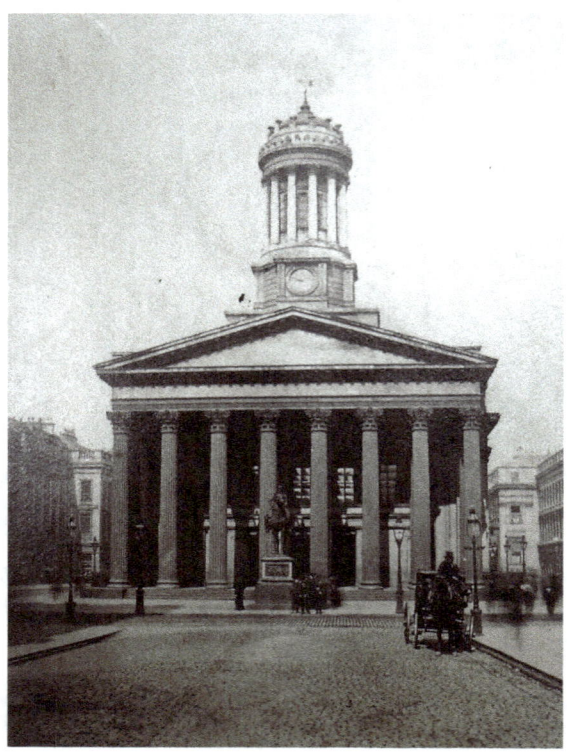

5:22 Thomas Annan, "Royal Exchange," from *Photographs of Glasgow*, Plate XIII. Albumen print. Courtesy of Fine Arts Library, Harvard University.

The Built Environment   87

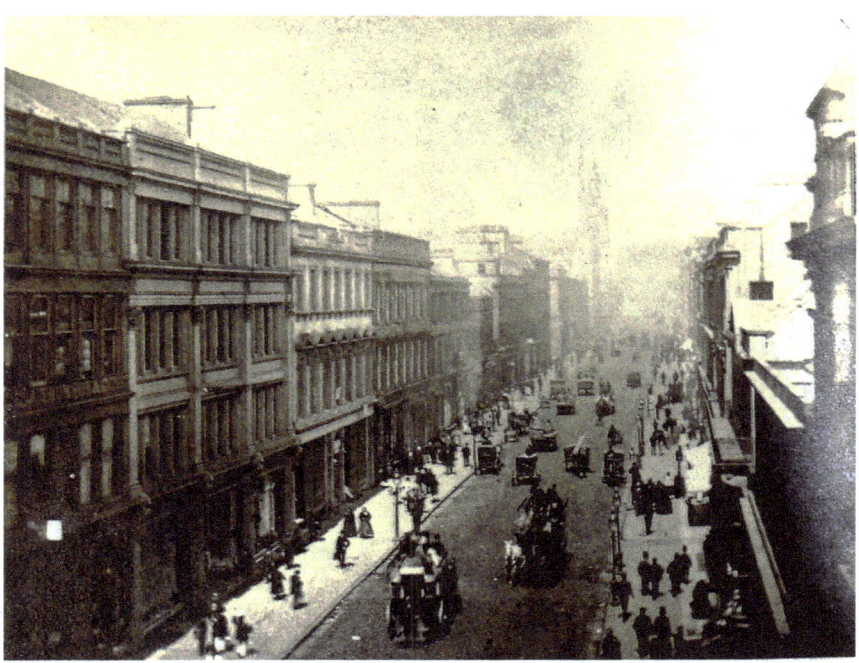

5:23 Thomas Annan, "Buchanan Street," from *Photographs of Glasgow*, Plate XII. Albumen print. Courtesy of Fine Arts Library, Harvard University.

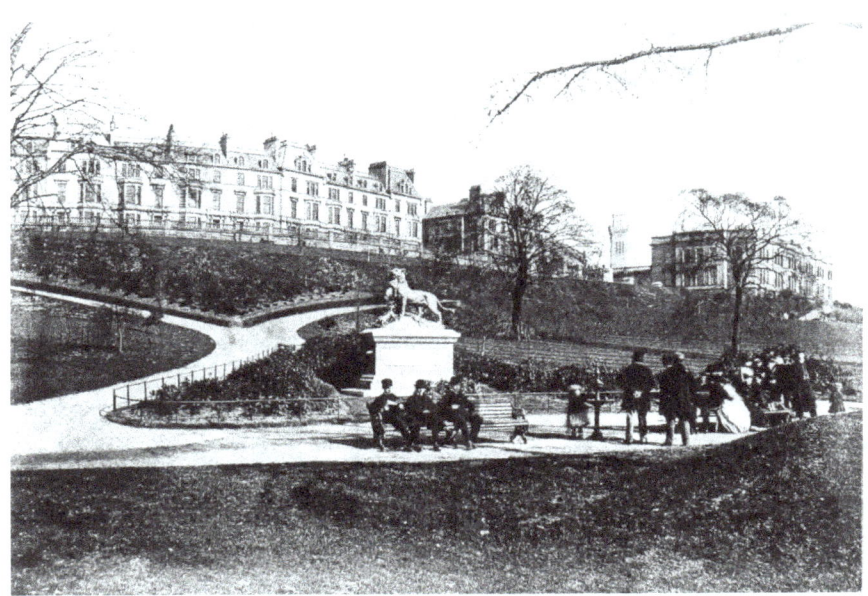

5:24 Thomas Annan, "West End Park," from *Photographs of Glasgow*, Plate X. Albumen print. Courtesy of Fine Arts Library, Harvard University.

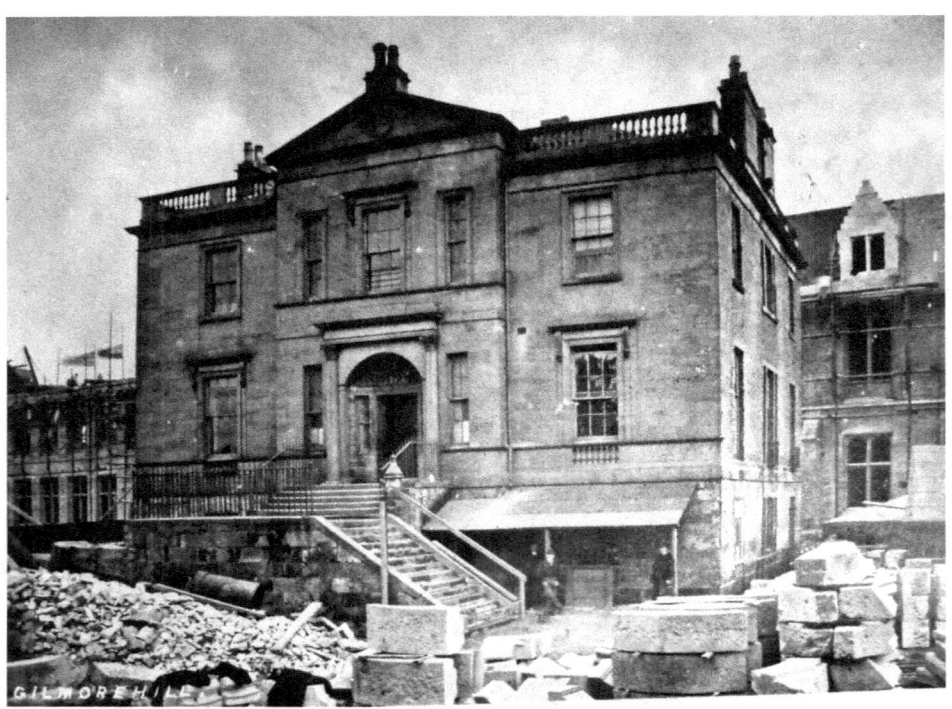

5:25 Thomas Annan, "Gilmorehill," from *The Old Country Houses of the Old Glasgow Gentry*, 2nd enlarged edition (Glasgow: James MacLehose, 1878). Carbon print. Graphic Arts Collection, Department of Rare Books and Special Collections, Princeton University Library.

6. *The Old Closes and Streets of Glasgow*

The best-known, most widely-admired, and most problematical of Annan's architectural photographs make up the collection known as *The Old Closes and Streets of Glasgow*. These photographs were commissioned by the City of Glasgow Improvement Trust, an agency set up to oversee the demolition, authorized by Act of Parliament in 1866, of a section of the old center of the city—in effect, a not insubstantial part of what Glasgow had been in Adam Smith's day. An informed understanding of this work of Annan's, which is still subject to divergent interpretations, requires some consideration of the conditions that obtained at the time of its commissioning.

Thanks to expanding trade with the New World and the rapid development of cotton spinning and tobacco processing in the eighteenth century, and of iron foundries, shipbuilding, locomotive building, and the chemical and machine industries in the nineteenth,[65] the population of Glasgow had grown from 12,000 at the time of the Treaty of Union with England in 1707, when Daniel Defoe described it as "one of the cleanest, most beautiful, and best built cities in Great Britain," to 100,000 in 1811 and 300,000 by the mid-1840s, when Engels wrote his *Condition of the Working Class in England in 1844* (Fig. 6:1).

By the end of the nineteenth century, the population had more than doubled to 761,000 and in 1912 it topped the million mark, making it one of the four or five most populous cities in Europe. "Between 1870 and 1914," in the words of the novelist and journalist Allan Massie, "Glasgow reached its apogee. Whatever its social problems, it was one of the richest and most splendid of European cities."[66]

Massive immigration from the Scottish countryside and especially from Ireland was both a condition and a consequence of the city's rapid industrialization and expansion.[67] The result, however, was the transformation of much of the old town—as the better-off residents and then the municipal buildings moved west—into a hugely overcrowded, fetid, dangerous and disease-ridden slum. Exploiting the desperate needs of impoverished immigrants, landlords turned the old multi-story townhouses (as Engels noted, "the houses in Scottish towns are generally four, five or six stories high")[68] into warrens of small, usually one-room apartments and, to make matters even worse, crammed additional jerry-built tenements into the former yards or gardens between them.

There are many harrowing contemporary descriptions of conditions in the slums of Glasgow in the mid-1800s. It is worth quoting from a few of them in order to convey an idea of the problem that prompted the city fathers to seek the authority to purchase and demolish entire streets of the old city.

In a *Report on the Sanitary Condition of the Labouring Population of Gt. Britain* that he presented to the House of Lords in 1842, Edwin Chadwick, Secretary to the Poor Law Commission, wrote that "it appeared to us [himself and his colleague, Dr. Neil Arnott, a Scottish-born and trained surgeon] that both the structural arrangements and the condition of the population in Glasgow was the worst of any we had seen in any part of Great Britain."[69] For his part, Engels quoted from a report in the new monthly periodical *The Artizan* (October 1843) in his *Condition of the Working Class in England in 1844*, published in the original German in 1845:

> The population in 1840 was estimated at 282,000, of whom about 78 percent belong to the working classes, 50,000 being Irish. Glasgow has its fine, airy, healthy quarters, that may vie with those of London and all wealthy cities; but it has others which, in abject wretchedness, exceed the lowest purlieus of St. Giles' or Whitechapel [. . .]—endless labyrinths of narrow lanes or wynds, into which almost at every step debouche courts or closes formed by old, ill-ventilated, towering houses crumbling to decay, destitute of water and crowded with inhabitants, comprising three or four families (perhaps twenty persons) on each flat, and sometimes each flat let out in lodgings that confine—we dare not say accommodate—from fifteen to twenty persons in a single room. These districts [. . .] may be considered as the fruitful source of those pestilential fevers which thence spread their destructive ravages over the whole of Glasgow.[70]

Finally, here is Jelinger Symons, an Assistant Commissioner on an official enquiry into the condition of handloom weavers in 1838:

> I have seen human degradation in some of its worst phases, both in England and abroad, but I can advisedly say that I did not believe until I visited the wynds of Glasgow, that so large an amount of filth, crime, misery, and disease

existed on one spot in any civilized country. [. . .] In the lower lodging-houses ten, twelve and sometimes twenty persons of both sexes and all ages sleep promiscuously on the floor in different degrees of nakedness. These places are, generally as regards dirt, damp and decay, such as no person of common humanity to animals would stable his horse in.[71]

By 1856, when Nathaniel Hawthorne, then U.S. Consul in Liverpool, visited the city, he commented on the "wide and regular" streets, the statuary in George Square and the "handsome houses and public edifices of a dark grey stone" in the newer sections, while on a second visit the following year he declared himself "inclined to think the newer portion of Glasgow [. . .] the stateliest of cities. The Exchange and other public buildings, and the shops in Buchanan Street are very magnificent; the latter especially excelling those of London." But when he went into the old city to view the University, he was appalled. It was "in a dense part of the town, and a very old and shabby part, too," he noted in his diary for May 10th, 1856. "I think the poorer classes of Glasgow excel even those in Liverpool in the bad eminence of filth, uncombed and unwashed children, drunkenness, disorderly deportment, evil smell, and all that makes city poverty disgusting." On his second visit, his impression had not changed: "The Trongate and the Salt-Market [. . .] were formerly the principal business streets, and, together with High Street, the abode of the rich merchants and other great people of the town. High Street, and, still more, the Salt-Market now swarm with the lower orders to a degree which I have never witnessed elsewhere; so that it is difficult to make one's way among the sullen and unclean crowd, and not at all pleasant to breathe in the noisomeness of the atmosphere. The children seem to have been unwashed from birth."[72]

Inevitably, disease was rampant, epidemics frequent, and crime endemic. There were outbreaks of typhus in 1818, 1832, 1837, 1847, and 1851-52; cholera epidemics in 1832, 1848-49, and 1853-54, the last two claiming almost 8,000 lives.[73] Though some of the better-off citizens were doubtless troubled in their Christian conscience by the inhuman conditions many of their fellow-creatures were living in, few ventured into the noisome and dangerous parts of their city.[74] However, a detailed account of these as a scene of hunger, drunkenness, promiscuity, prostitution, violence and crime was readily available to all in a widely-read book put out by a Glasgow publisher in 1858, just a couple of years after Annan opened his photographic business in the city. *Midnight Scenes and Social Photographs, Being Sketches of Life in the Streets, Wynds and Dens of the City* (Fig. 6:2) was divided into seven sections, each one describing a night in the slums, from Sunday, supposedly the Lord's day, until the following Saturday. The author apologized in his Preface for the gruesome picture his book presented of "the condition of the poor, and the classes generally inhabiting the lower depths of society," but insisted on its honest and unembellished realism. Though "the 'Photographs' present a tone painfully dark and gloomy [. . .], they are not creations of the brain, but so far as the writer's knowledge of the art extends—they are truthful [. . .]; as they occurred, so have they been given."[75]

The book's claim to realism was underscored not only by the use of the common Glasgow dialect among the characters encountered or interviewed by the narrator but, above all, by the photographic metaphor in the title, photographs being still widely considered impartial and objective copies of reality made with no input from the photographer other than his technical skill. The metaphorical function of the term "social photographs" is highlighted by the fact that there are no photographs in the book, its only illustration being a frontispiece engraving by the great caricaturist George Cruikshank which depicts a photographer taking pictures of scenes and situations described in the text (Fig. 6:3).

Local readers might also have come across some lines by the popular Kilmarnock-born and Glasgow-raised poet Alexander Smith (1829-1867), who had spent twelve years working long hours in a Glasgow factory and who in "A Boy's Poem," published in 1857, described living conditions in the city's slums in terms strikingly similar to those of *Midnight Scenes*:

>We crept into a half-forgotten street
>Of frail and tumbling houses propt by beams,
>And ruined courts which, centuries before,
>Rung oft to iron heels,—which palfreys pawed,
>As down the mighty steps the Lady came
>Bright as the summer morning,—peopled now
>By outcasts, sullen men, bold girls who sat
>Pounding sand in the sun. The day we came
>The windows from which beauty leant and smiled
>Were stuffed with rags, or held a withered stick
>Whence foul clothes hung to dry. Beneath an arch
>Two long-haired women fought; while high above,
>Heads thrust through broken panes, two shrill-voiced crones
>Scolded each other. Hell-fire burst at night
>Through the thin rind of the earth; the place was loud
>With drunken strife, hoarse curses; then the cry
>Of a lost woman by a ruffian felled
>Made the blood stop [. . .][76]

Alarmed by the threat to all the city's inhabitants—the well-to-do as well as the poor—from the filth, crime and disease at its very heart, the generally progressive city fathers moved to remedy the situation. The Loch Katrine Water Works project described earlier was a significant part of their improvement plan. Then, in 1862, the Glasgow Police Act allowed the municipality to regulate small dwelling places (under 3,000 cubic feet), assess the maximum number of inhabitants permitted in each (on the basis of 300 cubic feet per adult and 150 cubic feet per child), "ticket" the dwelling accordingly with a tinplate disc screwed to the door and have the sanitary police carry out inspections during the night to ensure that the "ticketed" maximum had not been overstepped.[77] Apparently this measure was not effective, for it was decided only three years later to proceed to a complete demolition of the dilapidated, overcrowded and filthy tenements as the only effective remedy.

In 1865, Provost John Blackie (a partner with his father in the notable Glasgow publishing firm of Blackie & Son) and the progressive City Architect John Carrick drew up the City of Glasgow Improvements Bill, the purpose of which was to authorize the Town Council to buy up and tear down properties in a designated area. The Bill was passed by Parliament the following year, making Glasgow "the first municipality to take such action on a large scale." "Indeed," one scholar writes, "the improvements scheme, embarked on under the City of Glasgow Improvements Act of 1866, was by far the largest and most comprehensive single undertaking of this kind in the nineteenth century."[78] As the area affected was also the oldest part of the city, the members of the City Improvement Trust resolved that, before demolition, photographs should be taken of the streets and their buildings to serve as a record of Old Glasgow. Thomas Annan was commissioned to carry out this assignment.

He began taking his photographs in 1868. When demolition began in 1871, he had taken over thirty. Despite the seemingly straightforward object of the commission, however—to create a record—these best-known of all Annan's photographic images have since been the topic of lively and continuing discussion and debate. Perhaps the first comprehensive collection of photographs ever made of slum properties, are they an early example of the so-called "social documentary" photograph—"the first major achievement of socially critical photography," in the words of a modern German scholar?[79] Did they appeal to the viewer's moral conscience in order to bring about an improvement in the slum-dwellers' lot? Or should they be viewed rather in the context of the esthetic of the "picturesque"—a mid-nineteenth-century anticipation, according to many scholars, of the Pictorialism advocated by

Alfred Stieglitz and Edward Steichen at the end of the century and in the early decades of the twentieth? Do they or do they not depict the extreme filth and squalor emphasized, as we have seen, by all those who wrote about Glasgow's slums, and if not, what to make of that fact? Was the photographer, in sum, moved primarily by esthetic considerations—composing a formally interesting photograph—rather than by purely documentary, let alone moral considerations? What, in particular, is the role of the human figures in many of the images? Are they a focus of interest in themselves or are they simply staffage, providing a sense of scale as in landscape paintings and photographs? Do they convey the alleged degradation and dehumanization of the slum's inhabitants or could they be intended, in contrast, to manifest the inhabitants' humanity? Critical opinion is divided or ambivalent on all those questions. In those cases where the inhabitants of the slums are distinctly portrayed—sometimes in groups—and must therefore, in view of the required long exposure times, have agreed to pose, how did Annan win their cooperation? Why are some of the scenes of notoriously teeming and horrifically overcrowded buildings shown as pure street architecture, devoid of any human presence? And how was this clearing of the streets accomplished? Was it by persuasion or with help from the city authorities (i.e. the police)? What, in short, was Annan's relation to the inhabitants of the old closes and streets? Did he view them simply as material for his camera or as forlorn objects of compassion and Christian charity? Or did he regard them, interact with them, and portray them as fellow human beings?

The problem of interpreting the photographs is compounded by two factors. First, Annan's own taciturnity. In the volumes on the country houses, the old College of Glasgow, and the Loch Katrine Water Works, the texts, as noted earlier, are by others. The photographs in the first two albums of *The Old Closes and Streets* (1871 and 1878) are unaccompanied by any text at all, other than simple identifying captions. The 1878 album was to have contained "an introductory and descriptive letterpress," but, in the event, it was put together without the planned text, which, in any case, would again not have been by Annan himself, but by the City Architect, John Carrick, an influential and energetic figure with strong ideas of his own. A volume published posthumously in a limited edition by Annan's son, James Craig Annan, did contain an introductory text by the local antiquarian and artist William Young, but it dealt mostly with the history of Glasgow and its various quarters and streets and had nothing to say about the photographs themselves, other than that their value "consists in their true presentation or suggestion of the seamy side of the city's life; in their depicting with absolute faithfulness the gloom and squalor of the slums" and thus affording "a peek into dark and dismal dens unvisited by the great purifying agencies of sun and wind."[80] Whereas Jacob Riis's photographs—published in the last decade of the nineteenth century in his book *How the Other Half Lives* and sometimes held to have been anticipated by those of Annan (Figs. 6:4-5)—are used to illustrate an extensive text in which the photographer-journalist himself exposes and denounces the squalid, inhuman conditions of life in the slums of New York, Annan offers no clue as to his own intentions or his own understanding of his work. Unlike those photographers who use text or extended captions to "'fix' the image, refusing it the right to vacillate between past and present, ideal and real," in the words of a scholar of our own time, Annan's silence, whether deliberate or fortuitous, places the burden of interpretation entirely on the viewer.[81]

A second difficulty in interpreting Annan's photographs in *The Old Closes and Streets* is presented by the different techniques which, over the years, were employed to produce them and the different publics for which they were produced. Though at least some of the prints were probably first issued singly (Glasgow's Mitchell Library has several in this form, a few with pasted-on title slips), a first folio album, bound in leather, was put together in 1871. This album, of which only four or five copies were produced and which has neither title page nor date, contained 31 albumen prints.[82] It was followed soon after, in 1878, by a second album, produced in response to a request from some members of the Improvement Trust that "a copy, in the form of an album, of the series of photographs taken some time ago of the more interesting portions of the City, since, to a great extent, demolished by the operations of the Improvement Scheme, should be furnished to each member of the Trust." This album, of which some sixty copies were produced in heavy crushed green morocco binding, included nine additional photographs. Instead of the albumen prints of the first album, however, Annan made use, for this second album, of Joseph Swan's carbon process.[83] Finally, in 1900, Annan's son, James Craig Annan, brought out a larger photogravure edition, referred to above (p. 7), with additional photographs by the Annan firm—but not by Thomas Annan himself. This was published by the T. & R. Annan Company in a limited edition of 100 copies and by James MacLehose, the University publisher, in an edition of 150 copies.[84]

Each of these print processes—albumen, carbon, photogravure—has its own particular characteristics.[85] To what degree do the changes resulting from the different processes both reflect and create varying expectations and responses on the part of viewers? Thus, for example, the "phantoms" or "blurred ghosts" caused by persons or objects having moved during the relatively long exposure time—and regarded by some viewers as contributing to the overall effect of the earlier albumen prints[86]—are removed from the photogravure edition of 1900. Thomas Annan himself added clouds to the carbon prints, which in general are more clearly outlined than the albumen prints and, correspondingly, lack some of the tonal qualities of the latter. The order and even the selection of the plates also vary from one edition to another. Does that have an effect on the viewer's reading of the series? How does history itself—the completely changed contexts in which the images have been encountered by members of the Improvement Trust in the 1870s, by readers of James Craig Annan's publication of 1900, by readers of the 1977 Dover Publications re-edition of the photogravure version and by twenty-first-century viewers of any of these—affect the way in which the images are experienced? The diminished, post-industrial, finance-, culture-, and tourism-oriented Glasgow of the twenty-first century, with its trendy bars and restaurants and lively pop music scene, is a very different place from the nineteenth-century "Second City of the Empire." As Ian Spring has pointed out,

> Today, in Glasgow shops you can purchase Annan's photograph of No. 65 High Street in postcard form.[. . .] The reverse gives some details under the heading "Art Cards." One generation's misery incarnate becomes another's consumable style. Today, shop windows are stocked with Annan prints framed for domestic consumption and countless city centre pubs and restaurants mount Glasgow's old streets and closes on their walls.[87]

I shall devote the remainder of this chapter to a closer consideration of two issues raised by the scholarly discussion of *The Old Closes and Streets*. First, should these striking photographs be seen as predominantly "documentary" or as predominantly "picturesque"? And second, is social documentary photography, as has sometimes been alleged, ultimately voyeuristic and exploitative, an act of aggression toward its "subjects"?

First then, "social documentary" or "picturesque"? Several critics have pointed out that the decision to demolish had already been taken before Annan moved in with his camera, and that his assignment was simply to record a significant piece of the city's past that was about to be destroyed.[88] Contrary to what is often argued or simply assumed,[89] it is thus unlikely, these critics hold, that he "used his camera as a social weapon," photographing the old closes and streets of Glasgow in order to draw attention to urban blight and promote action to correct it. In this respect, therefore, his work should probably not be seen as expressing the same concerns that animated Jacob Riis in his celebrated *How the Other Half Lives* (1890).[90] It is often pointed out that, unlike Riis, Annan did not photograph the interior of the slum dwellings and thus did not show the actual living conditions of the poor. The text accompanying Annan's 1868 album of *Photographs of Glasgow* would also seem to lend support to the view that the photographer's main objective in *The Old Closes and Streets* was not to expose and denounce a social evil but to make a record of what was about to vanish from view. "The High Street is the back-bone of the ancient city of St. Mungo," the author of the text, the liberally-minded Rev. A.G. Forbes, wrote. "But the old look is fast disappearing even here." Similarly, "the Saltmarket is not as it was, the domicile of provosts, bailies, and other civic dignitaries. [. . .] Eighty years ago it was otherwise. [. . .] In a house near the foot of Saltmarket, 'Silvercraig's land', Oliver Cromwell lodged while in Glasgow, as Darnley, the husband of Mary, also had lodged, in Rottenrow, off High Street." Forbes appears to have known of the upcoming demolition of the degraded buildings and to have accepted it as necessary for the health and wellbeing of their inhabitants and of the city as a whole. "One is sorry to lose the ancient landmarks." Nevertheless, "if ventilation and health, material and moral, be the result, no matter."[91]

If not motivated by social criticism, should Annan's work then be seen as closer in spirit and intent, albeit more modest in scale, to that of certain French contemporaries, such as the photographers of the *Missions héliographiques* (Baldus, Bayard, Le Gray, Le Secq, Mestral), who had been charged by the *Commission des monuments historiques* with making a photographic record of all the country's historic monuments, with special attention to those that were decayed or threatened with demolition; or, closer still, to the work of Charles Marville who, as official photographer for the city of Paris, had been commissioned in 1862 by the city's *Service des travaux historiques* to record not only the great sites of the capital and the grandiose achievements of Haussmann, but also old streets and buildings, particularly those slated for demolition? (Figs. 5:15-16).[92]

This connection is all the more plausible as Provost Blackie and John Carrick, who were behind the slum demolition plan and the commission to make photographic records of the condemned streets and wynds, were enthusiastic admirers of the redesigning of Paris under Napoleon III and Haussmann, and had led a civic delegation from Glasgow to the French capital in June 1866, the very year in which the City Improvements Act was passed. Moreover, Carrick's plans for the further development and reconstruction of the city incorporated wide and straight thoroughfares in the Haussmann style.[93] As Susan Sontag noted in her seminal work *On Photography* of 1973, referring in turn to Walter Benjamin's "Kleine Geschichte der Photographie" of 1931: "From the start, photographers not only set themselves the task of recording a disappearing world but were so employed by those hastening its disappearance."[94]

With all these officially appointed photographers, no less than with the artists employed by Taylor and Nodier in their multi-volume *Voyages pittoresques et romantiques dans l'ancienne France* (1820-1870), the goal of faithfully recording and documenting the national architectural heritage, or simply old buildings that had fallen into disrepair or were about to be torn down, was almost inevitably accompanied by a feeling for the "picturesque," inasmuch as the picturesque, from the outset, was associated with the old, the decaying, the neglected or unappreciated.[95] The beautiful, according to one writer at the end of the eighteenth century, depends on "ideas of youth and freshness," while the picturesque depends on "those of age, and even decay." Thus Archibald Burns, a successful photographer of old streets and buildings in Edinburgh, entitled his 1868 volume *Picturesque 'Bits' from Old Edinburgh*. As a modern scholar has put it, "the picturesque became generalized to that which is multifarious, irregular, unevenly lit, worn, and strange. Everything that appeared smooth, bright, symmetrical, new, whole, and strong, on the other hand, was placed in the categories of the beautiful or the sublime." Disengaged from notions of perfection and suitability and from such functions as moral enlightenment and edification (as in the formula of French classicism, "*plaire et instruire*"), rejecting established views of the beautiful and privileging the more refined esthetic sense required to appreciate unusual, non-traditional representations of the world, the "picturesque," in the view of the same scholar, was "based on an over-functionalization of the esthetic." As it is "more demanding to value something worn and decayed than to like [. . .] what is acknowledged as beautiful, [. . .] the picturesque provides a test of whether the spectator is always able to assume the perspective of 'disinterested pleasure' that Kant designated as a precondition of the esthetic attitude."[96] The purely documentary function of photography, the function most commonly attributed to the use of the camera, thus came to be associated, in the case of the documentation of old or decaying buildings, with a nascent counter-claim that photography is an artistic medium like painting.

The vogue of the "picturesque," in short, reinforced the efforts of some photographers to win respect for photography as an art, rather than a merely utilitarian instrument for accurately recording reality—"an essentially *indexed* medium, [. . .] a direct light imprint on the model of the fingerprint or the death mask," as one contemporary scholar has put it[97]—and for themselves as artists, more alert, in fact, than many academically trained painters to objects of unsuspected beauty and suggestiveness, rather than simply skilled technicians.[98] As suggested earlier, supporters of the calotype, as opposed to the more precise and detailed daguerreotype, had used the argument that Talbot's process left more room than Daguerre's for choice and decision-making on the part of the photographer. In *The Pencil of Nature* (1844) Talbot himself associated his work with that of the Dutch school of painters, among whom artistic sensitivity and technique were generally considered to have been combined with faithful representation of the real. "A painter's eye," Talbot wrote, "will often be arrested where ordinary people see nothing remarkable. A casual gleam of sunshine or a shadow thrown across his path, a time-withered oak, or a moss-covered stone may awaken a train of thoughts and feeling, and picturesque imaginings."[99] Many of Talbot's own photographs, such as "The Open Door" and "The Haystack," exemplify this approach (Figs. 1:1-2). In 1860, Thomas Sutton, the editor of *Photographic Notes*, the journal of the Photographic Society of Scotland and the Manchester Photographic Society, was more specific: "Although photography is certainly a mechanical means of representing nature, yet, when we compare a really fine photograph with an ordinary mechanical view, we are compelled to admit that it exhibits mind, and appreciation of the beautiful and skill of selection and treatment of the subject on the part of the photographer, to a degree that constitute him an artist in a high sense of the word."[100]

Photographers were even urged sometimes to model themselves on painters—though this strategy did not necessarily coincide with cultivation of the picturesque. "There will be perhaps photograph Raphaels, photograph Titians," *The Photographic Journal*, the organ of the Royal Photographic Society, predicted in 1857. The successful Swedish-born photographer Oscar Rejlander did indeed produce a photographic version ("The Virgin in Prayer" [1858-60]) of a mid-seventeenth-century Madonna by Sassoferrato, now in in the National Gallery of Victoria in Melbourne, and an elaborate photographic allegory ("Two Ways of Life" [1857]) inspired by Raphael's "School of Athens" (Figs. 6:6-7).

The portrait painter Sir William Newton, who also happened to be a vice-president of the Royal Photographic Society in the 1850s, urged photographers to seek artistic effects rather than a mere copy of nature. "The whole subject might be a little out of focus," he suggested, "thereby giving a greater breadth of effect, and consequently more suggestive of the true character of Nature."[101]

The view of photography as an art that must be guided by concerns similar to those of the painter was even more vigorously defended three decades later by Frank Sutcliffe, the admired photographer of the fishing town of Whitby and its inhabitants and an early member of the Linked Ring, the British group advocating what was shortly afterwards defined as Pictorialism: "A picture must have a pattern. And it is this pattern most of them lack. It is this pattern, or pleasing combination of line and mass, that the artist considers of greater importance than any historical facts which may be found in his subject, and he does not hesitate to sacrifice the latter to the former."[102] In short, the photograph is not simply a mechanical copy of the real: it can be manipulated, and therein lies its claim to be art. In France, in an 1851 article in *La Lumière*, the earliest of all photographic journals, Francis Wey explained that, unlike the daguerreotype, the calotype "works with masses, disdaining detail as a gifted master painter does [. . .] and choosing to emphasize formal qualities in one place and tonal qualities in another." That is why "the taste of the individual photographer can be discerned clearly enough in his work for the experienced amateur, on seeing a photograph produced by the paper process, to be able to identify the photographer that made it."[103]

Thomas Annan did not often express himself on the question whether photography is an art (though his better-known son James Craig Annan, another early member of the Linked Ring, asserted unequivocally that it is[104]). Still, in at least one case—a view of the Palace of Linlithgow—there is material evidence that he sketched the scene he wanted to photograph and made notes to himself about lighting conditions and the best times of day for camera work.[105] Even from a technical point of view, photographing in the dark closes of Glasgow must have required close attention to the conditions of light at different times of day and, in view of the long exposure times needed, to controlling the movement of people in order to avoid excessive blurring. In addition, the wet collodion process made necessary by the generally poor light conditions required a great deal of equipment, considerable preparation, and further work immediately after the pictures had been taken. The pictures were thus necessarily composed with care, and while it was not Annan's brief to depict the universally denounced squalor of the old closes and streets but only the closes and streets themselves, it is striking that, in the view of many (though by no means all) commentators, the photographs do not, on the whole, convey a deeply disturbing sense of squalor or degradation (with some notable exceptions, such as "Closes 97 and 103 Saltmarket")[106] (Fig. 6:8).

The alleys are dark and rundown, to be sure, but not especially dirty. On the contrary, there are few signs of refuse in them and the lines of washing hung out over them in many of the pictures—"Annan's slumdwellers are perplexingly fastidious launderers of linen," one scholar remarks[107]—not only suggest a concern with cleanliness on the part of the inhabitants but provide a formally effective horizontal complement to the high, somber and close-packed verticals of the walls. An occasional silvery rivulet running down a cobbled alleyway might have been the effluent deplored by sanitary inspectors rather than simply rain water, but it also functions to enliven the scene and guide the eye. Similarly, isolated figures in some of the photographs appear, with a few exceptions, fairly clean and decently, if not well, clothed (albeit the children are usually barefoot), bearing little resemblance to the wretched creatures described in the written reports on the slums. Often they seem strategically placed to draw the eye along in the direction desired by the photographer; in other cases, they are grouped or framed in such a way as to be themselves part of the formal design of the photograph—again bearing little resemblance to the destitute and degraded denizens of the published reports (Figs. 6:9-18).

In the words of the scholar who wrote the Introduction to the 1977 Dover Publications re-edition of *The Old Closes and Streets*, "Annan's approach was not what we would call straight." In the 1878 carbon prints, "he added clouds, which brighten the skies over Glasgow's slums, and he whitened the wash on the line. He did this for pictorial effect, for nice balance."[108] Among Annan's own contemporaries, the Rev. A.G. Forbes, author of the texts accompanying *Photographs of Glasgow* (1868), refers to him repeatedly as "our artist,"[109] while, as noted earlier in chapter 4, a reviewer of a Photographic Society show in London described Annan's landscapes as of such "high artistic merit" that their creator "must rank amongst our first class artists." As early as 1864, in a letter to the Photographic Society of Scotland on the occasion of his having been awarded the Society's silver medal for a photograph of Dumbarton Castle, Annan himself professed that "my constant aim is to make my Photographs like Pictures and I am happy to think that my efforts are not altogether unsuccessful." Two decades later, near the end of his life, in May 1884, he gave a lecture at a meeting of the Photographic Society in Edinburgh on the topic "Art in Photo Landscapes."[110] It is not implausible, in short, to argue that formal design was a concern of Annan's.[111]

The formal, esthetic impact of Annan's photographs of the old closes and streets has aroused puzzlement and even discomfort in some of the best informed and most experienced students of his work. Sara Stevenson, for instance, in the handsome brochure on Annan put out by the National Galleries of Scotland in its "Scottish Masters" series, notes that

> The photographs are undeniably beautiful. Annan used his knowledge and control of the collodion process to achieve the same kind of subtle light and detail that appear in his landscape photographs. He must have explored the wynds at length, waiting for the best time of day, when light crept in. He used the trickling gutters to make elegant lines of light. He relished the hanging washing which made the closes even more dark, and one or two of the photographs are more about these hanging clothes—the flapping shirts and the little lines of socks—than about the buildings he was paid to photograph. Annan may even have been thinking of Turner while taking these pictures, considering Turner's remark about the need to paint in the clothes hung by bargemen on their boats' shrouds 'to break the perpendicular and unpleasantly straight lines.' [. . .] Seeing beauty and poetry in photographs of slums makes us rightly uneasy and doubtful about the photographer—if the photographs are beautiful can he have been concerned about the squalor? [. . .] It is a disconcerting fact that pollution can be beautiful. Iridescent bubbles on a stream are magical until they are recognized as industrial effluent and become ugly.[112]

Ray McKenzie, the author of several illuminating essays on Annan, writing of the forty images of slum properties gathered in the 1878 album, acknowledges that "the tension between their function as documents and their status as aesthetic objects is [. . .] problematic. It is impossible to look at a photograph such as *Close, No. 80 High Street* without an uncomfortable sense of the ambiguity of our own position as contemporary observers; we are simultaneously appalled by what it tells us about a human situation and thrilled by its uniquely seductive qualities as a photographic print." (Fig. 6:15)[113] The late Margaret Harker considered that "the strange and lasting fascination of these photographs" is in fact due to the "curious combination between the picturesque and the sordid in Annan's interpretation of the Glasgow slums."[114] The ten-word e-mail reaction of a friend, the architect and photographer Alan Chimacoff, when I introduced him to *The Old Closes and Streets*, is by no means untypical: "Beautiful stuff . . . if that sort of stuff can be beautiful."[115]

In fact, Annan's concern with form and the "restraint" with which, in the view of some scholars,[116] he represented the filthy, degraded, violent reality of the old closes (as described by the reformers, missionaries and sanitary inspectors who dared venture into them) may well go hand in hand with a distinctive vision of the slum-dwellers themselves. Sometimes they do seem to be little more than staffage—of a piece with and virtually inseparable from the texture of the stone walls they are pressed against or enclosed by. But sometimes, as in "28 Saltmarket," "118 High Street" and "46 Saltmarket" (Figs. 6:16-18)—the last of these curiously not included by James Craig Annan in his 1900 photogravure edition—they have a simple dignity that is rarely evoked in the written reports of missionaries and reformers. The primary intent of Annan's photographs may well not have been—not, at least, in the first instance—that of a social reformer like Riis, namely to awaken the compassion of comfortably-off, middle-class viewers with a moral conscience for the victims of greedy landlords, or horror and indignation at the conditions in which the poor are obliged to live, or uneasiness and fear in the face of a threateningly alien environment.[117] Nor, in contrast to the engravings based on daguerreotypes by Richard Beard in Henry Mayhew's *London Labour and the London Poor* (1851) (Figs. 6:19-20) or even to the photographs by fellow-Scot John Thomson in his much admired *Street Life in London* (1878) (Figs. 1:24-25), does Annan exploit and update the traditional "Cries of London" genre: stereotypes of street people or "nomades," as Thomson describes them, such as the costermonger, the pie-man, the flower-seller, the sweep, the shoe-black, the rat-catcher, the "Jew old-clothes man"—all of whom, as Thomas Prasch has pointed out, represent "marginal" and "static forms of labor largely unchanged by the forces of industrial society."[118]

First and foremost, it seems to me, Annan's photographs ask us as viewers to *respect* the people in them, to recognize them, not as "the poor," or "street people," or "arabs"—the term by which the homeless and uprooted or the denizens of city slums were often referred to, as though to emphasize that they were virtually of a different "race" from "us"—but simply as human beings.[119] Annan's people, both singly and in groups are not "other" (to be pitied or assisted or feared) as in some "social documentary" photographs of the time. In the group portraits especially, the figures represented seem to assert their humanity, overwhelmed, hemmed in and rendered fragile as it is by the somber and oppressive mass of their stony environment.[120] Given that the unavoidably long exposure times required his human subjects to remain absolutely still for several minutes, Annan clearly had to win their goodwill and co-operation. That he apparently did so (albeit with understandably less success in the case of young children) would suggest that, instead of regarding him with suspicion, as they often looked on sanitary inspectors, advocates of church attendance and abstention from alcoholic drinks, and similarly well-meaning but interfering outsiders, the inhabitants of the closes (most of them probably poor Irish immigrants) may have seen him as a friendly figure and been pleased or flattered to be selected for portrayal in his photographs—unless, of course, though this seems unlikely, they were rewarded for their co-operation. It may even be that some of them—like the centrally positioned, self-assured male figures, especially the young boy with arms akimbo, looking directly, almost defiantly, at the camera in "Close, no. 46 Saltmarket"—took advantage of the opportunity provided by the photographer to assert themselves and challenge the viewer to acknowledge them, instead of playing only a passive role as the photographer's "subjects," in the full sense of that word. It may be, in other words, that there was a reciprocal relationship between the photographer and his "subjects," that they had their motives in posing for him just as he had his reasons for having them pose (Fig. 6:18).

Nevertheless—and this is the second of the two issues I would like to explore briefly—a major criticism remains to be considered, one that goes to the heart of any photography that presents itself as having a social documentary intent while at the same time pursuing formal and compositional goals, and that thus necessarily affects Annan's work in some measure. Hinted at in Ian Spring's reference to the vogue of Annan's photographs of the old closes in twenty-first-century, post-industrial Glasgow, this issue is raised and discussed by Susan Sontag in her now classic essays on photography. "There is an aggression implicit in every use of the camera," Sontag asserts. "To photograph people is to violate them, by seeing them as they never see themselves, by having knowledge of them that they can never have; it turns people into objects that can be symbolically possessed."[121]

The maker and the viewer of social documentary photographs, in short, easily become *voyeurs*, engaged by spectacle, sensitive to design and largely indifferent to the reality of which the photograph purports to provide a faithful representation: "Photographing is essentially an act of non-intervention. [. . .] The person who intervenes cannot record, the person who is recording cannot intervene." Even though "an event known through photographs certainly becomes more real than it would have been if one had never seen the photographs," in the end "images transfix. Images anaesthetize. [. . .] Aesthetic distance seems built into the very experience of looking at photographs, if not right away, then certainly with the passage of time."[122] Writing in the midst of a wave of reaction against the Pictorialism of Alfred Stieglitz and his successors, Sontag cites Walter Benjamin on photography's estheticizing tendency: "The camera is now incapable of photographing a tenement or a rubbish heap without transfiguring it, not to mention a river dam or electric cable factory; in front of these photography can only say 'how beautiful' [...] It has succeeded in turning abject poverty itself, by handling it in a modish, technically perfect way, into an object of enjoyment."[123] As a result, according to Sontag, "whatever the moral claims made on behalf of photography, its main effect is to convert the world into a department store or museum-without-walls in which every subject is depreciated into an article of consumption, promoted into an item for aesthetic appreciation."[124]

Among many examples of "documentary" photographs that have ceased to function as social criticism or even primarily as historical records and now function almost exclusively as art—or that were in fact always positioned astride the boundary separating documentation and art—one could cite the beautifully composed photographs of exploitative child labour by Lewis Hine in the early years of the twentieth century, some of the photographs taken by Dr. Barnardo and his missionaries in the last quarter of the nineteenth century, and the work of Depression-era photographers such as Dorothea Lange (Figs. 6:21-22).

An earlier, disturbing example of the "voyeuristic" character of seemingly social documentary photography is offered by Captain Willoughby Wallace Hooper's photographs of victims of the 1876-1879 Madras famine. A keen photographer who had contributed to the 468 images in an eight-volume work inspired by Lord Canning, Governor-General of India from 1856 to 1862 (*The People of India*, ed. John Forbes Watson and John William Kaye, London, 1868-1875), Captain Hooper took a number of powerful and horrifying but carefully-composed photographs of skeletal victims of the famine (Fig. 6:23).

These, it has been alleged, were "sold commercially" and "circulated in private photograph collections, commercially produced albums, and as postcards into the early twentieth century."[125] Whether they were ever primarily intended to provoke action in favor of the victims remains moot. Hooper is said to have had famine-stricken families brought to him to be photographed and to have then sent them away without feeding them. In addition, during the Third Burmese War (1885) he photographed prisoners he himself had ordered to be executed at the precise moment of their execution, planning to have the images produced commercially and offered for sale. It appears almost certain, in short, that there was little, if any, connection for this seemingly social documentary photographer between viewing and acting, recording and intervening.[126] Indeed, Hooper may well have come disturbingly close to the situation imagined by Guillaume Apollinaire in his short story, "Un beau film" of 1901, and by the French director Bertrand Tavernier in his mordant movie, "La Mort en direct," of 1980 ("shot," as it happens, in Glasgow), in which the desire to photograph real scenes of extreme human violence or anguish leads the artist wielding a camera to provoke such scenes for the purpose of recording them. In Apollinaire's story, the film-maker takes care to assure the public that the violent murder scene he set up and then captured on film was not simply staged but really took place. The public responds enthusiastically and the film becomes a huge financial success.[127]

The power relation underlying both the act of photographing social scenes and the viewing of such photographs is a central motif of recent critical writing on photography by the artist Martha Rosler and the critic John Tagg. "The insistence that the ordered world of business-as-usual take account of [. . .] a reality newly elevated into consideration simply by being photographed and thus exemplified and made concrete," Rosler notes, writing from what appears to be a Marxist or Benjaminian perspective, is not accompanied by any analysis of how the situation represented came about. "The meliorism of Riis, Lewis Hine, and others involved in social-work propagandizing argued [. . .] for the rectification of wrongs. It did not perceive these wrongs as fundamental to the social system that tolerated them. The assumption that they were tolerated rather than *bred* marks a basic fallacy of social work. [. . .] Documentary photography has been much more comfortable in the company of moralism than wedded to a rhetoric or program of revolutionary politics." Ultimately, "the exposé, the compassion and outrage of documentary fueled by the dedication to reform has shaded over into combinations of exoticism, tourism, voyeurism . . ."[128]

For his part, John Tagg, who acknowledges his indebtedness to Michel Foucault, sees "the insatiable appropriations of the camera" as one of the ways in which a power relationship is manifested and maintained.

> Whether it is John Thomson in the streets of London or Thomas Annan in the slums of Glasgow; [. . .] whether it is Jacob Riis among the 'poor,' the 'idle' and the 'vicious' of Mulberry Bend or Captain Hooper among the victims of the Madras famine of 1876: what we see is the extension of a 'procedure of objectification and subjection' [. . .]. Photography as such has no identity. [. . .] Its nature as a practice depends on the institutions and agents which define it and set it to work. [. . .] Photography does not transmit a pre-existent reality which is already meaningful in itself. As with any other discursive system, the question we must ask is not, 'What does this discourse reveal of something else?' but 'what does it do: what are its conditions of existence, [. . .] how does it animate meaning rather than discover it?' [. . .]
> Hence the questions:
> Why were photographs of working-class subjects, working-class trades, working-class housing, and working-class recreations made in the nineteenth century? By whom? Under what conditions? For what purposes?[129]

In Annan's case, an answer to Professor Tagg's questions has been provided, at least in some measure I hope, in the course of this essay. Annan's pictures of the old closes and streets were the product of a commission by the municipal authorities of Glasgow which sought to retain a record of the dilapidated old buildings in the city center, the demolition of which had been authorized at least as much in the interest of the health of the city as a whole as in the interest of the slum-dwellers themselves. (Provision for rehousing the latter was in fact inadequate; the new accommodations were too expensive for many of the displaced, and photographs taken decades later reveal slum conditions hardly improved over those photographed by Annan [Fig. 6:23].)

As urbanization proceeded apace in the nineteenth century and the traditional fabric and appearance of cities underwent drastic transformations, similar commissions were issued in other cities, notably Paris. Making, preserving and collecting records, written and visual, was in fact a major preoccupation of the century of revolutionary change. While conscientiously executing the task assigned to him, however, Annan also seems to have wanted to give a human face to the often luridly described inhabitants of the condemned tenements.

At the same time, it is certainly the case that Annan's work—particularly in *The Old Closes and Streets*—has come to be appreciated by later generations unfamiliar with the concerns of the photographer's contemporaries not only or mainly for its value as a record of a vanished past or as a testimony to its own time (that is, to the ideas and outlook of the photographer and his contemporaries), but for itself, for its timeless formal and evocative qualities, in other words, as art.[130] There is no strong evidence, as we saw, that Thomas Annan deliberately and consciously used his camera "creatively," to "make art"—as the Pictorialists were to do soon after him—rather than to record empirical reality. But as a landscape and portrait photographer, an experienced and much admired photographer of paintings, a good friend of several painters and an engraver of paintings before he took up photography, he almost inevitably had the painter's approach to landscapes, cityscapes and portraits in mind when making his photographs. As he himself declared in his letter to the Photographic Society of Scotland, quoted earlier: "My constant aim is to make my Photographs like Pictures."

Toward the end of the essay "Photographic Evangels" in her *On Photography*, Susan Sontag defines photography as a medium, like language, rather than an art form:

> Although photography generates works that can be called art—it requires subjectivity, it can lie, it gives esthetic pleasure—photography is not, to begin

with an art form at all. Like language it is a medium in which works of art (among other things) are made. Out of language one can make scientific discourse, bureaucratic memoranda, love letters, grocery lists, and Balzac's Paris. Out of photography one can make passport pictures, weather photographs, pornographic pictures, X-rays, wedding pictures, and Atget's Paris.[131]

If Sontag's view of photography as comparable to language has some merit, it may be useful to pursue it further. A verbal text does not have to be defined solely by its ostensible genre or function: some historical or biographical narratives, some works of political or economic theory or of philosophy are also, by common consent, great works of literature. One thinks immediately of Gibbon's *Decline and Fall of the Roman Empire*, Michelet's *Histoire de France*, Boswell's *Life of Johnson*, Montesquieu's *Spirit of the Laws* or Nietzsche's *Gay Science*, not to mention, in antiquity, Plutarch, Herodotus or Tacitus. In similar fashion, photographs may fulfil one or more functions of the medium. Roman Jakobson's six communication functions of the speech act would seem to apply equally to photography: "referential" (emphasis on the informational content of the message), "aesthetic or poetic" (emphasis on the message itself), "emotive or expressive" (emphasis on the sender and her or his feelings), "conative or vocative" (emphasis on persuading or arousing a response in the receiver or addressee), "phatic" (emphasis on the channel of communication) and "metalingual" (emphasis on the shared code of communication, "self-referential").[132] And in photography, as in any speech act or verbal text, while the emphasis may fall or be perceived to fall by the viewer, as by the listener or reader, on one or another of these functions, the others are not thereby abolished.

However conscientiously "referential" they may be in providing the record he was commissioned by the Improvements Trust to produce, Thomas Annan's photographs do not exclude or eliminate "aesthetic," "expressive" or "conative" functions. Different viewers at different times may focus on the information the photographs provide, their formal characteristics, the mood they manifest or seek to evoke, or the lesson they urge on us, and they may judge Annan to have himself emphasized one or another of these functions. The strength of Annan's work may well lie precisely in its ability to stimulate a variety of different readings and responses corresponding to the function that the viewer chooses to perceive as dominant.[133]

Nevertheless, as Roland Barthes has powerfully argued, the referential function in photography—where the referent, unlike the content of Jakobson's verbal message, is a particular, concrete object—is fundamental in a way that distinguishes photography from painting or discourse. As Barthes' argument seems to me relevant to the work of Thomas Annan, I will close this chapter by quoting from it at some length. "What the Photograph reproduces to infinity

The Old Closes and Streets of Glasgow 109

has occurred only once," Barthes writes. "The Photograph mechanically repeats what could never be repeated existentially. [. . .] It is the absolute Particular."[134]

> Photography's Referent is not the same as the referent of other systems of representation. I call "photographic referent" not the *optionally* real thing to which an image or a sign refers but the *necessarily* real thing which has been placed before the lens, without which there would be no photograph. Painting can feign reality without having seen it. Discourse combines signs which have referents, of course, but these referents can be and are most often "chimeras." Contrary to these imitations, in Photography I can never deny that *the thing has been there*. There is a superimposition here: of reality and the past. And since this constraint exists only for Photography, we must consider it, by reduction, as the very essence, the *noeme* of Photography. What I intentionalize in a photograph [. . .] is neither Art nor Communication, it is Reference, which is the founding order of Photography. [. . .]
>
> In the Photograph, what I posit is not only the absence of the object; it is also, by one and the same movement, on equal terms, the fact that this object has indeed existed and that it has been there where I see it.[135]

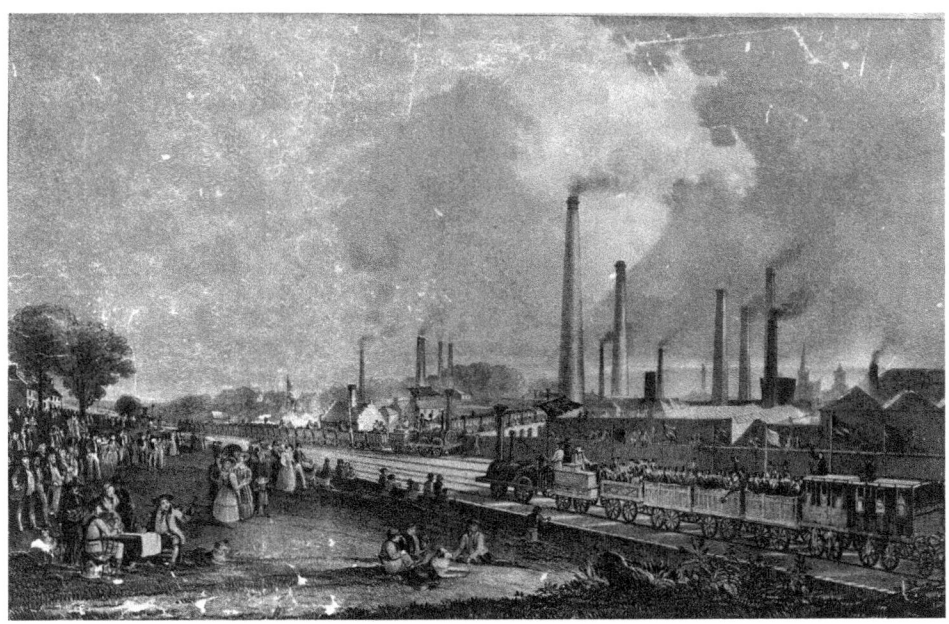

6:1 David Octavius Hill, "Opening of the Glasgow and Garnkirk Railway in 1831" with a view of the Tennant chemical works, St. Rollox. Lithograph after an original painting, from D. O. Hill, *Views of the Opening of the Glasgow and Garnkirk Railway* (Edinburgh: Alex Hill, 1832). ©CSG CIC Glasgow Museums and Libraries Collection: The Mitchell Library, Special Collections.

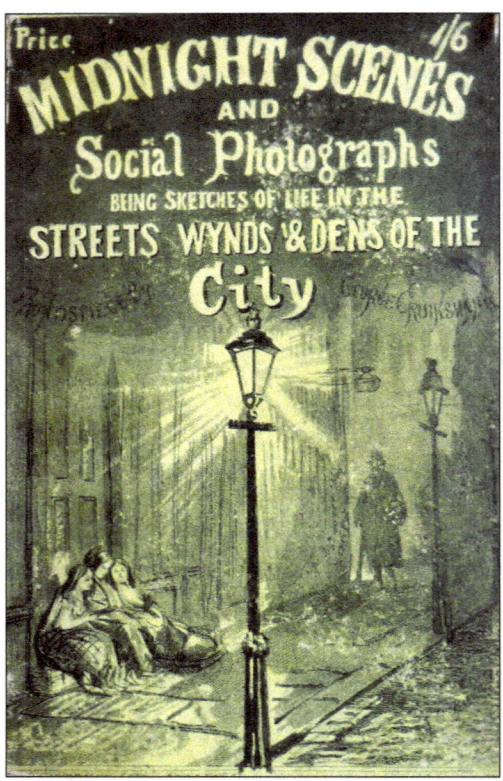

6:2 Shadow [Alexander Brown], *Midnight Scenes and Social Photographs being Sketches of Life in the Streets, Wynds and Dens of the City* (Glasgow: Thomas Murray, 1858). Cover design. Division of Rare Books, Department of Rare Books and Special Collections, Princeton University Library.

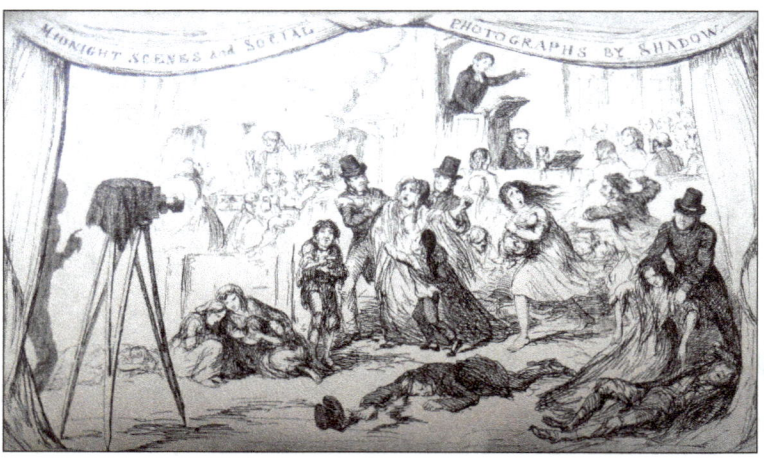

6:3 George Cruickshank, from *Midnight Scenes and Social Photographs*. Frontispiece. Division of Rare Books. Department of Rare Books and Special Collections, Princeton University Library.

The Old Closes and Streets of Glasgow   111

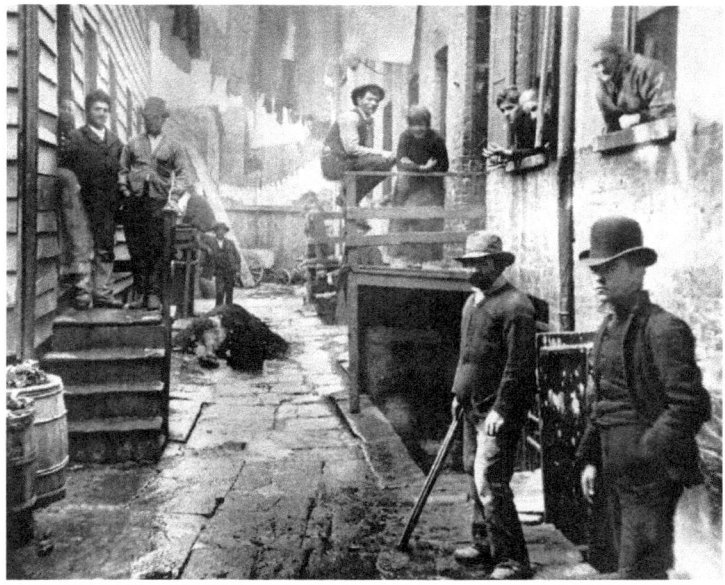

6:4 Jacob Riis, "Bandits' Roost," from his *How the Other Half Lives: Studies among the Tenements of New York, with Illustrations chiefly from Photographs taken by the Author* (New York: Charles Scribner's Sons, 1890), p. 63. Wikimedia.

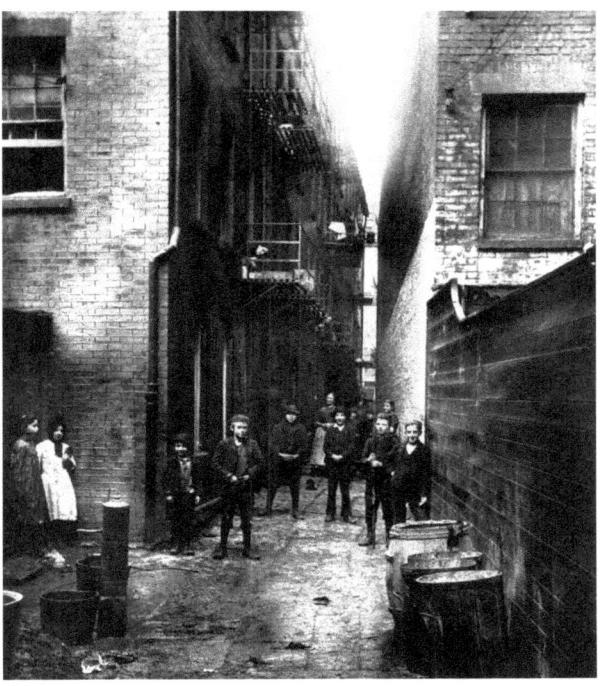

6:5 Jacob Riis, "Mullen's Alley, Cherry Hill." 1888. Museum Syndicate.

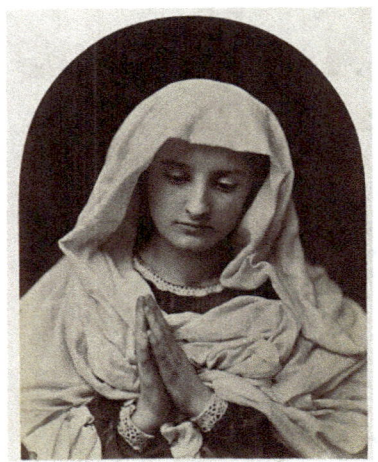 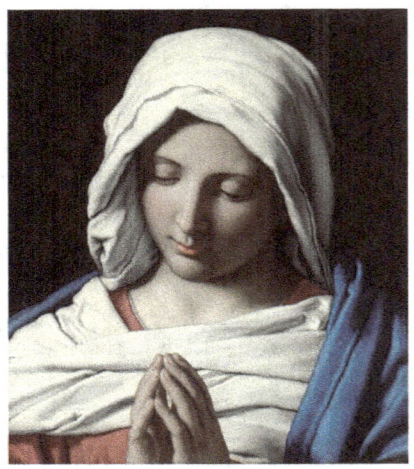

6:6 O.G. Rejlander, Swedish/English, 1813-1875, No title (The Virgin in Prayer). Ca.1858-60. National Gallery of Victoria Melbourne. Purchased 2002.

6:7 Sassoferrato, "The Virgin in Prayer." 1638-1652. Wikimedia.

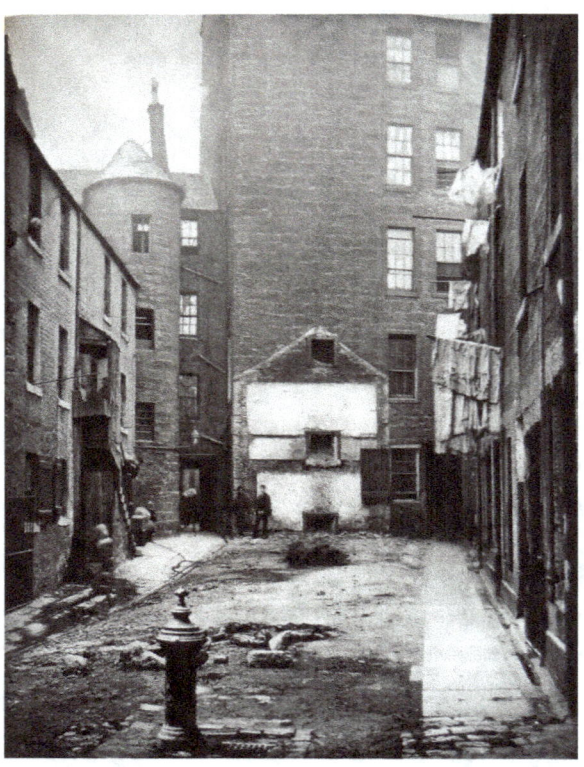

6:8 Thomas Annan, "Closes, Nos. 97 and 103 Saltmarket," from the album *Glasgow Improvements Act 1866. Photographs of Streets, Closes, &c. Taken 1866-71*, Plate 28. Albumen print. Graphic Arts Collection, Department of Rare Books and Special Collections, Princeton University Library.

The Old Closes and Streets of Glasgow   113

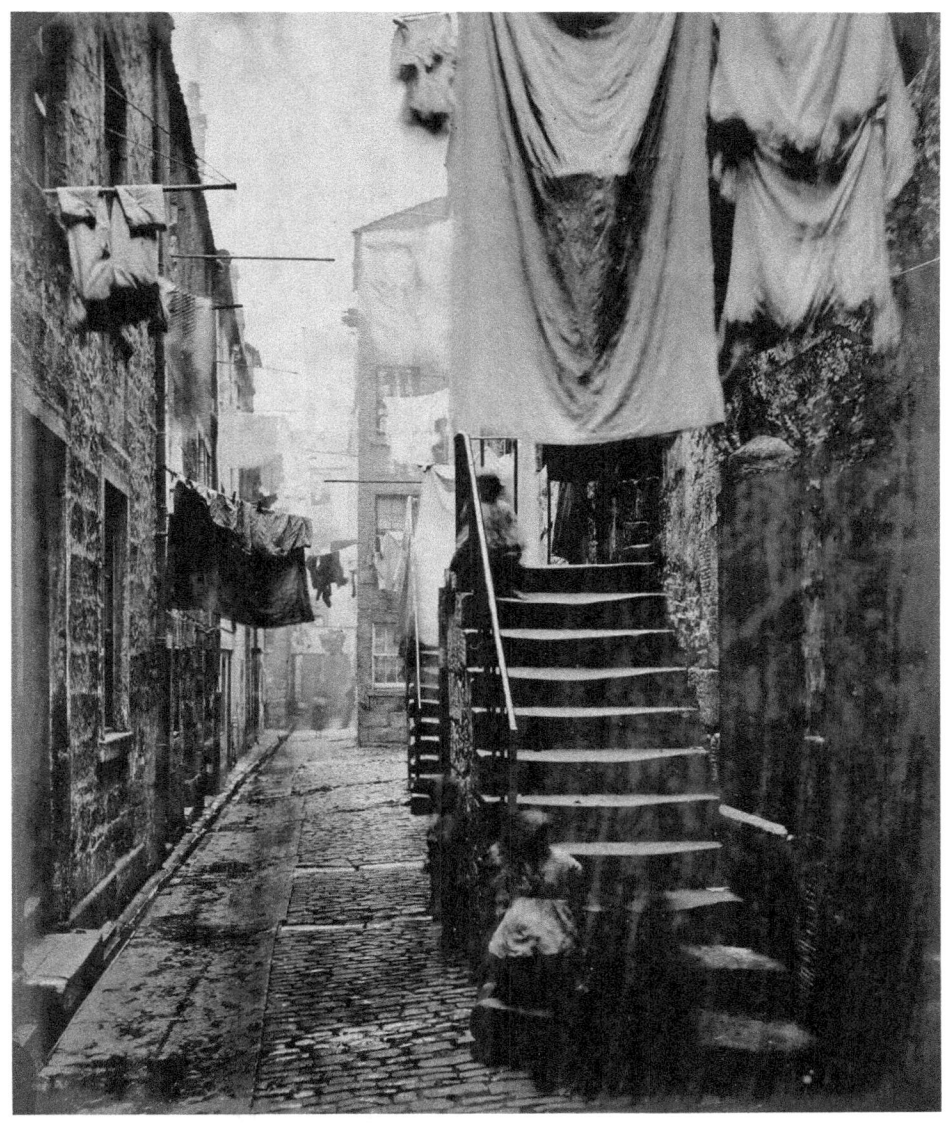

6:9 Thomas Annan, "Close, No. 93 High Street," from *Glasgow Improvements Act 1866*, Plate 9. Albumen print. Graphic Arts Collection, Department of Rare Books and Special Collections, Princeton University Library.

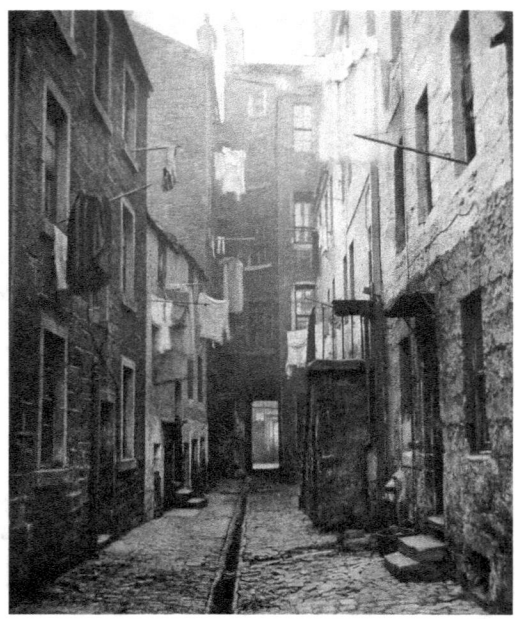

6:10 Thomas Annan, "Close, No. 75 High Street," from *Glasgow Improvements Act 1866*, Plate 7. Albumen print. Graphic Arts Collection, Department of Rare Books and Special Collections, Princeton University Library.

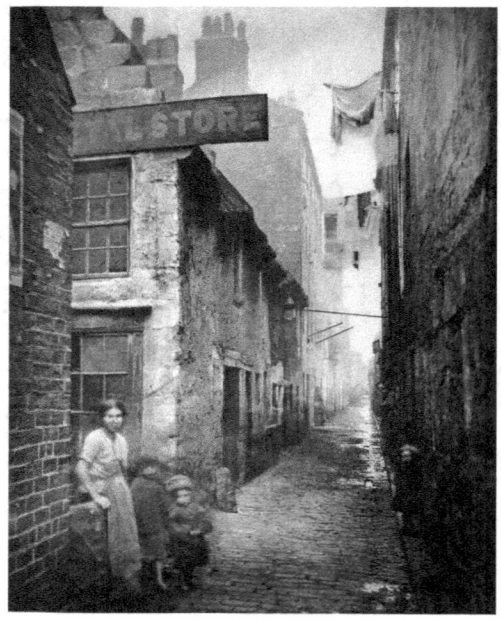

6:11 Thomas Annan, "Old Vennel off High Street," from *Glasgow Improvements Act 1866*, Plate 14. Albumen print. Graphic Arts Collection, Department of Rare Books and Special Collections, Princeton University Library.

The Old Closes and Streets of Glasgow 115

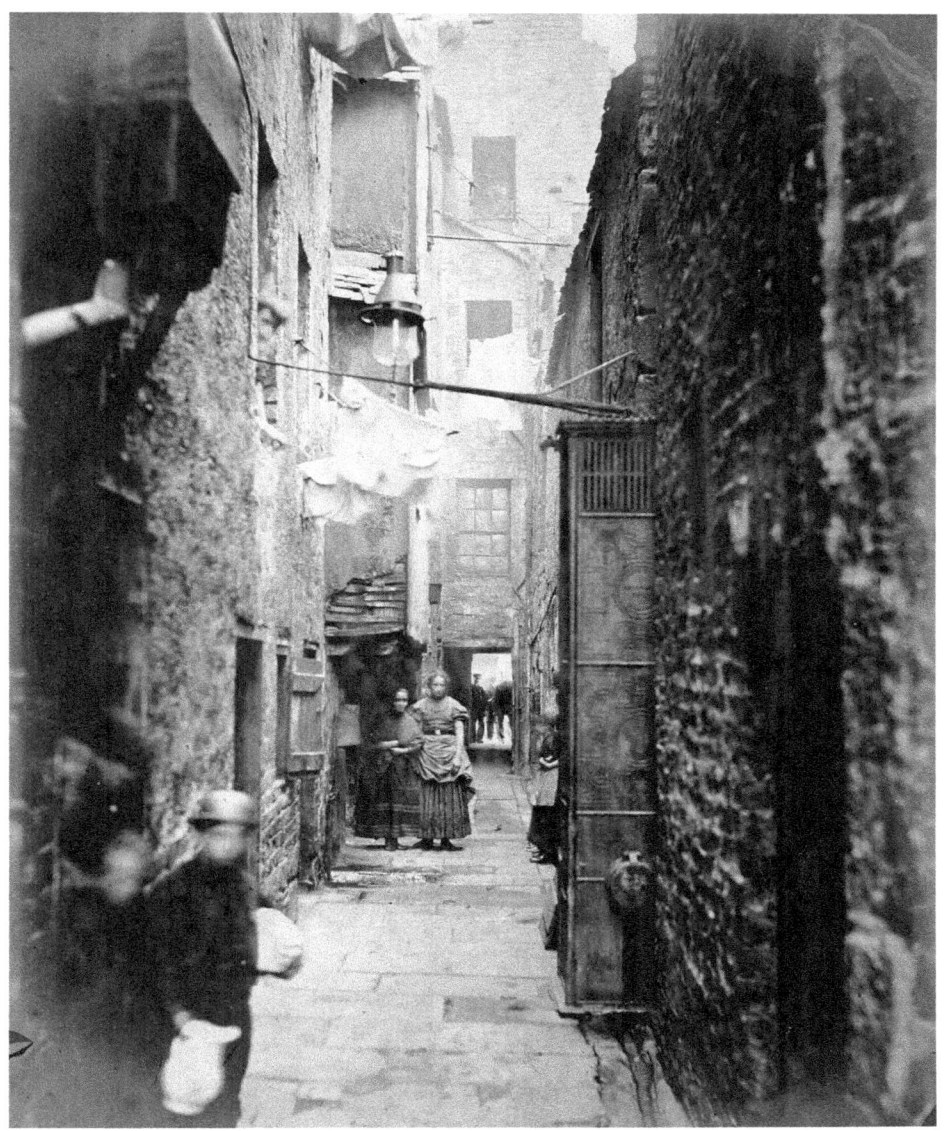

6:12 Thomas Annan, "Close, No. 37 High Street," from *Glasgow Improvements Act 1866*, Plate 5. Albumen print. Graphic Arts Collection, Department of Rare Books and Special Collections, Princeton University Library.

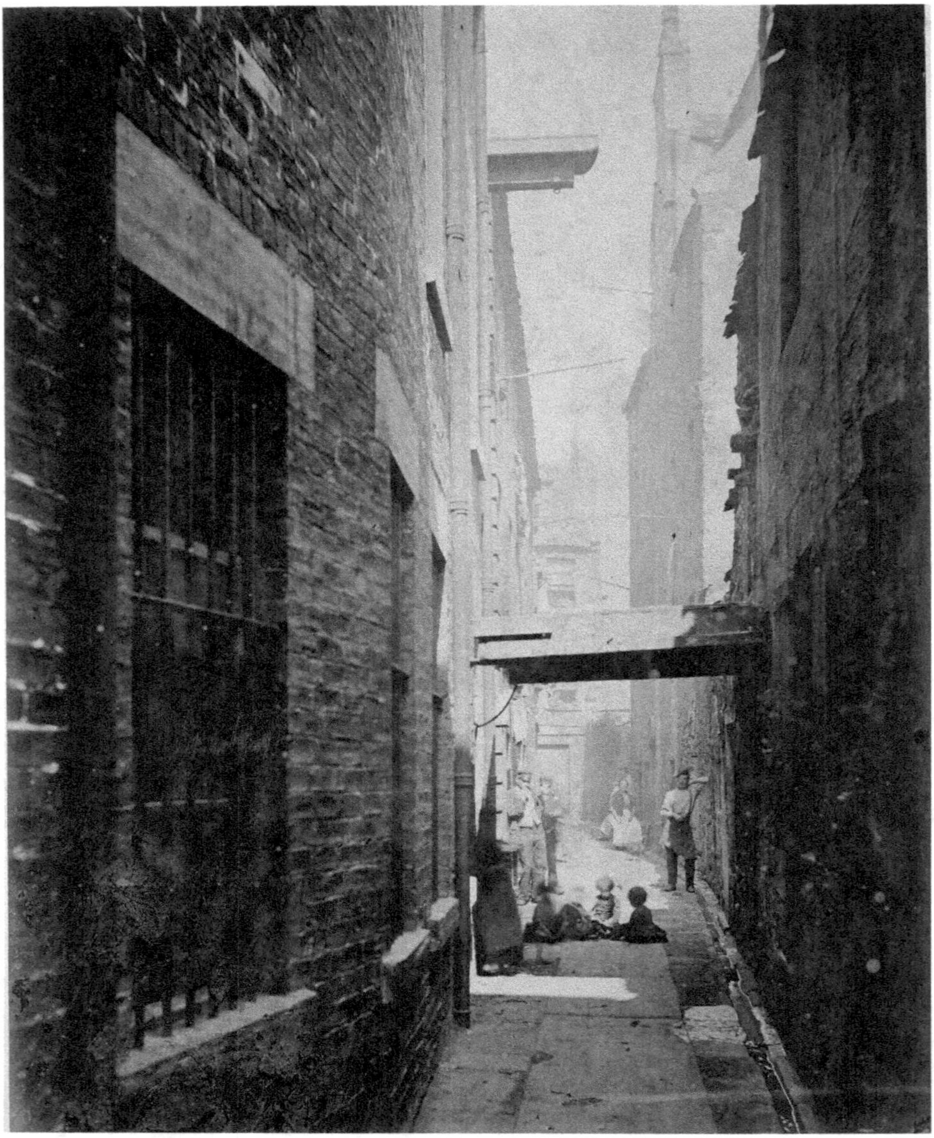

6:13 Thomas Annan, "Close, No. 29 Gallowgate," from *Glasgow Improvements Act 1866*, Plate 18. Albumen print. Graphic Arts Collection, Department of Rare Books and Special Collections, Princeton University Library.

The Old Closes and Streets of Glasgow 117

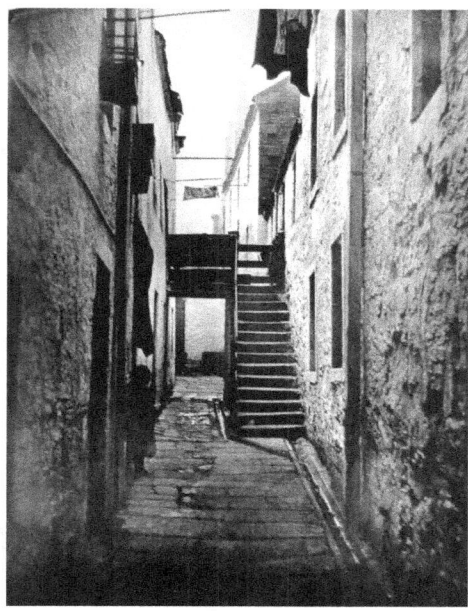

6:14 Thomas Annan, "Close, No. 128 Saltmarket," from *Glasgow Improvements Act 1866*, Plate 24. Albumen print. Graphic Arts Collection, Department of Rare Books and Special Collections, Princeton University Library.

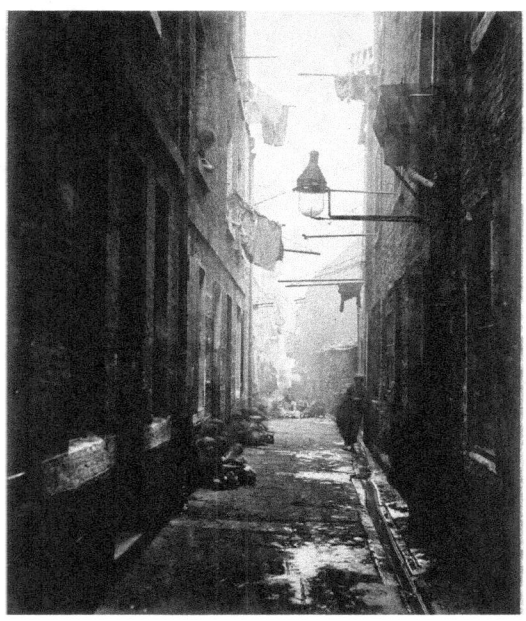

6:15 Thomas Annan, "Close, No. 80 High Street," from *Glasgow Improvements Act 1866*, Plate 13. Albumen print. Graphic Arts Collection, Department of Rare Books and Special Collections, Princeton University Library.

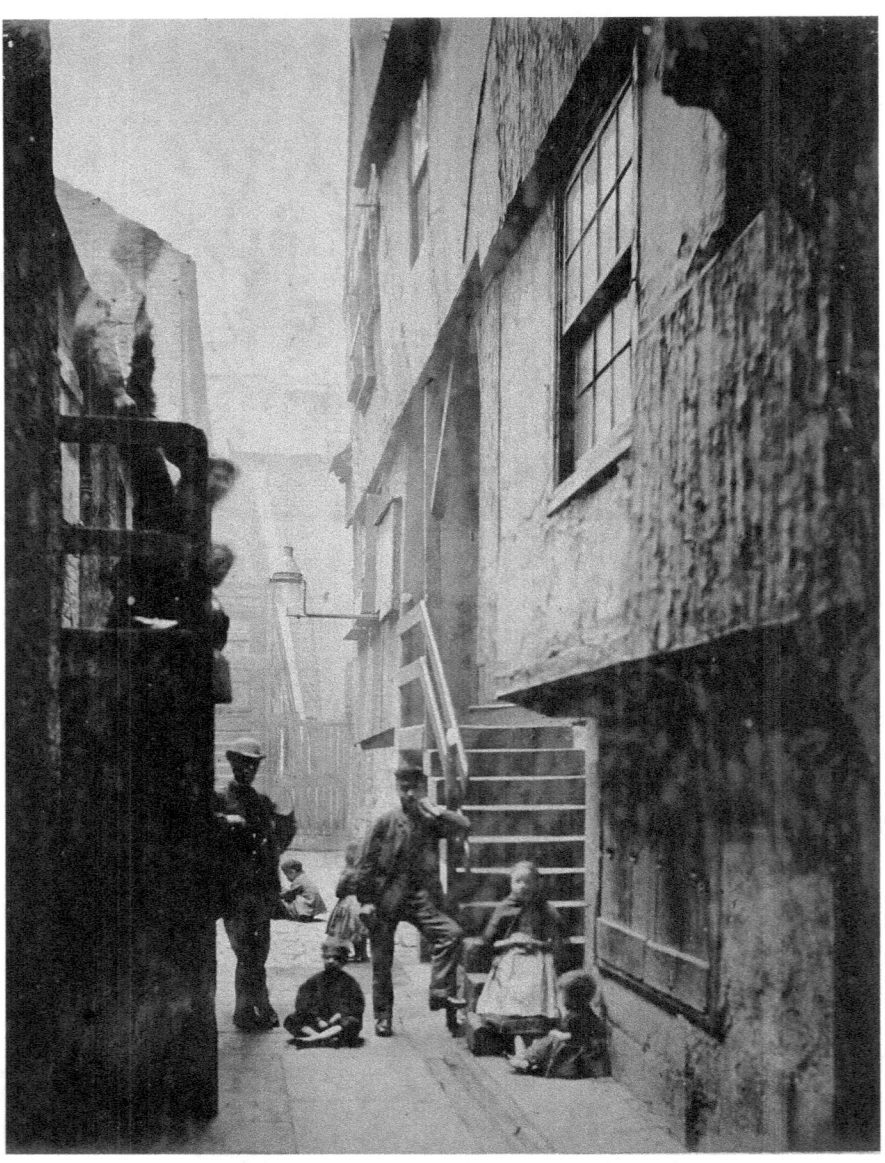

6:16 Thomas Annan, "Close, No. 28 Saltmarket," from *Glasgow Improvements Act 1866*, Plate 21. Albumen print. Graphic Arts Collection, Department of Rare Books and Special Collections, Princeton University Library.

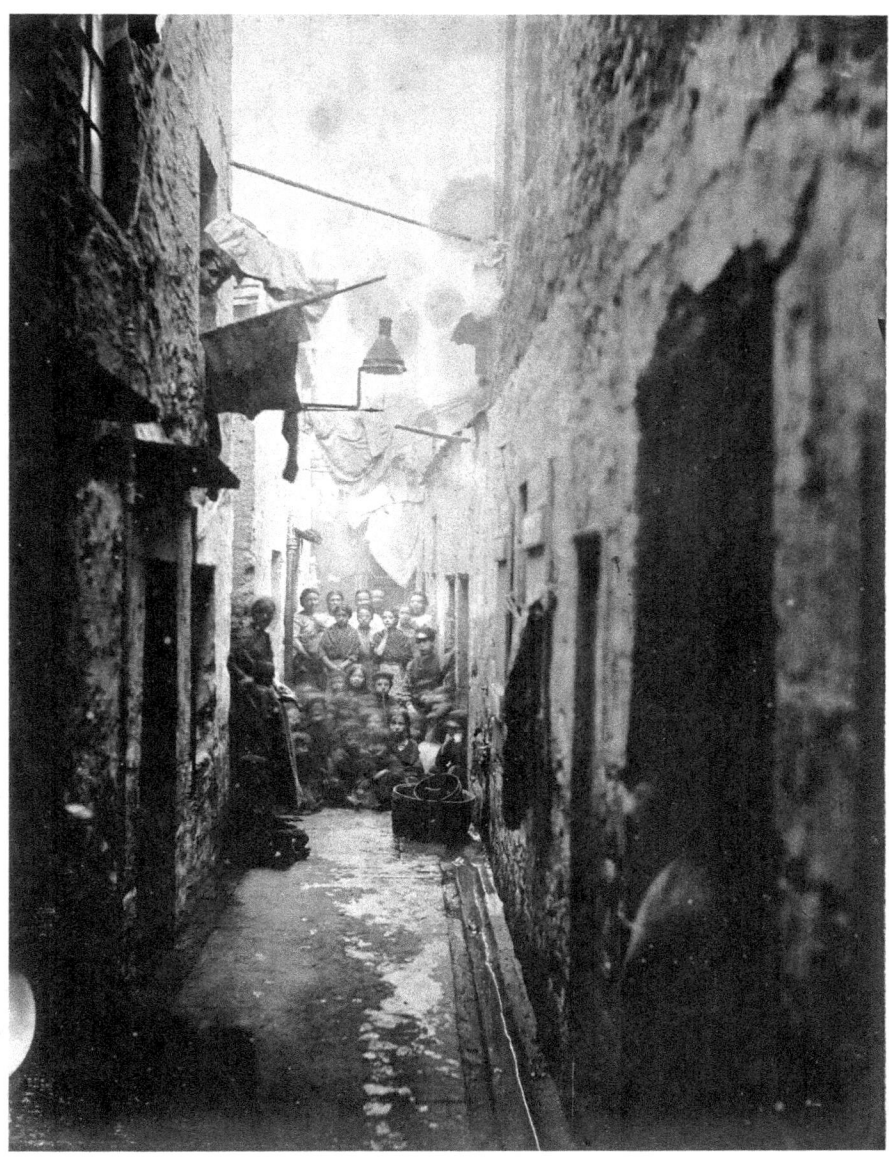

6:17 Thomas Annan, "Close, No. 118 High Street," from *Glasgow Improvements Act 1866*, Plate 15. Reproduced from the photogravure edition of 1900, *Old Closes and Streets: A Series of Photogravures 1868-1899* (Glasgow: T. & R. Annan & Sons, 1900), Plate 6. Graphic Arts Collection, Department of Rare Books and Special Collections, Princeton University Library.

6:18 Thomas Annan, "Close, No. 46 Saltmarket," from *Glasgow Improvements Act 1866*, Plate 22. Albumen print. Graphic Arts Collection, Department of Rare Books and Special Collections, Princeton University Library.

The Old Closes and Streets of Glasgow 121

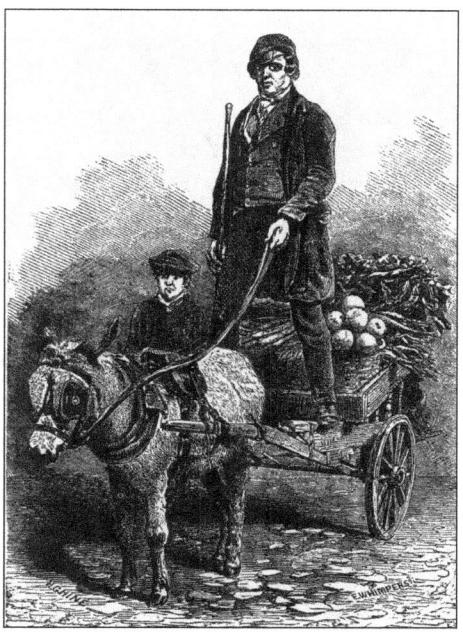

6:19 "The London Costermonger." Engraving of daguerreotype photograph by Richard Beard in Henry Mayhew, *London Labour and the London Poor: A Cyclopædia of the Condition and Earnings of those that will work, those that cannot work, and those that will not work* (London: Griffin, Bohn & Co., 1861), vol. 1, facing p. 12. Princeton University Library.

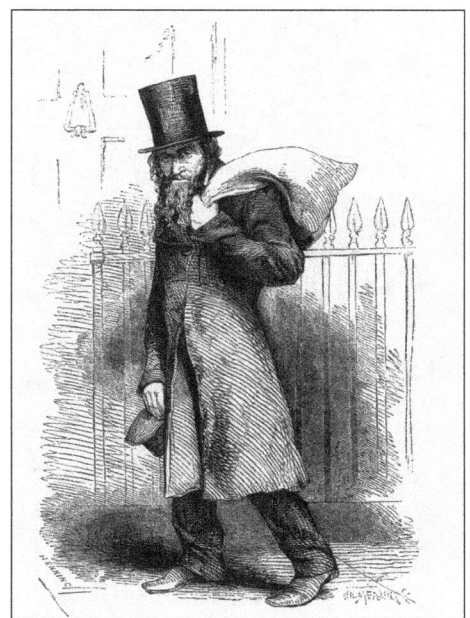

6:20 "The Jew Old-Clothes Man." Engraving of daguerreotype photograph by Richard Beard in Henry Mayhew, *London Labour and the London Poor*, vol. 2, facing p. 118.

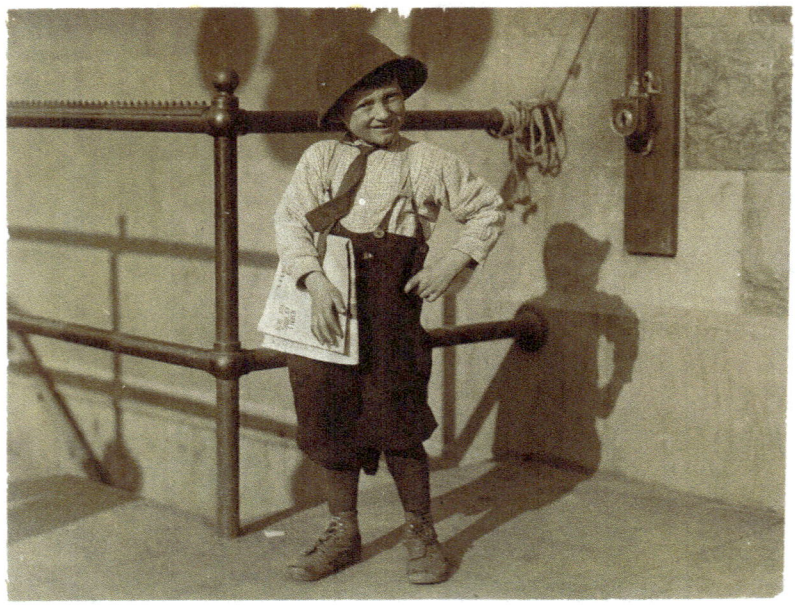

6:21 Lewis Hine, "Luigi, 6-years-old newsboy-beggar, Sacramento, California." 1915. Gelatin silver print. Wikimedia.

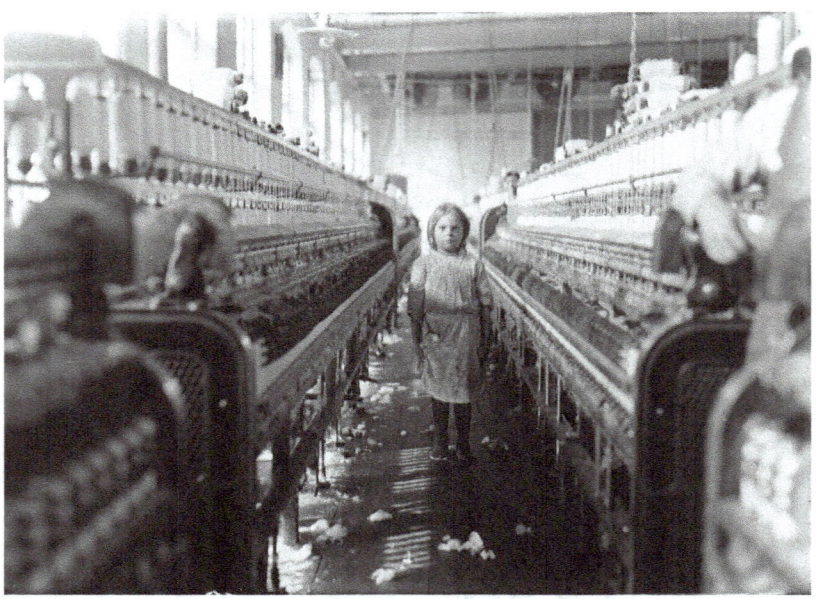

6:22 Lewis Hine, "Child-laborer." 1908. Digital file from original glass negative. Wikimedia.

The Old Closes and Streets of Glasgow   123

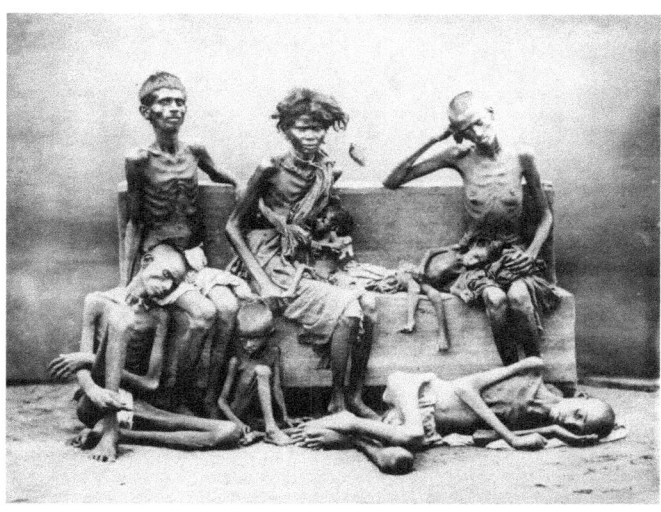

6:23 Colonel William Willoughby Hooper, "Victims of the Madras Famine." 1876. Albumen print. Museum Syndicate.

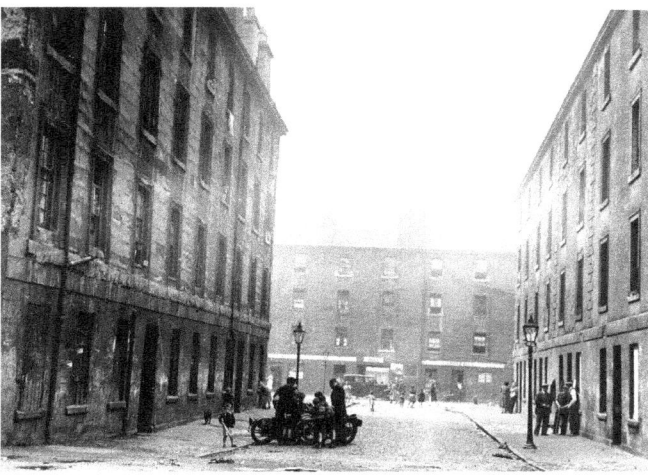

6:24 Glasgow Sanitary Department, "Roslin Place and Burnside Street near Garscube Road in Cowcaddens.' 1920s. Photograph reproduced by courtesy of Glasgow Museums Collection.

7. Epilogue

When the author of this short study was growing up in Glasgow in the 1930s and 1940s, "Clyde-built" referred to the ships built in the world-famous yards of Govan, Clydebank, Linthouse, Scotstoun, Whiteinch, Dumbarton, and other districts and suburbs of the city or nearby towns on the River Clyde. Though the industry was already in decline by that time, the term was used with pride throughout the West of Scotland. It denoted the honest, workmanlike products of inspired engineers and designers and skilled craftsmen (loftsmen, platers, welders, caulkers). As the Wikipedia article puts it, "*Clydebuilt* became an industry benchmark of quality."[136] It seems to me not inappropriate to use the term "Clyde-built" to describe Thomas Annan's work. It too is honest, straightforward, technically advanced, often strikingly well-designed and stirring, but not "artsy." As the writer of Annan's obituary in the *British Journal of Photography* for 23 December 1887 observed, "Honourable in feeling and fastidious in taste, he was utterly intolerant of sham and of everything below the best." At a time when many photographers were already producing work that would sell to the public—not only Valentine's and Wilson's landscapes, soon to be available as picture postcards, but even Hooper's horrific images of victims of the Madras famine—Annan worked to a great extent on commissions received from public agencies and institutions, as well as industries, book publishers, groups, and individuals. He carried out these commissions imaginatively but always conscientiously.

In "the shady commerce between art and truth" that characterizes photography for Susan Sontag,[137] Annan managed to maintain his honesty and integrity. If today we are impressed by the formal composition of his photographs, it does not appear that this quality took precedence for him as a photographer over other considerations. As far as one can judge, he remained committed to the idea of photography as a faithful, conscientiously-made representation of "reality" (including works of art created by others) and retained a naïve conviction—which was probably also that of William Henry Fox Talbot himself[138]—that the photograph can be at one and the same time an authentic historical record and a work of art. To be sure, in photographs of machines that were intended to explain or facilitate their workings, for instance, or in passport photographs, or in aerial photographs designed to assist bombing crews, the primary and dominant function will be that of replicating the object, though that function is always subject to supersession by other unintended functions. But a photograph of a landscape or a cityscape or a building or a person (a photographic portrait, as distinct from a simple mugshot), even if it aims at maximum fidelity, can hardly dispense with some attention to overall design and impact.

In the 1970s, Annan's conviction received something like an endorsement from an unexpected quarter. "The distinctive achievements of photographic seeing," Susan Sontag writes in what appears to be a modification of her critical judgment of the estheticizing effect of photography, "were until quite recently thought to be identical with the work of that relatively small number of photographers who, through reflection and effort, managed to transcend the camera's mechanical nature to meet the standards of art. But it is now clear that there is no inherent conflict between the mechanical or naïve use of the camera and formal beauty of a very high order [. . .]. This democratizing of formal standards is the logical counterpart to photography's democratizing of the notion of beauty. Traditionally associated with exemplary models (the representative art of the classical Greeks showed only youth, the body in its perfection), beauty has been revealed by photographs as existing everywhere."[139]

Endnotes

The following endnotes are often lengthy. My aim was to keep the main text uncluttered while providing additional relevant information and quotations from scholarly articles in the notes, along with abundant bibliographical indications to assist readers who might wish to pursue themes touched on in the text.

1. Brassaï, *Proust in the Power of Photography*, trans. Richard Howard (Chicago: University of Chicago Press, 2001; orig. French ed., 1997), p. xi. My thanks to my colleague Suzanne Nash for alerting me to Brassaï's book.

2. Thanks probably to an original donation by Princeton graduate David H. McAlpin 3rd, who also endowed the Chair of Photography in the Department of Art and Archaeology, Princeton University Library has an outstanding collection of rare albums and published volumes by Annan. Holdings include *The Old Closes and Streets of Glasgow* in both the extremely rare (four or five copies) album of 1871 and the very limited (100 copies) photogravure edition put out by Annan's son, James Craig Annan, in 1900; an album of *Photographs of Glasgow College* (1866), as well as copy no. 150 of *University of Glasgow Old and New* (1891), an updated edition in 350 copies, containing photogravure prints of many of Annan's original photographs in the 1866 album and in the later *Memorials of the Old College of Glasgow* (1871); *Photographs of the Clyde, with Descriptive Letterpress* (1867); *Illustrated Catalogue of the Exhibition of Portraits on Loan in the New Galleries of Art* (1868); *The Old Country Houses of the Old Glasgow Gentry* (both 1st ed., 1870 and 2nd ed., 1878); *Castles and Mansions of Ayrshire* (1885); and *Views on the Line of the Loch Katrine Water Works* (1859) in the later 1889 edition entitled *Photographic Views of Loch Katrine*.

3. On Swan, see George Fairfull Smith, "Joseph Swan (1796-1872) Engraver and Publisher," *The Private Library*, 4th Series, 10 (Summer 1997), 81-92. Among the richly-illustrated and well-selling books published by Swan are *Select Views of Glasgow and its Environs* (1828), *Select Views on the River Clyde* (1830) and *Select Views of the Lakes of Scotland* (1834). The engravings were based on drawings by Scottish artists (John Fleming, John Knox, Andrew Donaldson), and each engraving was accompanied by a descriptive and

historical text by John M. Leighton. Doubtless in order to benefit from tourist interest, the *Views of the Lakes* was also published in cheaper and handier editions, each one devoted to a different part of the country— Inverness-shire, Argyllshire, Perthshire, Selkirkshire, etc. In addition, Swan was commissioned to illustrate rare plants for the Glasgow Royal Botanic Institution and to supply engraved illustrations of mechanical inventions for *The Glasgow Mechanics' Magazine*.

4. "Talbot's technique was a two-step system: the picture exposed in the camera formed a negative image (black for white, and vice versa) on a transparent paper base; this negative image was then used as a filter through which a second piece of sensitized paper was exposed to the light, thus reversing the tonal values. Each daguerreotype was unique, but the calotype negative, like the etcher's plate, could be used to produce an indefinite number of prints. The calotype image was diffused slightly by the texture of the paper through which it was printed and consequently was less sharply detailed than the daguerreotype. But what [David Octavius] Hill had learned from the great dead painters allowed him to compose his pictures broadly and simply, and turn the limitations of the system to his advantage." (John Szarkowski, *Looking at Photographs: 100 Pictures from the Collection of the Museum of Modern Art* [New York: Museum of Modern Art, 1973], p. 16)

5. See Margaret Harker, "Scottish Contributions to Photography, 2: The Symposium," *British Journal of Photography*, 130 (13 May 1983), 492-93, 502 (p. 492), citing Anna Jameson (1794-1860), a British writer and art critic. On the use of the opposition of daguerreotype and calotype to help establish photography as an artistic medium reflecting the imagination and taste of the photographer and not simply a utilitarian instrument in which technical skill was the only discriminating factor, see also the important articles by Margaret Denton, "Francis Wey and the Discourse of Photography as Art in France in the Early 1850s: 'Rien n'est beau que le vrai; mais il faut le choisir'," *Art History*, 25.5 (November 2002), 622-48. http://dx.doi.org/10.1111/1467-8365.00348, and André Gunthert, "L'Institution du photographique: Le roman de la Société héliographique," *Études photographiques*, 12 (November 2002), 37-63. For a critique of the common opposition of daguerreotype and calotype as that of accurate mechanical representation and poetic emphasis on form, see Hans Rooseboom, "What's wrong with Daguerre?" in Tanya Sheehan and Andrés Maria Zervigán, eds., *Photography and its Origins* (New York and London: Routledge, 2015), 29-40. http://dx.doi.org/10.4324/9781315740096

6. Cit. Bodo von Dewitz and Karin Schuler-Procopovici, eds., *David Octavius Hill & Robert Adamson. Von den Anfängen der künstlerischen Photographie im 19. Jahrhundert*, exhibition catalogue, Museum Ludwig/Agfa Photo-Historama (Göttingen: Steidl, 2000), Introduction, p. 9. The King had been shown some calotypes by Principal David Brewster of St. Andrews University, who was himself keenly interested in photography and a

friend of Talbot's, and he had been encouraged by Talbot to stop off at the Hill and Adamson "atelier." Carus's response to photography was decidedly equivocal, however, and he compared it unfavourably with painting, expressing the view, common at the time, that it was a means of mechanically producing copies and thus in no way a true art. Assuredly, "such immediate copies of nature have given me ample materials for reflection." Still, "it is not easy to get a better idea of how much a real work of art—that is the representation of the idea in the soul of the artist [. . .]— must *of necessity* differ from nature than by comparing a really beautiful portrait—Raphael's Fornarina, for example—with a head copied by this process. The free work of art can and ought indeed to present everywhere *less* and at the same time *more* than nature. The mere copy gives the shadow of nature itself and therefore remains soulless, unsatisfying, and rigid. All this, however, does not prevent the neatness, exactness, perfectness, and the peculiar want of style, but at the same time want of affectation, of these latter specimens from possessing a peculiar charm for the artist." (Carl Gustav Carus, *The King of Saxony's Journey through England and Scotland in the Year 1844*, transl. By S.C. Davison [London: Chapman and Hall, 1846], pp. 336-37)

7. Bodo von Dewitz and Karin Schuler-Procopovici, eds., *David Octavius Hill & Robert Adamson*: "Die Bilder von Hill und Adamson nehmen heute unangefochten eine ästhetische und kulturgeschichtliche Spitzenposition in der Photographie des 19. Jahrhunderts ein, als die frühesten und brillantesten Zeugnisse des jungen Mediums. Sie sind Gegenstand ständiger auch noch heute relevanter Erkenntnisinteressen und sie haben durch eine langjährige Rezeption eine bahnbrechende Wirkung auf die jeweiligen künstlerischen Arbeiten mit Photographie gehabt." ["Today, as the earliest and most brilliant works bearing witness to the young medium, the pictures of Hill and Adamson occupy an undisputed highpoint in 19th-century photography from the point of view of both esthetics and cultural history. . ."] (Introduction by Bodo von Dewitz, p. 15); Helmut Gernsheim, *The History of Photography*, rev. ed. (London: Thames and Hudson, 1969 [orig. Oxford: Oxford University Press, 1955]), p. 168. In the same vein Sara Stevenson, *Facing the Light: The Photography of Hill and Adamson* (Edinburgh: Scottish National Portrait Gallery, 2002): "Hill and Adamson [. . .] produced some of the most beautiful and enduring images in the history of photography." (Foreword, p. 7) See also the no less admiring comments of Paul Strand, himself one of the great modern photographers, in "Photography and the New God," *Broom*, 5 (1922), 252-58: "Despite the primitive machine and materials with which [D.O. Hill] was compelled to work, the exposure of five to fifteen minutes in bright sunlight, this series of photographs has victoriously stood the test of comparison with nearly everything done in photography since 1845. They remain the most extraordinary assertion of the possiblity of the utterly personal control of a machine, the camera." (Reproduced in Nathan Lyons, ed., *Photographers on Photography* [Englewood Cliffs, N.J.: Prentice-Hall, 1966], 138-44 [p. 140])

8. On Wilson, see Roger Taylor, *George Washington Wilson, Artist and Photographer 1823-93* (Aberdeen: Aberdeen University Press, 1981); also Roddy Simpson, *The Photography of Victorian Scotland* (Edinburgh: Edinburgh University Press, 2012), pp. 115-24. http://dx.doi.org/10.3366/edinburgh/9780748654611.001.0001

9. On Valentine, see Simpson, *The Photography of Victorian Scotland*, pp. 124-28. On nineteenth-century Scottish photography, see also James Clement, "Scottish Contributions to Photography, 1: The Exhibitions," *British Journal of Photography*, 130 (6 May 1983), 467-68, and Margaret Harker, "Scottish Contributions to Photography, 2: The Symposium," *British Journal of Photography*, 130 (13 and 20 May 1983), 492-93, 502, 526-27, 530, 537. Princeton University's Graphic Arts Collection has 26 early Valentine photographs of landscapes and historical sites in Scotland and England.

10. On Scottish photographers active outside Scotland, see Simpson, *The Photography of Victorian Scotland*, pp. 90-114. On Notman, see
http://www.mccord-museum.qc.ca/notman_doc/pdf/EN/FINAL-NOTMAN-ENG.pdf
http://www.nfb.ca/film/notmans_world
http://www.biographi.ca/en/bio.php?id_nbr=6336
http://www.historytothepeople.ca/portrait-of-a-nation-the-photographs-of-william-notman-and-son-studios/
Princeton University's Graphic Arts Collection has a miniature advertising pamphlet from the Notman firm of 1867-70, in which Notman is described grandly as "Photographer to the Queen and under the patronage of the Emperor of France."

11. According to the Honorary Secretary of the Photographic Society of Great Britain, H. Baden Pritchard, "an inspection of a series of these [portraits] proclaims the master. The portraits are simple in pose—soft, and of exceeding brilliancy. Indeed we have rarely seen such brilliant photographs. They are without glaze, but printed, evidently, on very thickly albumenized paper, Mr. Fergus showing a predilection for a surface having a slightly roseate hue. Many of the portraits have plain backgrounds; none of them show elaborate accessories. Much taste is evident in the disposal of drapery, and the flowing robes of a model are marked with harmony and detail to the extreme margins of the picture. Yet it must not be thought that Mr. Fergus strives after effect by means of gorgeous raiment. The most charming study we saw was the simple portrait of a widow lady attired in weeds and crape-trimmed dress. The hair, streaked with silver, and the pale features, were limned with rare taste and delicacy, and in perfect harmony with the white cap and black dress; there was plenty of vigour and yet no violent contrasts." The design and outfitting of the "light and lofty studios" was also much admired, as was Fergus's own quiet modesty. (H. Baden Pritchard, *The Photographic Studios of Europe* [London: Piper and Carter, 1882], pp. 183-

87). Fergus must have had a fairly distinguished clientele, for in the 1880s he opened a branch studio in Cannes on the French Riviera. As the author of an article entitled "Glasgow Photographers" in the American journal *Wilson's Photographic Magazine*, put it in 1901: "Fergus is one of a small body of men whose work years ago led many wealthy English people to defer visiting a studio until they went north to Scotland. [. . . He] must be a photographer of the wealthy. Every picture of his is framed. There is one of the king, colored and brilliant in a frame of gold, and another colored one of a lady in a frame of ornate gilt gesso on an enamelled green flat." (vol. 31 [1901], p. 381) However, Fergus also made portraits of people distinguished in other ways, such as William Lloyd Garrison, the American abolitionist, Henry Morton Stanley, the explorer, and Lord Kelvin, the renowned scientist and professor at Glasgow University.

12. John Hannavy, *The Victorian Professional Photographer* (Aylesbury: Shire Publications, 1980), p. 6.

13. Her "gentle, yet paradoxically passionate images represent one of the most distinguished contributions to the development of High Victorian art photography." (Graham Ovenden, *Clementina, Lady Hawarden* [London: Academy Editions; New York: St. Martin's Press, 1974], p. 5) On Lady Hawarden, see also Julie Lawson, *Women in White: Photographs by Clementina, Lady Hawarden* (Edinburgh: Scottish National Portrait Gallery, 1997); Virginia Dodier, *Clementina, Lady Hawarden: Studies from Life 1857-1864* ([n.p.]: Aperture, 1999); and Roddy Simpson, *The Photography of Victorian Scotland*, pp. 157-61.

14. On Keith, see *Thomas Keith 1827-1895, Surgeon and Photographer: The Hurd Bequest*, ed. C.S. Minto (Edinburgh: Edinburgh Corporation Libraries and Museums Committee, 1972); John Hannavy, *Thomas Keith's Scotland: The Work of a Victorian Amateur Photographer 1852-57* (Edinburgh: Canongate, 1981); Roddy Simpson, *The Photography of Victorian Scotland*, pp. 55-60; and several essays devoted to Keith in *Studies in Photography*, 2007.

15. Cit. by Sara Stevenson in her *Thomas Annan 1829-1887*, Scottish Masters 12 (Edinburgh: National Galleries of Scotland, 1990), p. 8. On the growing number of professional photographers in Glasgow alone, see John Urie, *Reminiscences of Eighty Years* (Paisley: A. Gardner, 1908), pp. 114-29 and David Bruce, *Graetrex: Forger and Photographer* (Edinburgh: Renaissance Press, 2013), p. 31. For a complete list of Glasgow photographers from the 1840s to the early 1900s, with samples of their work, see http://www.thelows.madasafish.com/main.htm#mid Thirty are listed as being active or having opened in the 1850s alone.

16. *Photographs exhibited in Britain 1839-1865* (Ottawa: National Gallery of Canada, Occasional papers no. 5, [2002]), pp. 84-87. This text is also partly viewable online at http://peib.dmu.ac.uk where it is complemented by a convenient searchable database.

17. Business card reproduced in Margaret F. Harker, "The Annans of Glasgow," *British Journal of Photography* (12 and 19 October 1973), 932-35, 966-69 (p. 934). See also Rachel Stuhlman, "'Let Glasgow Flourish.' Thomas Annan and the Glasgow Corporation Waterworks," *Image*, 35 (1992), 38-51 (p. 47). In 1855, while it was still in the stocks, Annan photographed the new all-iron steamship "Persia," designed by Robert Napier of Glasgow for the Cunard line. It was the largest ship in the world at the time of its launch and the fastest trans-Atlantic liner. (See William Buchanan's entry on Thomas Annan in John Hannavy, ed., *Encyclopedia of Nineteenth-Century Photography*, vol. 1 [New York and London: Routledge, 2007], pp. 44-47. http://dx.doi.org/10.4324/9780203941782, and the same author's "Annans of Glasgow," *Studies in Photography* [2006], 20-29 [p. 20]).

18. Virginia Woolf, "Jane Austen," *The Common Reader: First Series* (New York: Harcourt Brace, 1948), p. 197.

19. Bingham's album was put out after Delaroche's death by the latter's dealer in Paris, the Goupil Gallery. See Stephen Bann, *Parallel Lines: Printmakers, Painters and Photographers in Nineteenth-Century France* (New Haven: Yale University Press, 2001), pp. 118-19; Laure Boyer, "Robert J. Bingham, photographe du monde de l'art sous le Second Empire," *Études photographiques*, 12 (November 2002), 127-41. Boyer notes that producing photographic reproductions of paintings was seen as a way for the photographer to win a respected place, as a successor to the engraver, in the world of art: "In an effort to win its title of nobility through the practice of reproducing great works of painting, photography positioned itself as the continuator of engraving. Viewed today simply as a document, the photographic reproduction of painting was seen at the time as an artistic practice as prestigious as engraving. Increasingly represented at exhibitions, the object of critical reviews and the winner of medals and prizes (Bingham was awarded a medal at the London International Exhibition of 1862), it was widely recognized in the 1860s as a particular artistic practice and by the end of the century it had replaced engraving." (pp. 132-33) Roddy Simpson observes that the earliest photographic illustrations of a book on painting are in *Annals of the Artists of Spain*, 3 vols. (London: John Ollivier, 1848) by Sir William Stirling-Maxwell, whose collection of Spanish paintings is preserved at the family's eighteenth-century home, Pollok House, now in the southern suburbs of Glasgow and open to the public. (*The Photography of Victorian Scotland*, p. 171; see also http://www.gla.ac.uk/schools/cca/research/instituteofarthistory/projectsandnetworks/stirlingmaxwellresearchproject/)

20. James Downs, "Out of the Shadows: István Szabó (1822-58), a Forgotten 'Photographic Luminary'," *Studies in Photography* (2008), 28-38 (pp. 31 and 37 [note 46]). Downs was probably referring to the text accompanying plate XXIII, "Hagar in the desert by Francesco Mola," in Talbot's *The Pencil of Nature*: "This plate is intended to show another important application of the photographic art. Fac-similes can be made from original sketches of

the old masters, and thus they may be preserved from loss, and multiplied to any extent" (pages unnumbered).

21. Mark Haworth-Booth and Anne McCauley, *The Museum and the Photograph* (Williamstown, MA: Sterling and Francine Clark Institute, 1998), pp. 11, 23, 34.

22. *Musée d'Anvers* (Brussels, Leipzig, Ghent: C. Muquard; Paris: Veuve Jules Renouard, 1862), pp. 10-11 (signed W.B. [Wilhelm Bürger]). On the fascinating history of the photographic reproduction of paintings, see the Introduction by Stephen Bann to his edited volume *Art and the Early Photographic Album* (Washington: National Gallery of Art; New Haven: Yale University Press, 2011), pp. 15-16. Bann observes that many notable artists (e.g. Ingres and Courbet) were keenly interested in photographic reproductions of their paintings and discriminated carefully between photographers whose work met their standards and those whose work did not; see Stephen Bann, *Parallel Lines*, pp. 158-68.

23. Grace Seiberling, *Amateurs, Photography, and the Mid-Victorian Imagination* (Chicago: University of Chicago Press, 1986), p. 86; Isobel Crombie, "The Madonnna of the Future: O.G. Rejlander and Sassoferrato," *Art Bulletin of the National Gallery of Victoria*, 43 (2003) at http://www.ngv.vic.gov.au/essay/the-madonna-of-the-future-o-g-rejlander-and-sassoferrato/

24. Obituary of T. Annan, *British Journal of Photography*, 34 (23 December 1887), 803. Commenting on Annan's photographs of paintings for the Glasgow Art Union, the *Photographic News* (6 November 1863) pronounced that "Mr. Annan confirms his position as one of our very finest masters of photographic reproduction." (Cited by William Buchanan, "The Annans of Glasgow," *Studies in Photography* [2006], 22)

25. As described by Stevenson, "The Art Unions were lotteries connected with the major art exhibitions; the successful subscribers won paintings, and every subscriber received an engraving. This encouraged artists and educated the public." (*Thomas Annan 1829-1887*, pp. 5-6)

26. Cited in Stevenson, *Thomas Annan*, p. 6. The positive view of photographs of paintings expressed by Millais and Paton was not shared by all. In the mid-1850s, David Octavius Hill had proposed replacing engravings of paintings with photographs for the annual awards to dues-paying members of the Edinburgh Association for the Promotion of the Fine Arts in Scotland, which he himself had founded in 1833. His proposal provoked an outcry in the *Art Journal* and a pamphlet entitled *Photography versus the Fine Arts* (1854), the author of which, representing the position that photography is a simple mechanical process devoid of any artistry, protested that "a photographic picture . . . is not Art, but the result of a scientific application of a natural element, no more allied to Art, except in this application, than is the steam engine or the electric telegraph."

Engravings continued to be the medium of choice well into the 1860s. (David and Francina Irwin, *Scottish Painters at Home and Abroad 1700-1900* [London: Faber and Faber, 1975], pp. 285-86)

27. *British Journal of Photography*, 10 (2 November 1863), 419. Cornell University Library's Division of Rare Books and Manuscripts holds a copy of the album containing the five plates in question. It is entitled *Bond and Free: Five Sketches Illustrative of Slavery by J. Noël Paton; Photographed by Thomas Annan* (Glasgow: Maclure and MacDonald, [1863]), cat. no.: Rare Books E433. P31+++. Other copies of this extremely rare work are in the rare books collection at Northwestern University, cat. no.: F 306.362 P312b, and in the Mitchell Library in Glasgow. For a close study of the work and the engravings drawn from it, see Susan P. Casteras, "Joseph Noel Paton's Bond and Free: Five Sketches Illustrative of Slavery," *Vital Resources: An International Journal of Documentation*, 27 (2011), 48-62. http://dx.doi.org/10.1080/01973762.2011.542354. Engravings of the first and last plates accompanied an anti-slavery poem, "The Song of the Freed Woman," by the Scottish poetess and early feminist Isa Craig (1831-1903) in the Christian *Sunday Magazine* (1 June 1865), 672-76.

28. Thus John Szarkowski in his classic *Looking at Photographs*, p. 16: "When the painting was finally finished in 1866, twenty-three years after the first photographs were made, it established Hill as one of the first artists to have converted good photography into bad painting." Malcolm Daniel of the Metropolitan Museum in a similar vein: "It was so easy to make the portrait 'sketches' by means of photography that Hill's painting was ultimately overburdened by a surfeit of recognizable faces: 450 names appear on his key to the painting. The final composition—not completed for two decades and as dull a work as one can imagine—lacks not only the fiery dynamism of Hill's first sketches of the event but also the immediacy and graphic power of the photographs that were meant to serve it." http://www.metmuseum.org/toah/hd/hlad/hd_hlad.htm#slideshow4. Not everyone entirely agrees. In an informal e-mail of 29/6/14 Ray McKenzie wrote to me: "D. O. Hill's Disruption painting is in the Free Presbytery Hall in Edinburgh. I went to see it with a group of colleagues [. . .] a few years ago and I thought it was nowhere near as bad as people [. . .] say it is. Sure, the composition is a bit clumsy, but with *that* many figures what do you expect? Hill was a more than competent painter, and if you can see past the spatial incongruities there is a lot to enjoy in it." See also a suggestive article by Duncan Macmillan, "The Disruption Painting," *Studies in Photography* (2002-03), 42-49 and John Wood and Sara Stevenson, *Printed Light: The Scientific Art of William Henry Fox Talbot and David Octavius Hill with Robert Adamson* (Edinburgh: H.M. Stationary Office, 1986). Wood and Stevenson reproduce (p. 157) an early sketch of the painting which "introduced a dramatic depth to the picture with a single high light-source" coming from the table at the centre, while a high arched top created a large space above the human figures. These features allowed for a more conventional composition.

29. Cited in Macmillan, "The Disruption Painting," p. 49.

30. Colin Ford, ed., *An Early Victorian Album: The Hill/Adamson Collection*, with a commentary by Roy Strong (London: Jonathan Cape, 1974), pp. 50-51. Ford cites a contemporary document: "It has been the ambition and aim of the Painter, to render his representation of the Disruption Assembly a desirable, if not indispensable heirloom in the homes of all Free Churchmen [. . .]. He has been careful to exclude from his canvas any episodical passage or incident which might by possibility have given offence to any individual or Church [and he] entertains the hope, therefore, that the representation [. . .] will find ready admission into the houses and Art Collections of men of all denominations of religious opinions, both in our own and other lands."

31. William Buchanan, ed., *J. Craig Annan: Selected Texts and Bibliography* (New York: G.K. Hall & Co., 1994), p. 1. On the planned formats of Annan's photograph of Hill's painting and their prices, see Ford, *An Early Victorian Album*, p. 52; William Buchanan, "The Annans of Glasgow," *Studies in Photography* (2006), 22, where it is asserted that each format was produced in an edition of 1,000; and especially the detailed account of formats and sales given by Roddy Simpson, "Subscribers to the Prints of the Disruption Painting," *Studies in Photography* (2008), 51-57.

32. The most quirky invention of John Kibble (1815-1894), the son of the owner of a wire and metal warehouse, was a floating bicycle, on which he is said to have cycled across Loch Long. As a photographer, he is best known for creating, in 1858, the world's biggest camera. It was mounted on a horse-drawn cart and had a lens with a diameter of 13 inches. The Kibble Palace, one of Glasgow's most popular attractions, was originally built by Kibble in 1865 as a large iron-framed conservatory at his home, Coulport House, on Loch Long. It was re-erected in 1871 in Glasgow's Botanical Gardens as the Kibble Crystal Art Palace and Royal Conservatory (www.glasgowbotanicgardens.com/the-gardens/history/kibble-palace/). House no longer exists; the entire village has been demolished to make way for the Royal Naval Armament Depot where nuclear weapons removed from nuclear submarines are stored while they are being serviced.
Turning from astronomical work to the design and making of photographic lenses, German-born John Henry Dallmeyer introduced improvements in both portrait and landscape lenses, in object-glasses for the microscope and in condensers for the optical lantern. He constructed photo-heliographs for the Wilna observatory in 1863, for the Harvard College Observatory in 1864 and for the British government in 1873. Dallmeyer's instruments took the highest awards at various international exhibitions and he was honored by both the Russian and French governments.

33. Margaret F. Harker, "Annans of Glasgow," *British Journal of Photography* (12 and 19 October, 1973), 933.

34. *Illustrations of Mary Queen of Scots, a poem by Henry Glassford Bell, being photographs from pictures painted for the Art Union of Glasgow by Robert Herdman, presented to the members for the year 1867-1868.* This work is held by only a small number of libraries in Great Britain and the U.S. and by the Rijksmuseum Library in Amsterdam. It should not be confused with a more widely distributed, later edition of Bell's poem, *Mary Queen of Scots: A Poem* (London: Raphael Tuck, [n.d.]), which was illustrated by the artist Walter G. Grieve and is more widely available at libraries in Britain, the U.S., Canada, the Netherlands, and at the Bibliothèque Nationale in Paris.

35. On the controversy over the Munich stained glass windows installed in Glasgow Cathedral, see the essays by Stephen Adam, a leading Glasgow artist in stained glass, *Stained Glass: Its History and Modern Development* (Glasgow: James MacLehose, 1877), pp. 17-24, 29, and "The Stained Glass Windows," in George Eyre-Todd, ed., *The Book of Glasgow Cathedral* (Glasgow: Morison Brothers, 1898), pp. 395-407; see also brief notes in George Fairfull Smith, "Glasgow Cathedral Windows" available at http://special.lib.gla.ac.uk/GlasgowCathedral/index.htm

36. In view of the cost at the time of illustrating them with mounted photographs, all these books appear to have been produced in very limited editions, with the result that they are currently held by only a few libraries in Britain, the U.S., Canada and the Netherlands. *The Scottish Bar Fifty Years Ago* is available online, however, at https://archive.org/details/cu31924024629853 and the photographs of the sketches at http://www.geni.com/projects/The-Scottish-Bar-Fifty-Years-Ago-Sketches-of-Scott-and-his-contemporaries/photos/15456 While Annan was selected to illustrate the paintings of Sir George Harvey, the sculptress Amelia Robertson Hill, the wife of Annan's friend David Octavius Hill, was commissioned to produce a head of the artist.

37. Lady Elizabeth Eastlake in *London Quarterly Review*, March 1857, article reproduced in Alan Trachtenberg, ed., *Classic Essays on Photography* (New Haven: Leete's Island Books, 1980), p. 41. Lady Eastlake, the former Elizabeth Rigby, was a talented writer and critic, and was herself the subject of portraits by Hill and Adamson. On the popularity of carte-de-visite portraits among "all classes and conditions of men and women," see John Urie, *Reminiscences of Eighty Years*, Chapter IX, p. 118.

38. *Historical Notices of the United Presbyterian Congregations in Glasgow*, edited by John Logan Aikman, with photographs by Thomas Annan (Glasgow: Thomas Annan, 1875). Copies of this rare publication are held by the National Library of Scotland; the British Library; the university libraries of Glasgow, Edinburgh, Strathclyde, St. Andrews and Aberdeen; the Pitts Theological Library, Candler School of Theology of Emory University, Atlanta, Georgia; the Rijksmuseum Library in Amsterdam; and the library of Keio University in Japan.

39. On the close connection between the styles of portraiture in painting and photography in the second half of the nineteenth century, see Elizabeth Anne McCauley, *A.A.E. Disdéri and the Carte de Visite Portrait Photograph* (New Haven: Yale University Press, 1985), especially ch. 6, "The Carte de Visite and Portrait Painting during the Second Empire."

40. For a positive view of Annan as a portrait photographer, see Margaret F. Harker, "Annans of Glasgow," *British Journal of Photography* (1973), 935, and Sara Stevenson, *Thomas Annan*, pp. 12-13. Harker reproduces one of Annan's more charming portraits: it shows his wife Mary at Talbot Cottage, with baby James Craig Annan on her lap, eldest son John reading by her side and Anna Mary, David Livingstone's daughter, standing and looking over John's shoulder (p. 933).

41. Helmut Gernsheim, *The History of Photography*, p. 304.

42. See Ray McKenzie, "A Love Affair with Loch Katrine: Problems of Representation in Early Scottish Landscape," *Scottish Photography Bulletin*, 1 (1990), 3-12 (pp. 3, 5-7). Of the 23 photographs in Talbot's *Sun Pictures in Scotland*, seven are devoted to Loch Katrine, the others to Abbotsford, Melrose, Dryburgh, the Scott Monument in Edinburgh and other scenes connected with Scott's life and work.

43. See Smith, "Joseph Swan (1796-1872) engraver and publisher," p. 92. Some of the photographs of landscapes in works by Annan, such as *Photographs of the Clyde* (Glasgow: Andrew Duthie, 1867) and *Photographs of Glasgow* (Glasgow: T.&R. Annan,1868), are in fact of subjects featured in Swan's *Select Views on the River Clyde, engraved by Joseph Swan from drawings by J. Fleming, with historical and descriptive illustrations by John M. Leighton* (Glasgow: Joseph Swan, 1830) and *Select Views of Glasgow and its Environs, engraved by Joseph Swan from drawings by Mr. J. Fleming and Mr. J. Knox, with historical and descriptive illustrations and an introductory sketch of the progress of the city by John M, Leighton, Esq.* (Glasgow: Joseph Swan, 1828).

44. Thus, for example, *Select Views of Glasgow and its Environs* (see note 43 above); *The Lakes of Scotland: A Series of Views from paintings taken expressly for the work by John Fleming, with historical and descriptive illustrations by John M. Leighton and remarks on the character of the Highland Scenery of Scotland by John Wilson* (Glasgow: Joseph Swan, 1834); *The Poetical Works of the Ettrick Shepherd* [James Hogg] *with an Autobiography and Illustrative Engravings, chiefly from Original Drawings by D.O. Hill, R.S.A.* (Glasgow: Blackie and Son, [1838]), 5 vols.; *The Land of Burns: A Series of Landscapes and Portraits illustrative of the life and writings of the Scottish poet by Professor John Wilson of the University of Edinburgh and Robert Chambers, Esq. The Landscapes from Paintings made expressly for the Work by D.O. Hill, Esq., R.S.A.* (Glasgow: Blackie and Sons, 1840).

45. Ray McKenzie, "Thomas Annan and the Scottish Landscape: Among the Gray Edifices," *British Journal of Photography*, 120 (12 October 1973), 40-49 (p. 42). For an overview of Annan's many landscape photographs, see the thumbnails in the online inventory of the extensive holdings of Annan photographs at the Mitchell Library in Glasgow: http://www.rls.org.uk/database/results.php?search_term=annan&x=26&y=7 on pp. 8-83. Unfortunately, they cannot be enlarged.

46. The 1857 and 1860 editions, from different Glasgow publishers, appear not to have included illustrations. In all of Annan's book publications, the photographs were still pasted in rather than printed along with the text. That possibility was not yet available in his time. Editions were therefore still restricted in number and copies expensive, but Annan was quick to realize the possibilities of the illustrated book. See on this topic Tom Normand, "The Book as Photography," in *The Edinburgh History of the Book in Scotland*, ed. David Finkelstein and Alistair McCleery, vol. 4 (Edinburgh: Edinburgh University Press, 2007), pp. 168-81.

47. Ray McKenzie, "Landscape in Scotland: Photography and the Poetics of Place," in *Light from the Dark Room: A Celebration of Scottish Photography*, ed. Sara Stevenson (Edinburgh: National Galleries of Scotland, 1995), p. 76; William Buchanan, entry on "Annan, Thomas," in John Hannavy, ed., *Encyclopedia of Nineteenth-Century Photography*, vol. 1, pp. 44-47. Journal passages cited in William Buchanan, "The Annans of Glasgow," *Studies in Photography* (2006), 21.

48. Quoted from the 1889 edition of *Photographic Views of Loch Katrine and of some of the principal works constructed for introducing the water of Loch Katrine into the city of Glasgow by T.& R. Annan and Sons, with descriptive notes by James M. Gale, M. Inst., C.E., Engineer to the Commissioners* (Glasgow: Printed by James C. Erskine). The earlier edition of 1877 (Glasgow: McLaren and Erskine) is held by the National Library of Scotland, the library of the Glasgow School of Art, the Library of Congress, the George Eastman House Museum, the library of the University of Guelph in Canada and the British Art Center at Yale. As far as I have been able to ascertain, the only accessible copy of the original 1859 album is held by the Mitchell Library of Glasgow.

49. Ibid., p. 9. The contrast between the traditional view of Loch Katrine, evoked by Annan himself in his album, and that presented by the photographs in *Views on the Line of Loch Katrine Water Works* is noted by Rachel Stuhlman in her article "'Let Glasgow Flourish': Thomas Annan and the Glasgow Corporation Waterworks," p. 43.

50. Ray McKenzie, "Thomas Annan and the Scottish Landscape: Among the Gray Edifices," *British Journal of Photography* (12 October 1973), p. 42.

51. Reported in *Illustrated London News* (22 October 1859), p. 404.

52. *Photographic Views of Loch Katrine and of some of the principal works constructed for introducing the water of Loch Katrine into the city of Glasgow* (as in endnote 48 above), p. 20. On Annan's *Photographic Views of Loch Katrine* as a "testament to the continuing will for civic improvement," see Stuhlman, "'Let Glasgow Flourish,'" p. 43. Growing up in Glasgow in the 1930s, 40s and 50s, the author of this essay remembers how much pride the citizens continued to take in their city's water—purer, they were convinced, than that of any other large city in the world. Bottled spring water was unheard of and, if it had been known, it would have been pronounced inferior.

53. Queen Victoria, *Our Life in the Highlands*, selected from *Leaves from the Journal of our Life in the Highlands* [London: Smith, Elder, 1868] and *More Leaves from the Journal of a Life in the Highlands*. [London: Smith, Elder, 1884] (London: William Kimber, 1968), pp. 129-30 (entry for Thursday, 2 September 1869). Queen Victoria seems not to have felt that the "steamer" she referred to was not exactly in harmony with the antique simplicity she so appreciated. A similar, even more striking unawareness is displayed in a report on a journey to Scotland undertaken by the well-known German art historian Gustav Friedrich Waagen in 1850: "By a happy combination of steamboat, railway and pedestrian journeys we managed to see Loch Lomond and Loch Long [. . .] in one day. Never before had I witnessed scenery which bore so strongly the impress of a grand melancholy. In those mists which never dispersed during the whole day, and veiled more or less the forms of the hills, I could well imagine the presence of those Ossianic spirits which pervade Macpherson's poems. Many parts also brought Scott's 'Lady of the Lake' vividly before me." (Cit. James Holloway and Lindsay Errington, *The Discovery of Scotland: The Appreciation of Scottish Scenery through Two Centuries of Painting* [Edinburgh: National Galleries of Scotland, 1978], p. 103). Holloway and Errington note that "Waagen's discrepant experience, the incongruity of which he seems not to have noticed, was matched by that of thousands of other nineteenth-century tourists who were enabled by the newly engineered communications systems to reach in easy journeys the most remote of Highland lochs and glens, but who, their goal attained, blotted the presence of steamboat, coach, and train from their vision and looked only for Ossian and Scott." Some, however, were keenly aware that the invasion of modernity undermined the Romantic view of Scotland. Lord Cockburn complained in 1844 that "from Edinburgh to Inverness the [. . .] country is an asylum of railway lunatics [. . .]. And anyone who puts in a word for the preservation of scenery, or relics, or ancient haunts, is put down as hostile [. . .] to 'modern improvement' and the 'march of intellect'." The railways, he protested, annihilated the scenic beauty they were designed to render available. "I never see a scene of Scotch beauty without being thankful that I have beheld it before it has been breathed over by the angel of mechanical destruction." (Cit. ibid.)

54. A modern edition of this work, in somewhat altered format, was published in 2004 by the Grimsay Press of Kilkerran, in south Ayrshire, Scotland, a publisher of books, new and old, on Scottish topics.

55. See the excellent article by Julie Lawson, "The Problem of Poverty and the Picturesque: Thomas Annan's *Old Closes and Streets of Glasgow* 1868-1871," *Scottish Photography Bulletin*, 2 (1990), 40-46.

56. Of *The Old Country Houses*, only about 120 copies of the 1870 edition were printed and the majority of the subscribers were the property-owners themselves, though several subscribers gave London as their residence, two Bombay, and one Edinburgh. 225 copies of the 1878 edition were printed and, once again, most of the subscribers were local, though one was a resident of Washington D.C. and another of New York City. Of *The Castles and Mansions of Ayrshire*, only 200 copies were printed, according to its 2004 republisher, the Grimsay Press.

57. "Memoir of the Author," signed G.N., in Mitchell's *Old Glasgow Essays* (Glasgow: James MacLehose and Sons; London: Macmillan, 1905), pp. xvii-xxviii (p. xxiv). The son of a city lawyer, Mitchell (b. 1826) was in the leather trade, but devoted much of his leisure time to antiquarian and local history pursuits. In recognition of these he was awarded an honorary LL.D. by Glasgow University.

58. Passages quoted are from the two Introductions, *Old Country Houses of the Old Glasgow Gentry*, 2nd ed. (Glasgow: James MacLehose, 1878), pp. ix-xvi. It should be noted that the conservatism of the editors extended well beyond a lament for the disappearance of the "old gentry." In their Introduction to the 1870 edition, they also noted with regret and concern the displacement by the expanding city of a class of smallholders who worked their own modest tracts of land: "There are other old country houses, scattered here and there round Glasgow, that it will never be worth any one's while to photograph, nor to decipher their trifling annals: little old one-storied farm-steadings, of the familiar Scotch type, with a but and a ben, a byre, a stable, may-be a cart-shed, and in the middle a through-gang to the kail-yard behind. They mostly stand alone: sometimes two or three nestle together into a little 'town.' Labourers, probably Irish, live in them, or they stand, with windows and thatch gone, like deserted shielings in a Highland glen. But a race once lived in them as proud as any Tobacco Lord [the 18th and early 19th century burgher aristocracy of Glasgow was largely composed of families active in tobacco importing and processing] of them all. For the few acres they laboured were their own, and had belonged to their forebears for generations back, and they knew that their class had done its full share in the making of Scotland. But the stars in their courses, on both sides of the Tweed, fight against the small proprietor, and, like the Yeomen and Statesmen of England, these Bonnet Lairds are mostly gone—gone and forgotten. Their little freeholds are broken up for villas, or lost in some bigger estate, the very names rubbed off the map." (p. xiii)

59. Thus the reader is informed in the entry on Craigpark House in the 1878 edition that "Provost McKenzie's house is gone" (p. 66); in the entry on

Meadow Park House that "Meadow Park house, like its stately neighbour Whitehill, has now made way for a row of 'flatted tenements'." (p. 179) Gairbraid House "is much altered since the photograph was taken. In fact the old place may be said to be gone. The magnificent avenue of beech trees has been cut down, the woods on the banks of the Kelvin have been ruthlessly swept away, and the old house now stands naked and forlorn amidst a wilderness of 'free coups,' broken bottles and bricks, pools of dirty water, clothes lines fluttering with parti-coloured rags and all the abominations of a new suburb. Instead of the singing of the birds and the music of the soft flowing Kelvin, the air is now vocal with the discordant voices of rough men, scolding women, and 'greeting bairns,' and with the clang of machinery and the hiss of the steam engine." (p. 102) As for Annfield, the editors had already noted in the text of the 1870 edition, reproduced in that of 1878, that it "was once a beautiful suburban villa, embosomed in trees, and perfectly retired. But the unceasing extension of the City has [...] completely changed its rural character. The gardens are now intersected by streets, both sides of the old highway built: and all that is recognizable of the Annfield of olden time is the house itself, yet lingering in a new street leading up to it from Gallowgate, but doomed to early destruction." (p. 3)

60. Margaret Harker, "From Mansion to Close: Thomas Annan, Master Photographer," *The Photographic Collector*, 5 (1984), 81-96 (p. 83). The Picturesque movement in photography is often considered a forerunner of the Pictorial movement at the end of the century and in the early decades of the twentieth century: i.e. it sought to establish photography as an art, by emphasizing the formal features of the images produced by the photographer and his own role in selecting them. See endnote 98 below.

61. "Historically, two distinct approaches to photographing architectural subjects can be identified. The early photography of architecture [...] was founded on an implicit trust in the medium's documentary veracity, and adhered to strict representational conventions intended to maintain its supposed neutrality and objectivity: the influential French *Commission des monuments historiques*, for example, began the process of documenting France's historical treasures with a strict set of rules for how its cathedrals and châteaux would be recorded. [...] An almost diametrically opposite approach [...] originates with the language of early art photography, which was very much indebted to the conventions of painting. [...] It was against the rules set out for the 'proper' documentation of architecture and monuments that many of the Pictorialists rebelled. The English photographer [Frederik] Evans thus chose to evoke rather than record the cathedrals of northern France in soft and atmospheric focus. In the United States, Paul Strand and Charles Sheeler moved towards a harder line in work which developed elements of the abstract." (Andre Higgott and Timothy Way, eds., "Introduction," *Camera Constructs: Photography, Architecture and the Modern City* [Farnham: Ashgate, 2012], pp. 11-12)

62. *Report of the Buildings of Glasgow University* appended to the *Report* of the Scottish Universities Commission of 1858, cited in J.D. Mackie, *The University of Glasgow 1451-1951: A Short History* (Glasgow: Jackson, 1954), p. 280. The report was published in 1863. See also J. Morrison in *Sanitary Journal*, 1 (1877), p. 268: "There was in the very heart of the city one of the foulest ulcers that ever disgraced a modern city. Every approach to the old University was through a moral sewer of a most loathsome description, crowded with population, showing by its physique the extent to which the human form divine could be degraded by drunkenness and every attendant form of vice and profligacy." (cit. by C.M. Allan, "The Genesis of British Urban Redevelopment with Special Reference to Glasgow," *Economic History Review*, new series, 18 [1965], 598-613 [pp. 602-03])

63. An updated edition of this work, limited to 350 sumptuously produced in-folio copies, with extensive and richly informed historical texts, additional photographs of the new University buildings and portraits of the current professors (i.e. heads of department) in each of the departments of the University's four faculties of Arts, Theology, Law and Medicine, was published by T. & R. Annan & Sons and James MacLehose & Sons in 1891, using the photogravure process, under the title *University of Glasgow Old and New*. Princeton University's Marquand Library owns copy number 150.

64. The previously mentioned (endnote 38) *Historical Notices of the United Presbyterian Congregations in Glasgow*, edited by John Logan Aikman, with photographs by Thomas Annan (Glasgow: Thomas Annan, 1875) contained over fifty photographs of the church buildings, along with portraits of the ministers.

65. As early as 1828, in the "Sketch of the Progress of Glasgow" that opened Joseph Swan's *Select Views of Glasgow and its Environs, engraved by Joseph Swan from drawings by Mr. J. Fleming and Mr. J. Knox* (Glasgow: Joseph Swan, 1828), John Leighton described the city's many "chemical manufactories," among which "the works of Messrs Charles Tennant & Coy are considered the largest in the world, and cover many acres of ground." (pp. ix-x) Two decades later James Pagan again referred to "the vast extent of the iron and engineering trades of Glasgow" and described Charles Tennant's St. Rollox chemical works, founded in 1800, as "the most extensive manufactory of the kind in the world, covering a space of upwards of ten acres"—soon to be 100 acres—and employing over a thousand workers (Fig. 6:1). The "monster chimney," erected in 1843 "for the purpose of carrying off any noxious gases which might arise in the process of their manufacture" and known as "Tennant's stalk"—one of hundreds that came to be part of the cityscape in those years—is said to have "stood 500 feet above the street" and was the tallest structure of its kind in the world (James Pagan, *Sketch of the History of Glasgow* [Glasgow: Robert Stuart, 1847], pp. 89-90). By 1870, 70% of all the world's iron vessels and two-thirds of all steamships were built on the Clyde (Allan Massie, *Glasgow: Portraits of a City* [London: Barrie & Jenkins, 1989], p. 54). In the years just before the First World War, 80%

of the world's sugar-refining machinery, 71% of its railway locomotives and 18% of its ships were built in Glasgow and Clydeside. (Seán Damer, *Glasgow: Going for a Song* [London: Lawrence and Wishart, 1990], pp. 39-40)

66. Allan Massie, *Glasgow: Portraits of a City*, p. 63. In 1891, the author of *Glasgow and its Environs: A Literary, Commercial and Social Review, Past and Present* (London: Stratten and Stratten, 1891) referred in the opening pages to "this large and stately city—the second in the British Empire [. . .], this great Scottish hive of industry," whose "wonderfully advanced municipal institutions have often been pointed out as models for the imitation of cities slower in growth, if more aristocratic in reputation." (p. 7) On the history of Glasgow in the nineteenth century, see Hamish Fraser and Irene Maver, eds., *Glasgow*, vol. II: 1830 to 1912 (Manchester: Manchester University Press, 1996), the richly documented general history of Irene Maver, *Glasgow* (Edinburgh: Edinburgh University Press, 2000), the last section of the handsomely illustrated architectural history by Carol Foreman, *Lost Glasgow: Glasgow's Lost Architectural Heritage* (Edinburgh: Birlinn, 2002), pp. 138-207 and the moving account of the transformation of the city, section by section, from its industrial heyday to the present in two books by Ian. R. Mitchell, *This City Now: Glasgow and its Working-Class Past* (Edinburgh: Luath Press, 2004) and *A Glasgow Mosaic: Explorations among the City's Architectural Icons* (Edinburgh: Luath Press, 2013). Population figures given by Rev. A.G. Forbes in the text accompanying Annan's *Photographs of Glasgow* (1868) were 12,700 in 1708, just after the Treaty of Union; 77,385 in 1801; 147,043 in 1821; 448,639 at the census of 1861 (4th unnumbered page of the Introduction). Until 1912, population figures did not include contiguous but still administratively independent areas such as Govan and Partick.

67. In one twelve-day period in 1847, no fewer than 12,940 poor Irish landed directly in Glasgow or in nearby Ardrossan (Damer, *Glasgow Going for a Song*, p. 54). In 1851, nearly 60,000 immigrants arrived from Ireland and Irish immigrants made up over 18% of the city's population (Fraser and Maver: Glasgow, vol. II, p. 149). In the words of Friedrich Engels, "the rapid expansion of British industry could not have taken place if there had not been available a reserve of labour among the poverty-stricken people of Ireland." (*The Condition of the Working Class in England in 1844*, trans. and ed. W.O. Henderson and W.H. Chaloner [Stanford, CA: Stanford University Press, 1968 (1958)], p. 104) While immigrants from other parts of Scotland tended to seek accommodation in newer tenements outside the city center, the totally impoverished Irish settled in their thousands in the cheapest dwellings they could find, that is, in the crowded tenements of the old city. (Michael Pacione, *Glasgow: The Socio-spatial Development of the City* [Chichester: John Wiley & Sons, 1995], p. 113)

68. Friedrich Engels, *Condition of the Working Class*, ed. cit., p. 42. Because of this feature of Scottish townhouses, the situation in the old town of Edinburgh in the nineteenth century, while not as acute as in Glasgow, also provoked horror and indignation in well-meaning visitors; see, for instance, George

Bell, M.D., *Day and Night in the Wynds of Edinburgh* (Edinburgh: Johnstone & Hunter, 1849 [3rd ed.]).

69. Edwin Chadwick, *Report on the Sanitary Condition of the Labouring Population of Gt. Britain*, with an Introduction by M.W. Flinn (Edinburgh: Edinburgh University Press, [1965]), p. 99. On the previous page Chadwick gives a gruesome account of his own inspection, with Dr. Neil Arnott, of dwellings in the rundown, poor sections of Glasgow: "'We entered a dirty low passage like a house door, which led from the street through the first house to a square court immediately behind, which court, with the exception of a narrow path around it leading to another long passage through a second house, was occupied entirely as a dung receptacle of the most disgusting kind. Beyond this court the second passage led to a second square court, occupied in the same way by its dunghill; and from this court there was yet a third passage leading to a third court, and third dungheap. There were no privies or drains there, and the dungheaps received all filth which the swarm of wretched inhabitants could give; and we learned that a considerable part of the rent of the houses was paid by the produce of the dungheaps. Thus, worse off than wild animals, many of which withdraw to a distance and conceal their ordure, the dwellers in these courts had converted their shame into a kind of money by which their lodging was to be paid. The interiors of these houses and their inmates corresponded with the exteriors. We saw half-dressed wretches crowding together to be warm; and in one bed, although in the middle of the day, several women were imprisoned under a blanket, because as many others who had on their backs all the articles of dress that belonged to the party were then out of doors in the streets. This picture is so shocking that, without ocular proof, one would be disposed to doubt the possibility of the facts."

70. "On the Health of the Working Classes in Large Towns," *The Artizan*, no. X (October 31, 1843), 228-31 (pp. 230-31), quoted by Engels, *Condition of the Working Class*, ed. cit., p. 45. See also the passage from J.C. Symons, *Arts and Artisans at Home and Abroad* (1839) quoted by the editors of the 1968 Stanford University Press edition of Engels on p. 46, footnote 2: "This district is bounded by the Clyde and the Trongate and extends in length from the Saltmarket to the Briggate. There are other similar districts skirting the High Street [...] The wynds near the Trongate are, however, the densest and the dirtiest . . . This quarter consists of a labyrinth of lanes, varying from 7 to 14 feet in width, out of which numberless entrances open into small square courts, appropriately designated 'closes', with houses, many of them in a dilapidated state [. . .], and a common dunghill, reeking with filth in the centre. Revolting as was the outward appearance of these places, I confess I was little prepared for the filth and destitution within. In some of these lodging rooms we found a whole lair of human beings littered along the floor, sometimes 15 and 20 in number, some clothed and some naked, men, women, and children, all huddled promiscuously together. Their bed consisted of a layer of musty straw, intermixed with ambiguous looking rags, of which it was difficult to discover any other

feature than their intense dirtiness." In the same vein, Dr. D. Smith, one of the city's District Surgeons, in 1843: "The tenements in which I have visited are occupied from the cellars to the attics. [. . .] The entrance to these abodes is generally through a close, not unfrequently some inches deep with water or mud, or the fluid part of every kind of filth, carelessly thrown down from unwillingness to go with it to one of the common receptacles; and in every close there is at least one of these places, situated immediately under the windows of the dwelling-houses, or together with byres, stables, etc., forming the ground floor, while the stench arising therefrom pollutes the neighbourhood and renders the habitations above almost intolerable." (Quoted by Damer, *Glasgow: Going for a Song*, p. 74)

71. Quoted by Engels, *Condition of the Working Class*, ed. cit., pp. 45-46.

72. *Notes of Travel*, 4 vols., vol. 2, pp. 110-11 (May 1, 1856) and pp. 378-79 (July 1, 1857) in *The Complete Writings of Nathaniel Hawthorne*, 22 vols., vol. 20 (Boston: Houghton, Mifflin and Company, 1900).

73. Damer, *Glasgow: Going for a Song*, p. 76; Michael Pacione, *Glasgow: The Socio-spatial Development of the City*, p. 117.

74. See Chadwick, *Report on the Sanitary Condition* (1842), p. 397: "When Dr. Arnott with myself and others were examining the abodes of the poorest classes in Glasgow and Edinburgh, we were regarded with astonishment; and it was frequently declared by the inmates, that they had never for many years witnessed the approach or the presence of persons of that condition" [i.e. "persons of the wealthier classes living in the immediate vicinity"].

75. Glasgow: Thomas Murray, 1858. Preface, p. v. The author's name, "Shadow," was a pseudonym of Alexander Brown, a local letterpress printer.

76. Alexander Smith, "A Boy's Poem," Part I, in his *City Poems* (Boston: Ticknor and Fields, 1857), pp. 122-23.

77. On measures taken to deal with slum conditions, both nationally and locally, in the first two-thirds of the nineteenth century, see C.M. Allan, "The Genesis of British Urban Redevelopment with special reference to Glasgow," pp. 599-602; on measures taken in Glasgow in particular, ibid., p. 603.

78. Ibid., p. 604. According to Carol Foreman, the area affected covered 90 acres, with a population of 50,000. "The Act empowered the Corporation to form thirty-nine new streets and to realign twelve others; to compulsorily acquire old properties and demolish them; to dispose of the ground released on lease or feu; and to control rebuilding. In addition, the Act allowed the Corporation to acquire land for the purposes of rehousing

the dispossessed tenants and to erect and maintain on any of the lands acquired by it such dwelling houses for mechanics, labourers and other persons of the working and poorer classes." (*Lost Glasgow*, pp. 143-44)

79. Wilfried Wiegand, *Frühzeit der Photographie 1826-1890* (Frankfurt: Societätsverlag, 1980), p. 217.

80. *The Old Closes and Streets of Glasgow* (Glasgow: J. MacLehose and Sons, 1900), p. 22.

81. On the use of text and captions by photographers to "'fix' the image, refusing it the right to vacillate between past and present, ideal and real," see the comments of Shelley Rice on Edward S. Curtis's monumental *The North American Indian* (twenty volumes of illustrated text and twenty supplementary portfolios of unbound gravures, 1907-1930) in her article "When Objects Dream," *The Book of 101 Books: Seminal Photographic Books of the Twentieth Century*, ed. Andrew Roth (New York: PPP Editions, 2001), pp. 3-33 (p. 5).

82. Though the album is untitled and undated, the front cover carries in gilt tooling, below the city's coat of arms, the notice "Glasgow Improvements Act 1866. Photographs of Streets, Closes &c. Taken 1868-71." See A.L. Fisher's three-part catalogue of *The Old Closes and Streets* in *Scottish Photography Bulletin*, Part I (Spring 1987), 4-8 (p. 5).

83. The passage quoted concerning the second album was put together from the Glasgow Town Council minutes for 15 July 1877 and cited by Fisher, p. 6, and by Anita Ventura Mozley in her Introduction to the 1977 Dover Publications edition of *The Old Closes and Streets* (*Thomas Annan: Photographs of the Old Closes and Streets of Glasgow 1868/1877, with a Supplement of 15 Related Views* [New York: Dover Publications, 1977]), p. v. For the numbers of sets produced, William Buchanan proposed a figure of "probably four" in 1871 and sixty in 1878 in his entry on Annan in John Hannavy's *Encyclopedia of Nineteenth Century Photography*, vol. 1, p. 45. I have accepted the numbers given by A.L. Fisher in *Scottish Photography Bulletin* (Spring 1987), 4-8 and 17-27 (pp. 6-7). According to Fisher, the extant copies of the 1871 album are held by the Mitchell Library, the library of the University of Glasgow, the library of the Scottish National Portrait Gallery, and the Canadian Centre for Architecture in Montreal. However, Princeton University's album of *The Old Closes and Streets*, which belonged at one time to the library of the Royal Faculty of Procurators in Glasgow, is also that of 1871. It may, in sum, be even harder than the texts of Buchanan or Fisher freely acknowledge to determine exactly how many albums were made in 1871, or even in 1878. Single albumen prints from 1871 and carbon prints from 1878, for instance, of which a fair number are still extant, might have been collected and bound together by individuals or institutions. The figure of sixty copies for the 1878 album may well be on the low side, according to Sonny Maley of Glasgow University

Library. (My thanks to Mr. Maley for sharing the results of his research with me in an e-mail of July 8, 2014.) In her Introduction to the 1977 Dover Publications edition (p. v and endnote 9 on p. xiii), Anita Ventura Mozley gives a figure of 100 copies for the 1878 album, citing information provided by Jerold C. Maddox, the Curator of Photography at the Library of Congress. According to Maddox, referring in turn to an article entitled "Notes from the North," in the *British Journal of Photography* for 19 April 1878, John Nicol, "who figures in the Trustees' requests to have prints of Annan's photographs made, 'had the pleasure of publishing a few notes of a late visit to the carbon printing establishment of Mr. Annan, of Glasgow, recently erected at Lenzie.' Annan showed Mr. Nicol [. . .] '3,000 prints from thirty negatives of the old closes and other interesting portions of Glasgow now removed by the Improvement Trust to make way for more modern erections.'" In contrast, in an illustrated catalogue of the prints from the 1878 album published by Lunn Gallery/Graphics International (Washington, D.C. [1976? 1980?]), Henry Lunn Jr. estimated that there were at most 25 to 40 sets of the 1878 album (misdescribed as the "1877" album). This low figure may, however, reflect the gallery's commercial interest in the rarity of the sets, since it was selling off single prints from a set that had come into its possession.

84. There is disagreement among the scholars even on the number of copies of the 1900 edition. The figures of 100 and 150 are those given by William Buchanan in John Hannavy's *Encyclopedia of Nineteenth-Century Photography*, vol. 1, p. 46. Other scholars give a figure of 100 copies each for both the Annan and the MacLehose publications. (David Bate, "Illuminating Annan," *Portfolio Magazine*, 3 [Spring/Summer, 1989], p. 19; Anita Ventura Mozley, Introduction to the 1977 Dover Publications edition, p. vi; Margaret Harker, "From Mansion to Close: Thomas Annan, Master Photographer," p. 94)

85. On these characteristics, see Robert Evans, "History in Albumen, Carbon, and Photogravure: Thomas Annan's Old Glasgow," in *Nineteenth-Century Photographs and Architecture*, ed. Micheline Nilson (Farnham: Ashgate, 2013), pp. 59-74.

86. See, for example, Ian Spring, *Phantom Village: The Myth of the New Glasgow* (Edinburgh: Polygon, 1990), p. 16; Rachel Stuhlman, "'Let Glasgow Flourish': Thomas Annan and the Glasgow Corporation Waterworks," p. 50. A similar appreciation of blur is expressed by Graham Bush in his edition of the photographs of old and threatened sites in London by Henry Dixon and the brothers Alfred and John Bool: "The photographs often contain activity. Figures stare at the camera, moving perhaps an arm to leave a smear on the plate. Some have obviously been told to stand still; others go about their business unconscious of the camera. Sometimes carts stay long enough to register on the plate, and sometimes they pass leaving tracks in the air. Fast emulsions would have lost these qualities, which for me are important. Photographers of that time, however, went to great lengths to keep their subjects still and exposures as short as possible." (*Old*

London, *photographed by Henry Dixon and Alfred & John Bool for the Society for Photographing Relics of Old London* [London: Academy Editions/New York St Martin's Press, 1975], p. 10)

87. Spring, *Phantom Village*, p. 31. Cf. Susan Sontag, *On Photography* (New York: Farrar, Straus and Giroux, 1977), p. 106: "One of the central characteristics of photography is that process by which original uses are modified, eventually supplanted by other uses—most notably by the discourse of art into which any photograph can be absorbed."

88. E.g. Julie Lawson, "The Problem of Poverty and the Picturesque," p. 40. Responding to interpretations of Annan's work "as polemical and reformatory in purpose," Lawson argues that "the historical facts of the matter inform us that the photographs were commissioned *after* the decision had been made to clear the slums: they were not part of the long and hard-won battle to prick the social conscience and bring about social amelioration." In a somewhat similar vein, Mozley (Introduction to the Dover Publications Edition of 1977, p. vii) states that "Annan was not a social reformer or investigator with a camera. He was no John Thomson, whose texts to *Street Life in London* (1877-1878) were vivified with quotations from nomads, cabmen, boardmen and flood victims. [...] His work is more like that of A. & J. Boole and Henry Dixon, who took photographs for the Society for Photographing Relics of Old London in the 1870's and 1880s." So too Wolfgang Kemp, "Images of Decay: Photography in the Picturesque Tradition," *October*, 54 (Autumn, 1990), 102-33 (p. 124): "It is certain that Annan did not take these photographs to facilitate or to justify the large-scale demolition of the old city center by illustrating its inhuman conditions. [...] He leaves more of the life that is crammed in these abysses to the spectator's imagination than he shows of it." (Original German text of this essay, 1978) For Eve Blau, on the other hand, "Annan did not shy away from showing the filth and degradation of the life lived within [these places], thereby providing implicit justification for tearing them down" (Eve Blau, "Patterns of Fact: Photography and the Transformation of the Early Industrial City," in Eve Blau and Edward Kaufman, eds., *Architecture and its Image* [Montreal: Centre Canadien d'Architecture/Canadian Centre for Architecture, 1989], pp. 36-57 [p. 48]). Likewise, the English Marxist historian Eric Hobsbawm used two of Annan's photographs from *The Old Closes and Streets* to illustrate his edition of Engels' *Condition of the Working Class in England in 1844* (Chicago: Academy Chicago, 1969).

89. See notably Elizabeth Lindquist-Cock, "Sentiment, Compassion, Straight Record: The Mid-Victorians," *The Massachusetts Review*, 19 (Winter 1978), special issue devoted to photography, 717-28: "Others, like Thomas Annan, attempted to rouse the public to the terrible conditions in Glasgow's slums by presenting stark and truthful images of the downtrodden poor in the dark tenement canyons"; (p. 717) "Thomas Annan used his camera as a social weapon..." (p. 723). Similarly for Wilfried Wiegand, *Frühzeit der Photographie 1826-1890)*, Annan's "Aufnahmen aus den Slums von Glasgow

(1866-1977) sind der erste Höhepunkt sozialkritischer Photographie" (p. 217). In a selection of Annan's photographs of Glasgow, James McCarroll compares Annan to Jacob Riis in his depiction of slum life: "His views of the closes are genuinely moving and full of pathos. They reveal the horrific living conditions endured by tens of thousands of Glaswegians in the midst of one of the world's most economically vibrant cities." (*Glasgow Victoriana: Classic Photographs by Thomas Annan* [Ayr: Fort Publishing Ltd., 1999], pp. 6-7) Such judgments are probably inevitable in view of the fact that "perhaps as a means of differentiating it from 'photojournalism,' to which it is closely related, modern definitions of documentary photography have focused less on its role in recording reality than on its ability to demonstrate the need for change." (Constance B. Schultz, "Documentary Photography," in *Oxford Companion to the Photograph*, ed. Robin Lenman and Angela Nicholson [Oxford: Oxford University Press, 2005], pp. 173-79), http://dx.doi.org/10.1093/acref/9780198662716.001.0001

90. Thus, according to Peter Baron Hales, reviewing possible anticipations of Jacob Riis's "social documentary" photographs in his *How the Other Half Lives*, "the purpose of [*The Old Closes and Streets*] might only loosely be considered sociological" (*Silver Cities: The Photography of American Urbanization 1839-1939* [Albuquerque: University of New Mexico Press, 2005], p. 297). See also Anita Mozley, "Thomas Annan of Glasgow," *Image*, 20, no. 2 (June 1977), 1-12 (p. 1). Riis was in any case likely to have been more aware of engravings made from photographs of slum tenements by the American photographer Edward Anthony than of Annan's work. These engravings were published in a *Report of the Council of Hygiene and Public Health of the Citizens' Association of New York* (New York: D. Appleton, 1865) several years before Annan began photographing the old closes and streets of Glasgow.

91. *Photographs of Glasgow* (Glasgow: Duthie, 1868), sections on "Trongate and Cross" and "The Parks: in connection with view of West-End Park."(Pages unnumbered)

92. On the "Missions héliographiques" and on Marville, see André Gunthert, "L'Institution du photographique: Le roman de la Société héliographique" (as in endnote 5 above); Eugenia Janis, "Demolition picturesque: Photographs of Paris in 1852 and 1858 by Henri Le Secq," in *Perspectives on Photography: Essays in Honor of Beaumont Newhall*, ed. P. Walch and T.F. Barnes (Albuquerque: University of New Mexico Press, 1986), pp. 33-66; Marie de Thézy, en collaboration avec Roxane Dubuisson, "Le Photographe des rues de Paris," in their *Marville Paris* (Paris: Éditions Hazan, 1994), pp. 28-36; and Patrice de Moncan, *Charles Marville: Paris photographié au temps d'Haussmann* (Paris: Éditions du Mécène, 2009). According to De Thézy, Marville's commission dated from 1865 and resulted within three years in an album of 425 images. A similar concern to inventory and record buildings and monuments, especially those under threat of decay or destruction, inspired the celebrated 24-volume *Voyages pittoresques et romantiques dans l'ancienne France* (1828-78) by Baron Taylor and the

poet Charles Nodier. On Annan and Riis, see Robert Evans, "History in Albumen, Carbon, and Photogravure: Thomas Annan's Old Glasgow," pp. 61-62. Ian Spring also makes the point that "Annan's work cannot be compared to other photographic projects directly involved in the legal process of instigating slum clearance—for example, the contemporary photographs of the Quarry Hill area of Leeds." (*Phantom Village*, p. 14) It does, however, seem somewhat comparable with that of fellow-Scot Archibald Burns, who was given a similar commission to Annan's by the Edinburgh Improvement Trust in 1871 and took 26 photographs of buildings in the old closes between the University and Cowgate shortly before they were demolished. It is entirely possible, of course, that other photographers learned from Annan's work to produce images with a reformist intent. Some of the photographs of Little Collingwood Street in Bethnal Green (ca.1900) by John Galt, a missionary with the London City Mission, bear a strong resemblance to Annan's *The Old Closes and Streets* in the 1900 photogravure edition created by James Craig Annan. (See, for instance, http://www.museumoflondonprints.com/image/141260/john-galt-residents-in-little-collingwood-street-c-1900)

93. Irene Maver, *Glasgow*, pp. v, 172-74. Cf. Carol Foreman, *Lost Glasgow*: "For the loss of so many of its historic buildings, Glasgow has only itself to blame. It has never been sentimental about its old buildings. It has been a point of civic pride to destroy and build better, and if old buildings got in the way of any new plan, they were swept away, supposedly in the name of progress. [. . .] Should we commend or condemn the Victorians for their redevelopment of the city? Probably a bit of both as they did make the town a more pleasant and much healthier place to live, and if, by removing the slums, which were the worst in the country, the picturesque was sacrificed, the means justified the end." (pp. vii and ix)

94. *On Photography*, p. 76. Sontag might have added that those who commissioned photographic records of what they themselves were destroying also used photography to record what they took pride in building. Hence Glasgow Corporation's commissioning Annan to record the construction of the Loch Katrine waterworks; the Canadian Grand Trunk Railway's commissioning William Notman to make a photographic record of the building of the Victoria Bridge over the St. Lawrence; or James Mayer de Rothschild's commissioning Édouard Baldus, around the same time, to record the construction of the railway from Boulogne to Paris, Lyon and the Mediterranean. In this respect, photography was taking over from prints and painting; Louis XIV had had his "battle painter" Adam Frans van der Meulen record a scene from the construction of Versailles in 1668, and Annan's friend D. O. Hill had made paintings of the Glasgow and Garnkirk railway in 1830-31, published in lithographic form as *Views of the Opening of the Glasgow and Garnkirk Railway* (Edinburgh: Alex Hill, 1832). The documentary photograph offered an age of revolutionary change, acutely aware of the transience of everything, a valued means of recording what was inevitably subject to the effects of time.

95. "The insistent recurrence of the word 'Old' in the titles of [Annan's] publications" was noted by Ray McKenzie in his article "Thomas Annan and the Scottish Landscape: Among the Gray Edifices," p. 47. Annan himself, as a young man working on the *Fife Herald*, wrote in February 1848 of his desire, with the coming of drier weather, to "get out to rove among the gray edifices of bygone years." (Cit. Sara Stevenson *Thomas Annan 1829-1887*, p. 4). In his essay "The Urban Landscape between Progress and Decay" (*Studies in Photography* [1998], 5-9) James Lawson argues that photography is by its very nature closely associated with time and change: "Photography [. . .] simultaneously affirms objective fact and draws attention to the contingent nature of that fact. It is obsessed by time. In its ability to record, it preserves, if not the substance of the thing, the image of a moment's existence. Thus, by its very nature, it forces acknowledgement that time changes things [. . .] Change being the condition of photography and the sense of the photographic image being something wrenched from the object and, with the passing of time, moving further and further from it, the recording of objects that already announced the erosive power of time was an obvious role for photography. The poetic photographer would seek out objects upon which time had done its work." (p. 7)

96. Wolfgang Kemp, "Images of Decay," pp. 104-05, 107. The late eighteenth-century quotation is from Sir Uvedale Price, *Essay on the Picturesque* (1794). Frank Sutcliffe, the still widely-admired photographer of the fishing town of Whitby and its inhabitants in the last decades of the nineteenth century, made the point forcefully in 1890: "Is it because we have been so in the habit of going only for the labelled objects that our eyes are not sufficiently alert and our senses properly tuned to respond to the greater charms of the rarer beauties?" (Cit. ibid., p. 111) The predilection of photography, from the outset, for the hidden, "the unofficial reality behind the façade of bourgeois life," for "uncovering a hidden truth, conserving a vanishing past," and for "discovering beauty in the humble, the inane, the decrepit" and in what was often seen as ugly, is, of course, a central theme of Susan Sontag's now classic *On Photography* (1973); see especially, pp. 15-16, 55-56, 76, 78-79, 89-90, 102. Sontag quotes with approval a remark by Princeton photographer Emmet Gowin: "Photography is a tool for dealing with things everybody knows about but isn't attending to. My photographs are intended to present something you don't see." (p. 200)

97. Neil Matheson, "Demand: Allegories of the Real and the Return of History," in *The State of the Real: Aesthetics in the Digital Age*, ed. Damian Sutton, Susan Brind, Ray McKenzie (London: I.B. Taurus, 2007), p. 38. Thus, for example, the Edinburgh newspaper *The Scotsman* in the mid-nineteenth century: "The artist cannot fail to tell; he can neither flatter nor detract from the appearance of the object which is presented to him; he is a secondary agent." (Cit. Hannavy, *The Victorian Professional Photographer*, p. 8)

98. As Ray McKenzie points out, the "Picturesque" fulfilled a function similar to that played by the more sophisticated, late nineteenth- and early twentieth-century concept of Pictorialism, represented by the work of the American photographers Alfred Stieglitz and Edward Steichen and, in Scotland, by Thomas Annan's own son James Craig Annan. It promoted "a particular understanding of how a picture can be made to evoke meanings beyond the mere 'facsimile' of an object's appearance" and, as A.J. Anderson put it in his *The Artistic Side of Photography in Theory and Practice* (London, 1910), can serve as "the outward and visible sign of an inward and spiritual meaning." See McKenzie, "Introduction: Pictorialism and its Malcontents," *Photography 1900: The Edinburgh Symposium (Proceedings of the Conference of the European Society for the History of Photography)*, ed. by Julie Lawson, Ray McKenzie, A.D. Morrison-Low (Edinburgh: National Museums of Scotland/National Galleries of Scotland, 1992), pp. 13-17 (p. 14). See likewise Shelley Rice's comment on the Pictorialists: "For these artists, the click of the shutter opened the door to eternity. The photographic image, rightly perceived, elevated reality to the level of symbol." ("When Objects Dream," p. 5)

99. William Henry Fox Talbot, *The Pencil of Nature* (London: Longman, Brown, Green, & Longmans, 1844), The text relates directly to Plate VI, "The Open Door." On the view of Talbot's calotype as facilitating the practice of photography as an art (in contrast to the mechanical accuracy of the daguerreotype), see Sara Stevenson, *The Personal Art of David Octavius Hill* (New Haven: Yale University Press, 2002), pp. 31-40. Stevenson quotes (p. 36) a remark by the history painter Benjamin Robert Haydon: "I am convinced that the Calotype is the greatest thing for Art since the Elgin Marbles."

100. Quoted by Alfred H. Wall in *British Journal of Photography*, 16 February 1863. Sutton's concern to promote photography as a creative art is demonstrated in his many practical manuals as well as in the Introduction he wrote for Louis-Désiré Blanquet-Evrard, *Intervention of Art in Photography* (London: Sampson Low, Son & Co., 1864), translated from French into English under Sutton's direction. When working with Blanquet-Evrard in Lille, Sutton explained, he came to admire "not only his great taste in matters relating to art, but his strenuous efforts to introduce, by legitimate means, artistic effects into the mechanical work of the camera and printing frame." (p. 3) Wall shared Sutton's understanding of photography: "No two trees or rocks are alike; light and shade change with every hour of the day, and with every such change the scene becomes a new one. [. . .] The finest and most beautifully varied scenery in the world may make and does commonly make the most uninteresting photographs, simply because the photographer [. . .] has neither chosen his point of view, his light and shade, nor his atmospheric effect with a proper care." ("On taking Picturesque Photographs" [1867], cit. in Kemp, "Images of Decay," pp. 109-10) Among many similar defenses of photography as an art and not simply a technique, see R.J. Chute, "Portrait Photography," *The Photographic World*, 24 (December 1872), p. 355: "Photographic chemistry,

with all its attendant processes and manipulations, may be easily learned; [. . .] but in reference to art there is something indefinable that cannot be told or written, it must be felt. As with music, there must be some inherent talent, some natural taste for it."

101. "Upon photography in an artistic view and its relation to the arts" (a talk given at the Royal Photographic Society, 3 February 1853), *Photographic Journal* (3 March 1853), quoted in Helmut Gernsheim, *Creative Photography: Aesthetic Trends 1839-1960* (New York: Dover, 1991 [orig. London, 1962], p. 74). See also Newton's complete text, reproduced in Bill Jay and Dana Allen, eds., *Critics 1840-1880* (Phoenix (?): Arizona Board of Regents, 1985), 49-52 (p. 50). In the same vein, Lady Elizabeth Eastlake in *London Quarterly Review* (March, 1857) — see endnote 37.

102. Cited in Kemp, "Images of Decay," p. 111. On the allegedly still influential (and in the writer's view deleterious) ambition of photography to be regarded in the same light as painting, see Paul Strand, "The Art Motive in Photography," *The British Journal of Photography*, 70 (1923), 612-15. According to Strand, a "generally erroneous notion of artist [namely, that 'everybody who slings a little paint is an artist'] has been and is the chief worry of photographers and their undoing. They too would like to be accepted in polite society as artists, as anyone who paints is accepted, and so they try to turn photography into something which it is not: they introduce a paint feeling. In fact, I know of very few photographers whose work is not evidence that at bottom they would prefer to paint if they knew how." (*Photographers on Photography*, ed. Nathan Lyons, pp. 144-54 [p. 145])

103. F. Wey, "De l'influence de l'héliographie sur les beaux-arts," *La Lumière*, 1 (9 February 1851), p. 3, cited in Gunthert, "L'institution du photographique," p. 20. *La Lumière*, the organ of the *Société héliographique*, was the first journal devoted to photography in Europe. Francis Wey's position was, in fact, complex; see the outstanding article by Margaret Denton, "Francis Wey and the Discourse of Photography as Art in France in the Early 1850s," *Art History*, 25 (November 2002), 622-48. Jules Champfleury, albeit one of the founding members of the *Société héliographique* (1851), still insisted on the "mechanical" character of photography: "Ten *daguerreotypeurs* meet up in the countryside and subject the scenery to the action of light. Beside them, ten students of landscape painting set to copying the same site. Once the chemical operation is complete, the ten plates are compared: they depict exactly the same landscape, without variation. On the other hand, after two or three hours at work the ten pupils [. . .] lay their sketches out next to each other. There is not a single similar one among them." (Cit. in Dominique de Font-Réaulx, *Painting and Photography 1839-1914* [Paris: Flammarion, 2012], p. 122) In our own time Susan Sontag has insisted that a distinctive individual style is less characteristic of photographers than of painters inasmuch as photography remains more bound to an impersonal representation of its subject matter: "A photographer is not like a painter, the role of the photographer being recessive in much of serious picture-

taking and virtually irrelevant in all the ordinary uses. So far as we care about the subject photographed, we expect the photographer to be an extremely discreet presence. [. . .] In the vast majority of photographs which get taken—for scientific and industrial purposes, by the press, by the military and the police, by families—any trace of the personal vision of whoever is behind the camera interferes with the primary demand on the photograph that it record, diagnose, inform. [...] It requires a formal conceit (like Todd Walker's solarized photographs [. . .]) or a thematic obsession (like Eakins with the male nude [. . .]) to make work easily recognizable. For photographers who don't so limit themselves, their body of work does not have the same integrity as does comparably varied work in other art forms." (*On Photography*, pp. 133-34) On continuing debate about the status of photography, see also in Pierre Bourdieu, ed., *Photography. A Middlebrow Art* (Stanford: Stanford University Press, 1990; orig. French, *Un Art moyen*, 1965) the articles by Pierre Bourdieu (pp. 13-72), Robert Castel and Dominique Schnapper (pp. 103-128), Jean-Claude Chamberdon (pp. 129-49) and Luc Boltanski and Jean-Claude Chamberdon (pp. 150-173).

104. In 1896 James Craig Annan was elected to the Brotherhood of the Linked Ring, the European equivalent of the American Photo-Secession. Both groups espoused the view of photography as art. In 1899 *Anthony's Photographic Bulletin* (no. 30, pp. 345-48) reported in detail on a lecture given by J.C. Annan to the Leeds Camera Club in 1899 on "Painters Who Have Influenced Me." A lecture on "Photography as a Means of Artistic Expression," given on 4 May 1910 to the Edinburgh Photographic Society, was published in December of the same year in Alfred Stieglitz's influential Photo-Secession journal *Camera Work* (no. 32, pp. 21-24), and in 1914 an entire number of the journal was devoted to J.C. Annan and his work. See William Buchanan, *James Craig Annan: Selected Texts and Bibliography* (New York: G.K. Hall, 1993).

105. For a reproduction of Annan's sketch, see Roddy Simpson, *The Photography of Victorian Scotland*, p. 151. Simpson observes that a note below the sketch "indicates Annan's concern about perspective and distance and the problem of relating foreground to middle and background, confirming his awareness of compositional rules in painting." Simpson devotes a section of his book (pp. 157-85) to the debate provoked in the nineteenth and early twentieth centuries by photography's claim to be art.

106. Among those impressed by the absence of images of extreme squalor, one could point to the following: David Bate, "Illuminating Annan," *Portfolio Magazine*, 3 (Spring/Summer, 1989), p. 19: "None of Annan's photographs actually represent the kind of overcrowding and 'squalor' described by official written accounts"; Kemp, "Images of Decay," p. 124: "Annan's photographs do not give the impression of a terribly overpopulated slum; instead we are given the feeling that the people are there to animate the scenery"; Julie Lawson, "The Problem of Poverty and the Picturesque," p. 45: ". . . his deliberate exclusion of some of the more shocking aspects of the place is important"; Ian Spring, "Midnight Scenes and Social Photographs," in Debra N. Mancoff and D.J. Trela, eds., *Victorian Urban*

Settings: Essays on the Nineteenth-Century City and its Contexts (New York and London: Garland, 1996), pp. 195-213 (pp. 201-02): "What we see is an illuminating but highly constructed view of these people. . .They appear perhaps disinterested, posed in a fashion, and docile. . . . .The exact antithesis of Cruikshank's engraving: no vice, no drunkenness, no crime, merely an orderly people, husbands, wives and children, all preoccupied with maintaining a degree of cleanliness." See also Evans, "History in Albumen, Carbon, and Photogravure," p. 64.

107. James Lawson, "The Urban Landscape between Progress and Decay," p. 5. "Signs of sickness and vice—to elicit the compassion and indignation of the social historian—are disappointingly absent," according to Lawson, from the street scenes of both Annan and his Edinburgh contemporary, Archibald Burns.

108. Mozley, Introduction, p. xi.

109. In the text accompanying Annan's photograph of George Square (the pages are unnumbered), Forbes refers to "the very distinct and otherwise excellent view presented by our artist"; in the text accompanying the photograph of the Royal Exchange, to "the beautiful view of the Exchange, here presented by our artist"; and in the text accompanying three photographs of the Cathedral, to "the third of these views presented by our artist."

110. See the final quotation at www.edinphoto.org.uk/3/3_pss_exhibitions_9th_dec_1864.htm under "Thomas Annan" On Annan's talk, see www.edinphoto.org.uk/PP/pp_annan_thomas_photographer.htm The master of this useful blog, contacted by e-mail, was unfortunately unable to locate a surviving text of Annan's talk.

111. Referring to post-World War I "social document" photography in Weimar Germany, Soviet Russia and Depression-era America, Jens Jäger drew attention to the difficulty of determining "from the images themselves whether the perspective of the photographers was conservative or socialist, or whether ultimately aesthetic considerations were decisive." (*Photographie: Bilder der Neuzeit* [Tübingen: Edition diskord, 2000], p. 111) A similar difficulty attends many earlier photographs. James Lawson makes the interesting argument that the seemingly contradictory "social-historical" and "art-critical" approaches to photography, especially documentary photography, reflect two essential aspects of the medium: its origin and its development. "The creation of records, substitutions and reproductions has been an important human ambition, and industry has historically seen the invention of a great variety of utilitarian machines and processes. [. . .] Stamping, casting, and die-making processes allowed for the imitation and reproduction of objects on an industrial scale. However, insofar as the mechanical process was recognized in the product, it was denied artistic credentials, and very many manufacturing processes never became artistic means. Photography, though, was different. [. . .] Despite the possibility of the photograph existing in multiple copies, [photography

is] not a process of mechanical reproduction in the sense in which stamping, casting and die-making are. [. . .] Perhaps the most salient difference is that it has no contact with the thing to be copied. [. . .] The notion of record remains embedded deep within the art of photography, but equally ineluctable is remoteness of object from process. The space separating the photograph from its object is occupied by factors making the object relative to conditions over which the process has no control. So, viewpoint limits the object to an aspect consisting in a singular configuration of planes, conditions of light make the object ontologically inconstant, and scale is inexplicit in relation to size." ("The Urban Landscape between Progress and Decay," pp. 6-7)

112. Sara Stevenson, *Thomas Annan 1829-1887*, p. 17.

113. Ray McKenzie, "Landscape in Scotland: Photography and the Poetics of Place," in *Light from the Dark Room: A Celebration of Scottish Photography. A Scottish-Canadian Collaboration*, ed. Sara Stevenson (Edinburgh: National Galleries of Scotland, 1995), p. 76. See also Ian Spring. "Midnight Scenes and Social Photographs," pp. 207-309, and Tom Normand, *Scottish Photography: A History* (Edinburgh: Luath Press, 2007), p. 91.

114. Margaret Harker, "From Mansion to Close," p. 91. For a similar judgment see Caroline Arscott, "The Representation of the City in the Visual Arts," in *The Cambridge Urban History of Britain*, vol. 3, ed. Martin Daunton (Cambridge: Cambridge University Press, 2001), pp. 811-832. http://dx.doi.org/10.1017/chol9780521417075. "Thomas Annan's photographs of Glasgow (1868-71) are haunting images of disease-ridden crumbling alleyways destined for demolition. The conundrum is the way the stained, seeping, closely spaced walls, signifiers of overcrowding, foul air, sewage and disease, are rendered in visually arresting form. The many similar closes generate varied compositions which balance blocks and patches of light and dark, the reflective and matt, and, above all, differentiate the textures of the stonework that dominates the environment." (p. 823)

115. E-mail of May 23, 2014. As it happens, there is sometimes a tension in Chimacoff's own photographic work that is strikingly similar to Annan's. An exhibition of his photographs at the Princeton Public Library in October 2014 highlighted the unsightliness and impracticality of the tangles of overhead wires and cables found in most American towns and suburbs. (Their vulnerability to extreme weather conditions results in frequent loss of power to thousands of homes.) Many of the photographs exhibited, however, were formally quite beautiful.

116. See especially Julie Lawson, "The Problem of Poverty and the Picturesque," pp. 42-43, on Annan's "quiet, contemplative photographs."

117. It would be rash to assert that such intentions played absolutely no role. Annan apparently shared the belief of many reform-minded Christians that education would help resolve the problem of poverty and had

considered opening a reading room for the poor (Stevenson, *Thomas Annan (1829-1887)*, p. 15). See also Julie Lawson, "The Problem of Poverty and the Picturesque": "Annan is known to have been a religious man, involved in the Church's effort to improve the lot of the inhabitants through voluntary education schemes. A man of liberal and Christian commitment, he would have welcomed the reforms and approved the legislation of the Civic Improvement Trust for whom he carried out the commission." (p. 43) See likewise Normand, *Scottish Photography: A History*: "Annan was a religious man, an advocate of abstention from alcohol, and something of a socially conscious reformer. His drive to reform was fundamentally shaped by his religious commitment and so the desires of Glasgow's Improvement Trust—sanitary housing, a disease-free environment, a policed inner city, a morally constructed community—were allied to Annan's views. In other words, Annan's 'documentary' photographs were 'political' only in the qualified sense that they proposed a paternalistic form of social engineering." (p. 97) Annan may well have shared the views of Rev. A.G. Forbes, who contributed the text to *Photographs of Glasgow* and who noted in his Introduction that the city had worked hard to remedy frequent fires and flooding and to deal with "riots among the people in seasons of famine or in circumstances of political discontent." He conceded that there is "poverty and crime," and attributed these to "a large amount of ignorance." Nevertheless, "there is also a pleasing extent of intelligence, and integrity, and charity." Ultimately, Forbes had confidence in the future of the city with its ever expanding trade and industry. Change is not to be feared. It is always "for the better [. . .] when it is the result of freedom and enlightened personal independence." The cure for poverty and crime lies in educating the poor and making them self-reliant.

118. Thomas Prasch, "Photography and the Image of the London Poor," in *Victorian Urban Settings: Essays on the Nineteenth-Century City and its Contexts*, pp. 179-94 (pp. 180-84). See also, on Beard and Thomson, Peter Baron Hales, *Silver Cities*, p. 297.

119. On this view of the poor and the working class as a "race apart," see George W. Stocking, *Victorian Anthropology* (New York: The Free Press, 1987), pp. 212-15. Stocking summarizes Engels' description of the working class (not without some exaggeration) as a "'race apart'—physically degenerate, robbed of all humanity, reduced morally and intellectually to near bestial condition, not only by economic exploitation, but by competition and association with the coarse, volatile, dissolute, drunken, impoverished Irish who slept with their pigs in the stinking slums of Manchester." (p. 213) Prasch quotes Mayhew's view of society as divided into "two distinct and broadly marked races, viz. the wanderers and the settlers—the vagabond and the citizen—the nomadic and the civilized tribes." ("Photography and the Image of the London Poor," p. 179)

120. See especially "28 Saltmarket," "46 Saltmarket," "37 High Street," "65 High Street," "118 High Street," "29 Gallowgate."

121. Sontag, *On Photography*, pp. 7, 14. A notable example of such symbolic appropriation might well be the celebrated twenty-volume masterpiece of the ethnologist and photographer Edward S. Curtis, *The North American Indian* (1907-1930). Financed in part by J.P. Morgan, this textual account of the native Americans, containing 1,500 small plates and 722 large gravures, "was printed on hand-made paper, [. . .] bound with irregularly grained Morocco leather, and published in a limited edition of 500 sets that sold for $5,000 each." As Shelley Rice observes, "The subjects of Curtis's photographs might be the dispossessed of American society but the intended audience certainly was not. [. . .] Consumers of such luxury items were also symbolically supporting a romantic, and equally fictitious, vision of their own past: their 'pure' civilization unravaged by the vulgar, mechanized masses." (Shelley Rice, "When Objects Dream," p. 4)

122. Sontag, *On Photography*, pp. 11-12, 20-21. See the summary of Sontag's position by Alexander Hutchison in *Porfolio Magazine*, 3 (Spring/Summer 1989): "For Sontag the person behind the camera is too often—maybe always—a 'voyeuristic stroller,' who is best characterized by words like 'acquisitive,' 'violating,' 'predatory'." (pp. 4, 10, 99) A recent incident, reported in the London *Daily Mail* of a woman being beaten to death by two other women, while bystanders, instead of going to her assistance, used their cell phones to videotape the scene, provides disturbing confirmation of Sontag's thesis. See http://www.dailymail.co.uk/news/article-2834199/Sentencing-set-fatal-nightclub-beating.html

123. Sontag, *On Photography*, p. 107. Cf. pp. 101-02: "The view of [Alfred] Stieglitz, [Paul] Strand and [Edward] Weston—that photographs should be, first of all, beautiful (that is, beautifully composed)—seems thin now, too obtuse to the truth of disorder. [. . .] Weston's images, however admirable, however beautiful, have become less interesting to many people, while those taken by the mid-nineteenth-century English and French primitive photographer [. . .] enthrall more than ever. [. . .] As these formalist ideals of beauty seem, in retrospect, linked to a certain historical mood, optimism about the modern age (the new vision, the new era), so the decline of the standards of photographic purity represented by Weston [. . .] has accompanied the moral letdown experienced in recent decades. In the present historical mood of disenchantment one can make less and less sense of the formalist's notion of timeless beauty. Darker, time-bound models of beauty have become prominent, inspiring a revaluation of the photography of the past; and, in an apparent revulsion against the Beautiful, recent generations of photographers prefer to show disorder."

124. Ibid., p. 110.

125. Zahid R. Chaudhary, *After-Image of Empire: Photography in Nineteenth-Century India* (Minneapolis: University of Minnesota Press, 2012), pp. 157-71. See also the entry on Hooper by Kathleen Howe in John Hannavy, ed., *Encyclopedia of Nineteenth-Century Photography*, vol. 1, pp. 713-14.

126. The Victorians themselves, Annan's contemporaries, appear to have anticipated to some extent the contemporary debate about documentary photographs that depict famine, poverty, war and other forms of human misery. Hooper's devastating photographs of the Madras famine victims provoked controversy at the time: "The Victorians debated whether taking these pictures was an exploitation of people's suffering and whether detachment created by cameras is a craven excuse for apathy. Others maintained that the photographs raised awareness; a contemporary paper reported: 'People who still delude themselves with the idea that the famine, if it has any existence at all, has been greatly exaggerated, could see [the photos], and they would lay aside that notion for good ... Their knowledge will enable them to testify that these photographs are not representations of exceptional cases of suffering, but are typical of the actual conditions of immense numbers of people in the Madras Presidency.' But soon, news came out that after taking such photos, Hooper would send the famine victims back to the countryside without giving them food, treatment or help. For this astonishing cruelty Hooper was roundly skewered in the British press." (Alex Selwyn-Holmes at http://iconicphotos.wordpress.com/2011/08/27/w-willoughby-hooper-on-famine/) See also Chaudhary, *After-Image of Empire*, loc. cit.

127. My thanks to my colleague Suzanne Nash for directing me to Apollinaire's story. The brilliant and powerful Tavernier film, entitled *Death Watch* in its original English-speaking version, is an early denunciation of the TV "reality" show.

128. Martha Rosler, "In, Around, and Afterthoughts (on documentary photography)," in Martha Rosler, *Works* (Press of the Nova Scotia College of Art and Design, 1981, repr. 2000). Cf. a similar comment on the iconography of famine in Africa, which belatedly purports to stir the conscience of viewers and has turned the popular image of the continent into one of "a desperate, poor, passive victim": "We can easily lament the limitations of famine iconography, especially the way it homogenises, anthropomorphises, infantilises and impoverishes. But above all else we have to understand it is a visual sign of failure. The recourse to the stereotypes of famine is driven by the complex political circumstances photography has historically been unable to capture. This means that when we see the images of distressed people, feeding clinics and starving babies, we are seeing the end result of a collective inability to picture causes and context." (http://www.david-campbell.org/2011/07/16/thinking-images-v-20-famine-iconography-failure/) See also Walter Benjamin, "Little History of Photography": "The creative in photography is its capitulation to fashion. The world is *beautiful*—that is its watchword. In it is unmasked the posture of a photography that can endow any soupcan with cosmic significance but cannot grasp a single one of the human connections in which it exists [. . .]. As Brecht says: '[...] a photograph of the Krupp works or the AEG tells us next to nothing about these institutions." (*Selected Writings*, ed. by Michael W. Jennings, Howard Eiland and Gary Smith, vol. 2, 1927-1934 [Cambridge, MA: Harvard University Press, 1999], p. 526)

129. John Tagg, *The Burden of Representation: Essays on Photographies and Histories* (Basingstoke: Macmillan Education, 1988), pp. 92, 118-19, 150-51. In a similar vein, Victor Burgin, ed., *Thinking Photography* (London: Macmillan, 1982). According to David Levi Strauss ("The Documentary Debate: Aesthetic or Anesthetic," in *Between the Eyes: Essays on Photography and Politics*, ed. D. Levi Strauss [New York: Aperture, 2003], pp. 3-11), Rosler's and Tagg's critiques, "focussing on the aestheticization of the documentary image [. . .] were accepted and absorbed into mainstream writing on photography." (p. 5) He quotes from an article severely critical of the great Brazilian photographer Sebastião Salgado in *The New Yorker* (9 September 1991): "Salgado is too busy with the compositional aspect of his pictures and with finding the 'grace' and 'beauty' in the twisted forms of his anguished subjects. And this beautification of tragedy results in pictures that ultimately reinforce our passivity toward the experience they reveal. [. . .] Beauty is a call to admiration, not to action." Similarly, in the catalogue of a 1990 exhibition of Salgado's work at the San Francisco Museum of Modern Art, the Uruguayan writer Eduardo Galeano acknowledged that "as an article of consumption poverty [. . .] is a commodity that fetches a high price on the luxury market" at the present time, even while arguing that Salgado's work transcends this exploitation of misery: "From their mighty silence these images, these portraits, question the hypocritical frontiers that safeguard the bourgeois order and protect its right to power and inheritance." (Both passages cited on pp. 5-7)

130. Annan's destiny was by no means unique. As noted, the work of Hine and Riis also came to be valued more for its formal than for its documentary qualities. It has been argued that the work of the celebrated late nineteenth- and early twentieth-century French photographer Eugène Atget was perceived differently by his French contemporaries and by later admirers in the United States. Atget, it is claimed, "was a commercial image-maker" whose "photographs and albums were sold to artists, libraries, and historical societies eager to preserve the past. [. . .] This artist chose to capture the Old Paris, to hold on to the relics of the past overwhelmed by the speeding traffic of the present day: the narrow cobblestone streets, the horse-drawn carts, the poor peddlers hawking their wares." His images "were produced as documents, recording monuments and sites that were clearly identified by their image-maker; but they were published in the United States, after the photographer's death, as art objects in a large and beautiful volume, where the images are severed from the captions that 'fix' them in historical time and space (the captions are listed in a separate section discreetly hidden at the back of the book)." American Pictorialism, in short, transformed the perception of the original, primarily documentary images. "The Old Paris, like Curtis's Navajo tribe, drifted into eternity once it reached American shores." (Shelley Rice, "When Objects Dream," p. 11) The painter and stained glass artist Brian Clarke expresses regret that photography has "become part of the system that

fifty years ago it seriously questioned," photographers having also come to adopt "galleries and museums" as "in many cases the singular end and goal to which they aspire." ("Toward a New Constructivism," in Brian Clarke, ed., *Architectural Stained Glass* [London: John Murray, 1979], p. 17)

131. *On Photography*, p. 148.

132. See "The Speech Event and the Functions of Language," in R. Jakobson, *On Language*, ed. Linda R. Waugh and Monique Monville-Burston (Cambridge, MA: Harvard University Press, 1990), pp. 69-79. Jakobson's text was written at a much earlier date, ca.1956.

133. Naomi Rosenblum catches something of this polyvalence in a brief comment on Annan's *The Old Closes and Streets* in her *World History of Photography* (New York: Abbeville Press, 2007): "A project that originated in the desire to make a record of slum buildings slated for demolition in central Glasgow also helped establish the documentary style even though its purpose was nostalgic rather than reformist. [. . .] Because the project was not conceived in a reformist spirit, no statistical information about living conditions or comments by the inhabitants—who appear only incidentally in the images—were included. Nevertheless, Annan's images might be seen as the earliest visual record of what has come to be called the inner city slum—in this case one that excelled in 'filth . . . drunkenness . . . evil smell and all that makes city poverty disgusting.' The vantage points selected by the photographer and the use of light to reveal the slimy and fetid dampness of the place transform scenes that might have been merely picturesque into a document that suggests the reality of life in such an environment. Whatever the initial purpose of the commission and despite their equivocal status as social documentation, many of Annan's images are surprisingly close in viewpoint to those of Jacob Riis, the first person in America to conceive of camera images as an instrument for social change. Sensitivity to the manner in which light gives form and dimension to inert object also links Annan's work with that of French photographers Charles Marville and Eugène Atget, and supplies further evidence that the documentary style in itself is not specific to images commissioned for activist programs." (pp. 358-59)

134. Roland Barthes, *Camera Lucida*, trans. Richard Howard (New York: Hill and Wang, 1981), p. 4.

135. Ibid., pp. 76-77, 115. Cf. a comment by Annan's son, James Craig Annan, in a talk printed in Stieglitz's *Camera Work* in December 1910. Though he was one of the early adherents of the Pictorial school in photography, Annan expresses opposition to the manipulating of images captured by the camera: "The peculiar quality of a gum print is that at one stage of the process of production the print is in such a soft state, somewhat analogous to a recently painted oil picture, and while it is in this state liberties may

be taken with it by rubbing off portions of the semi-fluid picture. [. . .] Interesting as these gum prints may be, I am rather inclined to believe that the most perfect work has been and will be done in pure photography, for the reason that by pure photography one may reproduce objects, with all their contours, tones, and modelling with absolute fidelity." ("Photography as a Means of Artistic Expression," in William Buchanan, ed., *J. Craig Annan: Selected Texts and Bibliography* [see endnote 31 above], pp. 124-25) Similar reservations had been expressed by the poet and critic Sadakich Hartmann, a frequent contributor to Stieglitz's *Camera Work*, in "A Plea for Straight Photography" (1904), reproduced in Peter Bunnell, ed., *A Photographic Vision: Pictorial Photography, 1889-1923* (Salt Lake City: Peregrine Smith, 1980), pp. 148-67.

136. https://en.wikipedia.org/wiki/Economic_history_of_Scotland#Ships Accessed 3.3.2015

137. Sontag, *On Photography*, p. 6.

138. See, for instance, the text accompanying Plate X, "The Haystack," in *The Pencil of Nature*: "One advantage of the discovery of the Photographic Art will be, that it will enable us to introduce to our pictures a multitude of minute details which add to the truth and reality of the representation, but which no artist would take the trouble to copy faithfully from nature. Contenting himself with a general effect, he would probably deem it beneath his genius to copy every accident of light and shade; nor could he do so indeed, without a disproportionate expenditure of time and trouble, which might be otherwise much better employed. Nevertheless, it is well to have the means at our disposal of introducing these minutiae without any additional trouble, for they will sometimes be found to give an air of variety beyond expectation to the scene represented." On Talbot's hesitation between an "indexical definition" of the photograph and a "hesitant" claim, made in connection with three plates in *The Pencil of Nature* (VI, "The Open Door"; X, "The Haystack"; and XIV, "The Ladder") "about the art-rivaling potential of photography," between emphasis on the reproducibility of the photographic image and appreciation of the "variability of the print" in relation to the negative, see Carol Armstrong, *Scenes in a Library: Reading the Photograph in the Book 1843-1875* (Cambridge, MA: MIT Press, 1998), pp. 107-08, 115, 123-24, 160-65.

139. *On Photography*, p. 103. David King's extraordinary *Ordinary Citizens: The Victims of Stalin* (London: Francis Boutle, 2003), consisting entirely of full-page reproductions of mugshots from the interrogation files of individuals arrested and shot during Stalin's reign of terror from the late 1920s until his death in 1953, demonstrates vividly that in certain circumstances (here the use of natural light and longer time exposure) even the mugshot can be movingly expressive and esthetically engaging.

List of Illustrations

1:1 William Henry Fox Talbot, "The Open Door," from *The Pencil of Nature* (London: Longman, Brown, Green & Longmans, 1844), Plate VI. Salted paper print. Rare Book Division, Department of Rare Books and Special Collections, Princeton University Library.   9

1:2 William Henry Fox Talbot, "Haystack," from *The Pencil of Nature*, Plate X. Salted paper print. Rare Book Division, Department of Rare Books and Special Collections, Princeton University Library.   9

1:3 William Henry Fox Talbot (attributed to), "The Fruit Sellers." 1844. Salted paper print. Metropolitan Museum of Art. Gilman Collection, Purchase, Harriette and Noel Levine Gift, 2005, Accession Number 2005.100.607. ©Metropolitan Museum. http://www.metmuseum.org/collection/the-collection-online/search/283067   10

1:4 David Octavius Hill, "Dunstaffnage," from *The Poetical Works of the Ettrick Shepherd. With an autobiography; and illustrative engravings, chiefly from original drawings by D.O. Hill. R.S.A*, vol. 3 (Glasgow, Edinburgh and London: Blackie and Son, [1838]). Frontispiece. Princeton University Library.   10

1:5 D.O. Hill, "Loch Lomond," from *The Land of Burns. A Series of Landscapes and Portraits Illustrative of the Life and Writings of the Scottish Poet. The landscapes made expressly for the work by D.O. Hill, Esq., R.S.A*, vol. 2 (Glasgow: Blackie and Son, 1840), facing p. 45. Princeton University Library.   11

1:6 D.O. Hill, "Scene on the Girvan," from *The Land of Burns*, vol. 1, facing p. 66. Princeton University Library.   11

1:7 D.O. Hill, "Feu de joie-Taymouth Castle." 1835. Oil on panel. Courtesy of Perth Museum & Art Gallery, Perth & Kinross Council.   11

1:8 D.O. Hill and Robert Adamson, "Edinburgh Ale: James Ballantine, Dr. George William Bell and David Octavius Hill." Ca.1844. Salted paper print. Wikimedia. http://commons.wikimedia.org/wiki/File:Edinburgh_Ale_by_Hill_%26_Adamson_c1844.png   12

1:9   Hill and Adamson, "Presbytery of Dumbarton." 1843-1847. Salted paper print. Metropolitan Museum of Art. Gift of Mrs. Pirie MacDonald and Mr. and Mrs. Everett Tutchings, 1943, Accession Number 43.10.49. ©Metropolitan Museum. http://www.metmuseum.org/collection/the-collection-online/search/268803?rpp=30&pg=1&ft=presbytery+of+dumbarton&pos=1   12

1:10 Hill and Adamson, "Newhaven Fishermen." 1845. Salted paper print. Metropolitan Museum of Art. Harris Brisbane Dick Fund, 1937, Accession Number: 37.98.1.78. ©Metropolitan Museum. http://www.metmuseum.org/collection/the-collection-online/search/268457   13

1:11 Hill and Adamson, "Newhaven Fisher Girls." 1843-1847. Salted paper print. Wikimedia. http://commons.wikimedia.org/wiki/Category:Hill_%26_Adamson#/media/File:Newhaven_fishergirls.jpg   13

1:12 Hill and Adamson, "A Newhaven Pilot." Ca.1845. Salted paper print. Wikimedia. http://commons.wikimedia.org/wiki/Category:Hill_%26_Adamson#/media/File:%27A_Newhaven_Pilot%27.jpg   14

1:13 Hill and Adamson, "Willie Liston: Redding the Line." 1845. Salted paper print. Wikimedia. http://commons.wikimedia.org/wiki/File:Willie_Liston,_'Redding_(cleaning_or_preparing)_the_line',_Newhaven_fisherman.jpg   14

1:14 Hill and Adamson, "His Faither's Breeks." 1844. Salted paper print. Wikimedia. http://commons.wikimedia.org/wiki/Category:Hill_%26_Adamson#/media/File:His_Faither%E2%80%99s_Breeks.jpg   14

1:15 Hill and Adamson, "Lady Ruthven." Ca.1845. Salted paper print. Metropolitan Museum of Art. The Rubel Collection, Purchase, Manfred Heiting and Lila Acheson Wallace Gifts, 1997, Accession Number 1997.382.18. ©Metropolitan Museum. http://www.metmuseum.org/collection/the-collection-online/search/282021?rpp=30&pg=1&ft=lady+ruthven&pos=1   14

1:16 Thomas Rodger, "Four Generations of Rodger." 1856. Collage of four photographic portraits. St. Andrews University Photographic Collection, ALB-49-56. Courtesy of St. Andrews University Library.   15

1:17 Thomas Rodger, "Thomas Rodger senior playing the bellows with Hungarian violinist Eduard Remeny." In album. St. Andrews University Photographic Collection, ALB-49-12. Courtesy of St. Andrews University Library.   15

1:18 George Washington Wilson, "Queen Victoria on 'Fyvie' with John Brown." 1863. Carte-de-visite. Wikimedia. http://commons.wikimedia.org/wiki/File:Queen_Victoria,_photographed_by_George_Washington_Wilson_(1863).jpg   16

1:19 George Washington Wilson, "Castle Urquhart." 1867. Albumen print. *Photographs of English and Scottish Scenery* (Aberdeen: Printed by John Duffus, 1866-1868). British Library. http://www.bl.uk/onlinegallery/onlineex/earlyphotos/c/largeimage53419.html   16

List of Illustrations 165

1:20   George Washington Wilson, "Pass of Beal Ach Nam Bo." 1868. 16
       Albumen print. *Photographs of English and Scottish Scenery*. British
       Library. http://www.bl.uk/onlinegallery/onlineex/earlyphotos/t/006
       tro10370cc35u00012000.html

1:21   James Valentine, "In the Vault, Dundee." 1878. Gelatin dry plate 17
       negative. St. Andrews University Photographic Collection, JV-916A.
       Courtesy of St. Andrews University Library.

1:22   James Valentine, "Jedburgh Abbey, Norman doorway." 1878. 17
       Sepiatype (Vandyke Print). St. Andrews University Photographic
       Collection, JV-366. Courtesy of St. Andrews University Library.

1:23   James Valentine, "Newport Arch, Lincoln." 1865-1880. Albumen print. 17
       Wikimedia. http://commons.wikimedia.org/wiki/File:Newport_Arch,
       _late_19th_century.jpg

1:24   John Thomson, "Halfpenny Ices," from J. Thomson, F.R.G.S. and 18
       Adolph Smith, *Street Life in London* (London: Samson Low, Marston,
       Searle, & Rivington, 1877). Woodburytype. The London School of
       Economics and Political Science Digital Library, CC BY-NC-SA.
       http://digital.library.lse.ac.uk/objects/lse:gox325doj

1:25   John Thomson, "The Temperance Sweep," from *Street Life in London*. 18
       Woodburytype. The London School of Economics and Political
       Science Digital Library, CC BY-NC-SA. http://digital.library.lse.
       ac.uk/objects/lse:qav226jay

1:26   John Thomson, "Amoy Boys," from *Illustrations of China and its People*, 18
       vol. 2 (London: Samson Low, Marston, Low, and Searle, 1873), Plate
       XIV. Woodburytype. MIT Visualizing Cultures, CC BY-NC-SA. http://
       ocw.mit.edu/ans7870/21f/21f.027/john_thomson_china_03/ct_gal_02_
       thumb.html

1:27   Alexander Gardner, "Abraham Lincoln and His Second Son Thomas 19
       (Tad)." Albumen print. Wikimedia. http://commons.wikimedia.
       org/wiki/File:Alexander_Gardner_(American,_born_Scotland_-_
       (Abraham_Lincoln_and_His_Second_Son_Thomas_(Tad))_-_
       Google_Art_Project.jpg

1:28   Alexander Gardner, "Ditch at Antietam." 1862. Albumen print. 19
       Library of Congress, LC-DIG-cwpb-01088. http://lcweb2.loc.gov/
       service/pnp/cwpb/01000/01088v.jpg

1:29   Alexander Gardner, "Washington Navy Yard, District of Columbia. 20
       Lewis Payne, in sweater, seated and manacled." 1865. Albumen
       print. Library of Congress, LC-DIG-cwpb-04212. http://www.loc.gov/
       pictures/item/cwp2003006172/PP/

1:30   William Carrick, "Knife Grinder." Russia, 1870. Albumen print. 20
       Wikimedia. http://commons.wikimedia.org/wiki/File:Carrick,_Knife-
       grinder.jpg

1:31   Robert Macpherson , "Museo Chiaramonti, Vatican." 1872. Albumen print. Wikimedia. http://commons.wikimedia.org/wiki/File:MacPherson,_Robert_(1811-1872)_-_Museo_Chiaramonti_-_Vatican.jpg   21

1:32   William Notman, "Jefferson Davis and Mrs Davis." 1867. Albumen print. McCord Museum, Montreal, QC. ©McCord Museum, I-28147.1. CC BY-NC-ND. http://www.mccord-museum.qc.ca/scripts/large.php?accessnumber=I-28147.1&zoomify=true&Lang=1&imageID=166927   21

1:33   Horatio Ross, "Stag in Cart." 1858. Albumen print. Metropolitan Museum. Gilman Collection, Museum Purchase, 2005, Accession Number 2005.100.16. ©Metropolitan Museum. http://www.metmuseum.org/collection/the-collection-online/search/283088?rpp=30&pg=2&ft=horatio+ross&pos=35   21

1:34   John Moffat, "William Henry Fox Talbot." 1864. Albumen print. Wikimedia. http://commons.wikimedia.org/wiki/Category:Henry_Fox_Talbot#/media/File:William_Henry_Fox_Talbot,_by_John_Moffat,_1864.jpg   22

1:35   Archibald Burns, "Cardinal Beaton's House, Cowgate, Edinburgh," from *Picturesque "bits" from old Edinburgh: a series of photographs, with descriptive and historical notes by Thomas Henderson* (Edinburgh: Edmonston and Douglas, 1868). Albumen print. Graphic Arts Collection, Department of Rare Books and Special Collections, Princeton University Library.   22

1:36   Clementina Fleeming, Lady Hawarden, "Studies from Life; Isabella Grace and Clementina Maude, 5 Princes Gardens." 1863. Albumen print from wet collodion on glass negative. Given by Lady Clementina Tottenham. Victoria and Albert Museum, London, PH267. ©Victoria and Albert Museum. http://collections.vam.ac.uk/item/O72732/studies-from-life-or-photographic-photograph-hawarden-clementina-viscountess/   23

1:37   Clementina Fleeming, Lady Hawarden, Untitled (Clementina and Isabella Grace). 1863-1864. Albumen print. Given by Lady Clementina Tottenham, Victoria and Albert Museum, London, PH266-1947. ©Victoria and Albert Museum. http://collections.vam.ac.uk/item/O1047886/photograph-clementina-lady-hawarden/   23

1:38   Thomas Keith, "Unidentified Close" (probably Reid's Close). 1854-1856. Paper negative. City of Edinburgh Council —Libraries. (www.capitalcollections.org.uk). By kind permission of the City of Edinburgh Council.   24

1:39   Thomas Keith, "Tower of St Giles from Parliament House, Edinburgh." Paper negative. City of Edinburgh Council—Libraries. (www.capitalcollections.org.uk). By kind permission of the City of Edinburgh Council.   24

List of Illustrations   167

2:1   Joseph Noël Paton, "The Capture or The Slave Hunt," from *Bond and*   33
      *Free: Five sketches illustrative of slavery by J. Noël Paton; photographed
      by Thomas Annan* (Glasgow: Maclure and MacDonald, 1863), Plate 3.
      Reproduced in Alfred T. Story, "Sir Noël Paton: His Life and Work,"
      The Art Journal (1895), 97-128 (p. 98). Marquand Library, Princeton
      University.

2:2   Joseph Noël Paton, "Freedom," from *Bond and Free*, Plate 5.   33
      Reproduced in *Sunday Magazine* (1 June 1865, pp. 672-76). Princeton
      Theological Seminary Library.

2:3   David Octavius Hill, "In Memoriam: The Calton." 1862. Oil on   34
      panel. City Art Centre: Edinburgh Museums and Galleries. By kind
      permission of Edinburgh Museums and Galleries. http://www.bbc.
      co.uk/arts/yourpaintings/paintings/in-memoriam-the-calton-93390

2:4   Thomas Annan, Photograph of D. O. Hill's "Disruption" painting   35
      ("First General Assembly of the Free Church of Scotland. Signing the
      Act of Separation and Deed of Demission at Tanfield, Edinburgh, May
      1843"). 1868. Carbon print. By kind permission of the photograph's
      owner, Roddy Simpson, who also generously provided a high
      resolution digital copy of the print.

2:5   Sir George Hayter, "The House of Commons, 1833." 1833-1843. Oil   36
      on canvas. ©National Portrait Gallery, London, Asset no. 54. By kind
      permission of the National Portrait Gallery.

2:6   William Powell Frith, "The Marriage of H.R.H. the Prince of Wales   36
      with Princess Alexandra of Denmark, St. George's Chapel, Windsor,
      10 March, 1863." Oil on canvas. 1865. Wikimedia. http://commons.
      wikimedia.org/wiki/File:William_Powell_Frith_-_The_Marriage_of_
      the_Prince_of_Wales,_10_March_1863.JPG

2:7   George Washington Wilson, "Aberdeen Portraits No. 1." 1857.   37
      Albumen silver print. Metropolitan Museum. The Horace W.
      Goldsmith Foundation Fund, through Joyce and Robert Menschel,
      2011, Accession Number 2011.424. ©Metropolitan Museum.
      http://www.metmuseum.org/collection/the-collection-online/
      search/298968?rpp=30&pg=1&ft=george+washington+wilson&pos=4

2:8   John Trumbull, "The Declaration of Independence." 1818. Oil on   37
      canvas. Installed in Rotunda of U.S. Capitol, Washington, D.C., 1826.
      Architect of the Capitol. http://www.aoc.gov/capitol-hill/historic-
      rotunda-paintings/declaration-independence.

3:1   Thomas Annan, Portrait of David Livingstone. 1864. Carbon print.   41
      Wikimedia. http://commons.wikimedia.org/wiki/Category:David_
      Livingstone?uselang=de#mediaviewer/File:David_Livingstone_by_
      Thomas_Annan.jpg

3:2   Thomas Annan, Portrait of Horatio McCulloch, from Alexander Fraser, *Scottish Landscape: The Works of Horatio McCulloch, R.S.A.* (Edinburgh: Andrew Eliot, 1872). Frontispiece. Carbon print. British Library. http://www.bl.uk/catalogues/photographyinbooks/Photo.ASP?PhotoID=3536   42

3:3   Thomas Annan, Portrait of William T. Gairdner, Professor of the Practice of Medicine, from *Memorials of the Old College of Glasgow* (Glasgow: Thomas Annan; James MacLehose, 1871), Plate XVI. Albumen print. Courtesy of University of Glasgow Library, Department of Special Collections. http://encore.lib.gla.ac.uk/iii/encore/record/C__Rb1168827?lang=eng.com/imageview.php?inum=TGSD00018   42

3:4   Thomas Annan, Portrait of Thomas Barclay, Principal of Glasgow University 1858-1873, from *Memorials of the Old College of Glasgow.* Unnumbered plate. Albumen print. Courtesy of University of Glasgow Library, Department of Special Collections. http://encore.lib.gla.ac.uk/iii/encore/record/C__Rb1168827?lang=eng.com/imageview.php?inum=TGSD00018   43

3:5   John Fergus of Largs, William Lloyd Garrison (American abolitionist). Albumen cabinet card. 1870s. National Portrait Gallery, London. Asset Number x28191. ©National Portrait Gallery. By kind permission of the National Portrait Gallery.   43

3:6   John Fergus of Largs, carte-de-visite portrait of Henry Morton Stanley (Explorer). Carbon print published by Eglington & Co., 1890. National Portrait Gallery, London, Asset Number Ax5497. ©National Portrait Gallery. By kind permission of the National Portrait Gallery.   44

3:7   Sir Henry Raeburn, "Francis Horner." 1812. Oil on canvas. National Portrait Gallery, London, Asset Number 485. ©National Portrait Gallery, London. By kind permission of the National Portrait Gallery.   44

3:8   D.O. Hill and Robert Adamson, Portrait of D.O. Hill. 1843-1847. Salted paper print. Wikipedia. http://en.wikipedia.org/wiki/David_Octavius_Hill#/media/File:Hill_%26_Adamson_(Scottish,_active_1843_-_1848)_-_D._O._Hill_-_Google_Art_Project.jpg   45

3:9   D.O. Hill and Robert Adamson, Portrait of Mrs. Anna Brownell Jameson. 1844. Salted paper print. Wikimedia. http://commons.wikimedia.org/wiki/Category:Hill_%26_Adamson#/media/File:Anna_Brownell_Jameson_1844.jpg   46

3:10   Dr. John Adamson, "Potato Head." 1855. Salted paper print. St. Andrews University Photographic Collection, ALB-6-158. Courtesy of St. Andrews University Library.   46

3:11   Dr. John Adamson, "The Sick Baby" (Professor Hugh Lyon Playfair and Professor William Macdonald). 1855. Salted paper print. St. Andrews University Photographic Collection, ALB-6-131-1. Courtesy of St. Andrews University Library.   47

List of Illustrations 169

3:12 Thomas Rodger, Portrait of Thomas Rodger Senior in Fishwives' Costume. 1860. In album. St. Andrews University Photographic Collection, ALB-49-11. Courtesy of St. Andrews University. 47

4:1 "Château de Dunderaw sur le Lac Fine," from François-Alexandre Pernot and Amédée Pichot, *Vues pittoresques de l'Écosse* (Paris: Charles Gosselin et Lami-Denozan, 1826; Brussels: A. Wahlen, A. Dewasme, 1827). Courtesy of Ancestry Images. http://www.ancestryimages.com/proddetail.php?prod=e9765 55

4:2 D.O. Hill, "Drumlanrig Castle," from *The Land of Burns* (as in Fig.1:6), vol. 2, facing p. 20. 55

4:3 John Fleming, "Loch Maree," from *Select Views of the Lakes of Scotland: from Original Paintings by John Fleming engraved by Joseph Swan; with historical and descriptive illustrations by John M. Leighton* (Glasgow: J. Swan, [1834-1840]). Princeton University Library. 55

4:4 "The Saltmarket," from James Pagan, *Sketch of the History of Glasgow* (Glasgow: Robert Stuart, 1847), facing p. 161; originally plate 20 of "Illustrated Letterpaper comprising a Series of Views in Glasgow" (Glasgow: Allen and Ferguson, 1843). https://archive.org/stream/sketchhistorygl00pagagoog#page/n210/mode/2up 56

4:5 Thomas Annan, "Stonebyres Linn," from his *Photographs of the Clyde* (Glasgow: Andrew Duthie, 1867). Graphic Arts Collection, Department of Rare Books and Special Collections, Princeton University Library. 56

4:6 Thomas Annan, "Hamilton Palace," from his *Photographs of the Clyde*. Graphic Arts Collection, Department of Rare Books and Special Collections, Princeton University Library. 56

4:7 Thomas Annan, "Bothwell Castle," from his *Photographs of the Clyde*. Graphic Arts Collection, Department of Rare Books and Special Collections, Princeton University Library. 57

4:8 Thomas Annan, "Castle, Little Cumbray," from John Eaton Reid, *History of the County of Bute and Families connected therewith* (Glasgow: T. Murray and Son, 1864). British Library, London. http://www.bl.uk/onlinegallery/onlineex/earlyphotos/c/largeimage54199.html 57

4:9 Thomas Annan, "Loch Ranza Castle," from *History of the County of Bute*. British Library, London. http://www.bl.uk/onlinegallery/onlineex/earlyphotos/l/largeimage54202.html 58

4:10 Thomas Annan, "Tomb, St. Mary's Chapel, Rothesay," from *History of the County of Bute*. British Library, London. http://www.bl.uk/onlinegallery/onlineex/earlyphotos/t/largeimage54195.html 58

4:11 John Knox, "The Head of Glen Sannox." Oil on canvas. Wikimedia. http://commons.wikimedia.org/wiki/File:Knox_John_Glen_Sannox.jpg 58

170   Thomas Annan of Glasgow

4:12 Thomas Annan, "Glen Sannox," from *History of the County of Bute*. 59
British Library, London. http://www.bl.uk/onlinegallery/onlineex/
earlyphotos/g/largeimage54200.html

4:13 Thomas Annan, "Dumbarton Castle." Exhibited 1864. ©CSG CIC 59
Glasgow Museums and Libraries Collection: The Mitchell Library,
Special Collections.

4:14 John Knox, "Landscape with tourists at Loch Katrine." Ca.1820. 60
Oil on canvas. Wikimedia. http://commons.wikimedia.org/wiki/
File:John_Knox_-_Landscape_with_Tourists_at_Loch_Katrine_-_
Google_Art_Project.jpg

4:15 W. Miller, "Loch Katrine," engraving by W. Miller after painting 60
by J.M.W. Turner. Published in *The Poetical Works of Sir Walter Scott,
Bart*. (Edinburgh: Robert Cadell & Whittaker, 1833-1834). Wikimedia.
http://commons.wikimedia.org/wiki/File:Loch_Katrine_engraving_
by_William_Miller_after_Turner_R507.jpg

4:16 William Henry Fox Talbot, "Loch Katrine," from H. Fox Talbot, 60
Esq., F.R.S., *Sun Pictures in Scotland* (London: [n. pub.], 1845), Plate
16. Salted paper print. Division of Rare Books, Marquand Library,
Princeton University.

4:17 Alexander Nasmyth, "Landscape, Loch Katrine." 1862. Oil on canvas. 60
Kelvingrove Art Gallery, Glasgow. Courtesy of Glasgow Museums
Collection.

4:18 Horatio McCulloch, "Loch Katrine." 1866. Oil on canvas. Courtesy of 61
Perth Museum & Art Gallery, Perth & Kinross Council.

4:19 Thomas Annan, "Loch Katrine and Ellen's Isle and Ben Venue," from 61
*Glasgow Corporation Water Works. Photographic Views of Loch Katrine,
and of some of the principal works constituted for introducing the water
of Loch Katrine into the city of Glasgow* (Glasgow: Printed by James C.
Erskine, 1889). Albumen print. (Original photograph, 1859). Graphic
Arts Collection, Department of Rare Books and Special Collections,
Princeton University Library.

4:20 Thomas Annan, "Aqueduct Bridge near Duntreath Castle, 22 62
miles from Loch Katrine," from *Glasgow Corporation Water Works*.
Albumen print. (Original photograph, 1859). Graphic Arts Collection,
Department of Rare Books and Special Collections, Princeton
University Library.

4:21 Thomas Annan, "Endrick Valley looking South," from *Glasgow* 62
Corporation Water Works. Albumen print. (Original photograph, 1859).
Graphic Arts Collection, Department of Rare Books and Special
Collections, Princeton University Library.

4:22 Thomas Annan, "Glasgow Corporation Water Commissioners at Loch Katrine, 1886," from *Glasgow Corporation Water Works*. Albumen print. Graphic Arts Collection, Department of Rare Books and Special Collections, Princeton University Library.   63

4:23 Thomas Annan, "Glasgow Water Commissioners at Loch Katrine, 1878," from *Glasgow Corporation Water Works*. Albumen print. Graphic Arts Collection, Department of Rare Books and Special Collections, Princeton University Library.   63

4:24 Thomas Annan, "Glasgow Water Commissioners at opening of a new aqueduct, 1886," from *Glasgow Corporation Water Works*. Albumen print. Graphic Arts Collection, Department of Rare Books and Special Collections, Princeton University Library.   64

4:25 Engraving from a photograph by Annan in *Illustrated London News*, 15 October 1859. Princeton University Library.   64

4:26 "Views of the Loch Katrine water works," *Illustrated London News*, 22 October 1859. Princeton University Library.   65

4:27 George Washington Wilson, "Loch Katrine. The Silver Strand," from *Photographs of English and Scottish Scenery*, vol. 11 (Aberdeen: Printed by John Duffus, 1865-1868). Albumen print. Also in Sir Walter Scott, *The Lady of the Lake* (Edinburgh: Adam and Charles Black, 1869). British Library, London. http://www.bl.uk/onlinegallery/onlineex/earlyphotos/t/largeimage53432.html   66

4:28 George Washington Wilson, "Ellen's Isle, Loch Katrine." 1870s. Albumen print. Smith College Art Museum, SC 1982-38-565. Purchased with Hillyer-Tryon-Mather Fund, with funds given in memory of Nancy Newhall (Nancy Parker, class of 1930) and in honor of Beaumont Newhall, and with funds given in honor of Ruth Wedgwood Kennedy. Courtesy of Smith College Art Museum.   66

4:29 James Valentine, "Loch Katrine. Trossachs from Roderick Dhu's Watch Tower." 1878. Gelatin dry plate negative. St. Andrews University Photographic Collection, JV-270.A. Courtesy of St. Andrews University Library.   66

5:1 Thomas Annan, "Bedlay," from *The Old Country Houses of the Old Glasgow Gentry*, 2nd enlarged edition (Glasgow: James MacLehose, 1878). Carbon print. (The photographs in the first edition of 1870 are albumen prints.) Graphic Arts Collection, Department of Rare Books and Special Collections, Princeton University Library.   76

5:2 Thomas Annan, "Cochna," from *The Old Country Houses*. Carbon print. Graphic Arts Collection, Department of Rare Books and Special Collections, Princeton University Library.   76

5:3 Thomas Annan, "Craighead," from *The Old Country Houses*. Carbon print. Graphic Arts Collection, Department of Rare Books and Special Collections, Princeton University Library. 77

5:4 Thomas Annan, "Hunterston Castle, West Kilbride," from *Castles and Mansions of Ayrshire, illustrated in seventy views* (Edinburgh: W. Paterson, 1885). Albumen print. Graphic Arts Collection, Department of Rare Books and Special Collections, Princeton University Library. 77

5:5 Thomas Annan, "Mount Charles," from *Castles and Mansions of Ayrshire*. Albumen print. Graphic Arts Collection, Department of Rare Books and Special Collections, Princeton University Library. 78

5:6 Thomas Annan, "Ardeer," from *Castles and Mansions of Ayrshire*. Albumen print. Graphic Arts Collection, Department of Rare Books and Special Collections, Princeton University Library. 78

5:7 Thomas Annan, "The College from College Street," from the album *Photographs of Glasgow College* (Glasgow: T. Annan, [1866?]). Albumen print. Graphic Arts Collection, Department of Rare Books and Special Collections, Princeton University Library. 79

5:8 Thomas Annan, "The Outer Court with the great stair leading to the Fore-Hall," from *Photographs of Glasgow College*. Albumen print. Graphic Arts Collection, Department of Rare Books and Special Collections, Princeton University Library. 79

5:9 Thomas Annan, "The Outer Court from the top of the Fore-Hall stair," another view, from *Photographs of Glasgow College*. Albumen print. Graphic Arts Collection, Department of Rare Books and Special Collections, Princeton University Library. 80

5:10 Thomas Annan, "Archway in Inner Court looking towards the Outer Court with Zachary Boyd's bust," from *Photographs of Glasgow College*. Albumen print. Graphic Arts Collection, Department of Rare Books and Special Collections, Princeton University Library. 80

5:11 Thomas Annan, "Hunterian Museum," from *Memorials of the Old College of Glasgow* (Glasgow: Thomas Annan; James MacLehose, 1871), reproduced in *University of Glasgow Old and New, illustrated with views and portraits in photogravure* (Glasgow: T.&R. Annan & Sons; James MacLehose, 1891), Plate 16. Division of Rare Books, Marquand Library, Princeton University. 81

5:12 Thomas Annan, "The Professors' Court," from *Photographs of Glasgow College*. Albumen print. Graphic Arts Collection, Department of Rare Books and Special Collections, Princeton University Library. 81

5:13 Thomas Annan, "Interior of Hunterian Museum," from *Memorials of the Old College of Glasgow,* reproduced in *University of Glasgow Old and New,* Plate 17. Division of Rare Books, Marquand Library, Princeton University. 82

5:14 Thomas Annan, Portrait of Professor Allan Thomson, Professor of Anatomy at Glasgow from 1848 to 1877, from *Memorials of the Old College of Glasgow*. Albumen print. Courtesy of University of Glasgow Library, Department of Special Collections. http://encore.lib.gla.ac.uk/iii/encore/record/C__Rb1168827?lang=eng.com/imageview.php?inum=TGSD00018 82

5:15 Charles Marville, "Impasse Briare." 1868. Albumen print. Wikimedia. http://commons.wikimedia.org/wiki/File:Charles_Marville,_Impasse_Briare_(de_la_Cit%C3%A9_Coquenard).jpg 83

5:16 Charles Marville, "Rue Traversine (from the rue d'Arras)." Ca.1868. Albumen print. Metropolitan Museum, Gift of Howard Stein, 2010. Accession Number 2010.513.2. ©Metropolitan Museum. http://www.metmuseum.org/collection/the-collection-online/search/233713?rpp=30&pg=2&ft=marville%2c+charles&pos=33 83

5:17 Eugène Atget, "Hôtel de Sens, rue de l'Hôtel de Ville." Early 1900s. Albumen print. Metropolitan Museum. The Rubel Collection, Gift of William Rubel, 1997. Accession Number 1997.398.2. ©Metropolitan Museum. http://www.metmuseum.org/collection/the-collection-online/search/282111?rpp=30&pg=1&ft=atget+hotel+de+sens&pos=1 84

5:18 Henry Dixon, "Old Houses in Drury Lane." 1880. Albumen print. British Library, London. http://www.bl.uk/onlinegallery/onlineex/earlyphotos/o/largeimage54365.html 84

5:19 Thomas Annan, "Glasgow Bridge and Harbour," from *Photographs of Glasgow, with descriptive letterpress by Rev. A.G. Forbes* (Glasgow: Andrew Duthie, [1868]), Plate III. Albumen print. Courtesy of Fine Arts Library, Harvard University. 85

5:20 Thomas Annan, "Trongate and Cross," from *Photographs of Glasgow*, Plate IX. Albumen print. Courtesy of Fine Arts Library, Harvard University. 85

5:21 Thomas Annan, "George Square," from *Photographs of Glasgow*, Plate II. Albumen print. Courtesy of Fine Arts Library, Harvard University. 86

5:22 Thomas Annan, "Royal Exchange," from *Photographs of Glasgow*, Plate XIII. Albumen print. Courtesy of Fine Arts Library, Harvard University. 86

5:23 Thomas Annan, "Buchanan Street," from *Photographs of Glasgow*, Plate XII. Albumen print. Courtesy of Fine Arts Library, Harvard University. 87

5:24 Thomas Annan, "West End Park," from *Photographs of Glasgow*, Plate X. Albumen print. Courtesy of Fine Arts Library, Harvard University. 87

5:25 Thomas Annan, "Gilmorehill," from *The Old Country Houses of the Old Glasgow Gentry*, 2nd enlarged edition (Glasgow: James MacLehose, 1878). Carbon print. Graphic Arts Collection, Department of Rare Books and Special Collections, Princeton University Library. 88

6:1 David Octavius Hill, "Opening of the Glasgow and Garnkirk Railway in 1831" with a view of the Tennant chemical works, St. Rollox. Lithograph after an original painting, from D. O. Hill, *Views of the Opening of the Glasgow and Garnkirk Railway* (Edinburgh: Alex Hill, 1832). ©CSG CIC Glasgow Museums and Libraries Collection: The Mitchell Library, Special Collections. 109

6:2 Shadow [Alexander Brown], *Midnight Scenes and Social Photographs being Sketches of Life in the Streets, Wynds and Dens of the City* (Glasgow: Thomas Murray, 1858). Cover design. Division of Rare Books, Department of Rare Books and Special Collections, Princeton University Library. 110

6:3 George Cruickshank, from *Midnight Scenes and Social Photographs*. Frontispiece. Division of Rare Books. Department of Rare Books and Special Collections, Princeton University Library. 110

6:4 Jacob Riis, "Bandits' Roost," from his *How the Other Half Lives: Studies among the Tenements of New York, with Illustrations chiefly from Photographs taken by the Author* (New York: Charles Scribner's Sons, 1890), p. 63. Wikimedia. http://commons.wikimedia.org/wiki/File:Jacob_Riis_-_Bandits'_Roost.jpg 111

6:5 Jacob Riis, "Mullen's Alley, Cherry Hill." 1888. Museum Syndicate. http://www.museumsyndicate.com/item.php?item=42940 111

6:6 O.G. Rejlander, Swedish/English, 1813-1875, No title (The Virgin in Prayer). Ca.1858-60. Albumen silver photograph. 20.2 x 15.4 cm irreg. (image and sheet). National Gallery of Victoria Melbourne. Purchased 2002. 112

6:7 Sassoferrato, "The Virgin in Prayer." 1638-1652. Wikimedia. http://commons.wikimedia.org/wiki/File:Sassoferrato_-_Madonna_in_prayer_-_Google_Art_Project.jpg 112

6:8 Thomas Annan, "Closes, Nos. 97 and 103 Saltmarket," from the album *Glasgow Improvements Act 1866. Photographs of Streets, Closes, &c. Taken 1866-71*, Plate 28. Albumen print. Graphic Arts Collection, Department of Rare Books and Special Collections, Princeton University Library. 112

6:9 Thomas Annan, "Close, No. 93 High Street," from *Glasgow Improvements Act 1866*, Plate 9. Albumen print. Graphic Arts Collection, Department of Rare Books and Special Collections, Princeton University Library. 113

6:10 Thomas Annan, "Close, No. 75 High Street," from *Glasgow Improvements Act 1866*, Plate 7. Albumen print. Graphic Arts Collection, Department of Rare Books and Special Collections, Princeton University Library. 114

List of Illustrations   175

6:11   Thomas Annan, "Old Vennel off High Street," from *Glasgow*   114
       Improvements Act 1866, Plate 14. Albumen print. Graphic Arts
       Collection, Department of Rare Books and Special Collections,
       Princeton University Library.

6:12   Thomas Annan, "Close, No. 37 High Street," from *Glasgow*   115
       Improvements Act 1866, Plate 5. Albumen print. Graphic Arts
       Collection, Department of Rare Books and Special Collections,
       Princeton University Library.

6:13   Thomas Annan, "Close, No. 29 Gallowgate," from *Glasgow*   116
       Improvements Act 1866, Plate 18. Albumen print. Graphic Arts
       Collection, Department of Rare Books and Special Collections,
       Princeton University Library.

6:14   Thomas Annan, "Close, No. 128 Saltmarket," from *Glasgow*   117
       Improvements Act 1866, Plate 24. Albumen print. Graphic Arts
       Collection, Department of Rare Books and Special Collections,
       Princeton University Library.

6:15   Thomas Annan, "Close, No. 80 High Street," from *Glasgow*   117
       Improvements Act 1866, Plate 13. Albumen print. Graphic Arts
       Collection, Department of Rare Books and Special Collections,
       Princeton University Library.

6:16   Thomas Annan, "Close, No. 28 Saltmarket," from *Glasgow*   118
       Improvements Act 1866, Plate 21. Albumen print. Graphic Arts
       Collection, Department of Rare Books and Special Collections,
       Princeton University Library.

6:17   Thomas Annan, "Close, No. 118 High Street," from *Glasgow*   119
       Improvements Act 1866, Plate 15. Reproduced from the photogravure
       edition of 1900, *Old Closes and Streets: A Series of Photogravures 1868-
       1899* (Glasgow: T. & R. Annan & Sons, 1900), Plate 6. Graphic Arts
       Collection, Department of Rare Books and Special Collections,
       Princeton University Library.

6:18   Thomas Annan, "Close, No. 46 Saltmarket," from *Glasgow*   120
       Improvements Act 1866, Plate 22. Albumen print. Graphic Arts
       Collection, Department of Rare Books and Special Collections,
       Princeton University Library.

6:19   "The London Costermonger." Engraving of daguerreotype   121
       photograph by Richard Beard in Henry Mayhew, *London Labour and
       the London Poor: A Cyclopædia of the Condition and Earnings of those that
       will work, those that cannot work, and those that will not work* (London:
       Griffin, Bohn & Co., 1861), vol. 1, facing p. 12. Princeton University
       Library.

6:20   "The Jew Old-Clothes Man." Engraving of daguerreotype photograph   121
       by Richard Beard in Henry Mayhew, *London Labour and the London
       Poor* (as in Fig. 6:19 above), vol. 2, facing p. 118.

6:21 Lewis Hine, "Luigi, 6-years-old newsboy-beggar, Sacramento, California." 1915. Gelatin silver print. Wikimedia. http://commons.wikimedia.org/wiki/File:Lewis_Hine,_Luigi,_6_years_old,_newsboy-beggar,_Sacramento,_California,_1915.jpg   122

6:22 Lewis Hine, "Child-laborer." 1908. Digital file from original glass negative. Wikimedia. http://commons.wikimedia.org/wiki/File:Child_laborer.jpg   122

6:23 Colonel William Willoughby Hooper, "Victims of the Madras Famine." 1876. Albumen print. Museum Syndicate. http://www.museumsyndicate.com/images/7/65024.jpg   123

6:24 Glasgow Sanitary Department, "Roslin Place and Burnside Street near Garscube Road in Cowcaddens." 1920s. Photograph reproduced by courtesy of Glasgow Museums Collection.   123

Index of Names

Adamson, John 3-4, 40-41
Adamson, Robert 2-4, 6-7, 28, 40, 129-130, 136
Albert, Prince 75
Allan & Ferguson 50
Anderson, Thomas 40
Annan, James Craig 2, 6, 94-96, 100, 103, 127, 137, 150, 152-154, 161-162
Anthony, Edward 149
Apollinaire, Guillaume 105, 159
Arnott, Neil 90, 144-145
Arscott, Caroline 156
Atget, Eugène 74, 108, 160-161

Bain, James 51
Baldus, Édouard 97, 150
Bann, Stephen 133
Barclay, Thomas 43-44
Barnardo, Thomas John 105
Barthes, Roland 108
Bateman, John Frederick 52, 53
Baudelaire, Charles 40
Bayard, Hippolyte 97
Beard, Richard 103-104, 157
Bell, Henry Glassford 31
Benjamin, Walter 98, 104, 106, 159
Bingham, Robert Jefferson 25
Blackburn, Hugh 40
Blackie, John 10, 50, 93, 97, 137
Blanquet-Evrard, Louis-Désiré 152
Blau, Eve 148
Boswell, James 108
Brady, Matthew 4

Brewster, Sir David 3-4, 128
Brown, Alexander ("Shadow") 91, 145
Burns, Archibald 5-6, 98, 150, 155
Burns, Robert 4, 50, 70

Caird, Edward 40
Caird, John 40
Carrick, John 93, 94, 97
Carrick, William 4
Carus, Carl Gustav 2, 129-130
Chadwick, Edwin 90, 144-145
Chimacoff, Alan 102, 156
Clarke, Brian 160
Clark, William Donaldson 30
Cockburn, Henry Thomas 139
Corot, Jean-Baptist-Camille 40
Cromwell, Oliver 97
Cruikshank, George 92, 155
Curtis, Edward S. 146

Daguerre, Louis 1, 99, 128
Dallmeyer, John Henry 30, 135
Darnley, Henry Stuart, Lord 97
David, Jacques-Louis 29
Defoe, Daniel 89
Delaroche, Paul 25, 132
Dewitz, Bodo von 129
Dickson, Alexander 40
Dixon, Henry 147-148
Donaldson, Andrew 127
Doré, Gustave 40
Dumas, Alexandre 40
Duthie, Andrew 50-51, 75, 137

Eastlake, Lady Elizabeth 136. *See also* Rigby, Elizabeth, Lady Eastlake
Edward, Prince of Wales, future Edward VII 4
Engels, Friedrich 89-90, 143-145, 148, 157
Evans, Frederik H. 141

Fenton, Roger 26
Fergus, John 5, 40, 130
Fierlants, Edmond 25
Fleming, John 127
Forbes, Rev. A.G. 50, 85, 97, 101, 143, 155, 157
Foreman, Carol 150
Foucault, Michel 106
Fraser, Alexander 32, 50
Friedrich August II, King of Saxony 2, 128
Frith, William Powell 29

Gairdner, William Tennent 40
Galt, John 150
Gardner, Alexander 4
Garrison, William Lloyd 131
Gernsheim, Helmut 2, 6, 40, 153
Gibbon, Edward 108
Gladstone, William Ewart 29
Gowin, Emmet 151

Harker, Margaret 72, 102, 128, 132, 137, 156
Harvey, George 31, 136
Haussmann, Georges-Eugène, Baron 97
Hawarden, Clementina, Lady 5, 23, 131-132
Hawthorne, Nathaniel 91
Hayter, Sir George 29
Hegel, Georg Wilhelm Friedrich 40
Herdman, Robert 30, 136
Herodotus 108
Hill, Amelia Robertson 136
Hill, David Octavius 2-4, 5, 6-7, 28-31, 40, 45, 50, 109, 111, 128-129, 133-137
Hine, Lewis 105-106, 160
Hogg, James 4, 50, 137
Hooper, Willoughby Wallace 105-106, 125, 159

Jakobson, Roman 108-109
Jameson, Anna Brownell 46, 128

Keith, Thomas 5, 131
Kemp, Wolfgang 148, 154
Kibble, John 30, 135
Klič, Karl 7
Knox, John (painter) 50, 127, 137, 142

Lange, Dorothea 105
Lawrence, Sir Thomas 31
Lawson, James 101, 151, 155-156
Lawson, Julie 148, 154, 156
Le Gray, Gustave 6, 97
Le Secq, Henri 97
Livingstone, David 39-41, 137

MacDonald, Hugh 50
MacGregor, John 4
MacLehose, James 40, 74, 95
Macpherson, James ("Ossian") 4, 139
Macpherson, Robert 4-5
Maley, Sonny 146
Marochetti, Carlo 75
Marville, Charles 26, 74, 97, 149, 161
Mary, Queen of Scots 30, 97
Massie, Allan 89, 142
Matheson, Neil 99
Mayhew, Henry 103, 157
McAlpin, David H. 127
McCulloch, Horatio 39, 40, 42
McKenzie, Ray x, 49, 52, 102, 134, 140, 151-153
McLellan, Archibald 31
Melbourne, Lord 29
Mestral, Auguste 97
Michelet, Jules 108
Millais, J.E. 26, 133
Millar, Alexander Hastie 68
Mitchell, John Oswald 68-72, 140
Moffat, John 5-6
Moncrieff, Robert Scott 31
Montesquieu, Charles-Louis de Secondat, Baron de la Brède et de 108
Moore, Sir John 75
Mozley, Anita Ventura 101, 146-148, 155

Nadar (Gaspard-Félix Tourachon) 40
Napoleon III 97
Nash, Suzanne 127, 159

Newton, Sir William 99
Nietzsche, Friedrich 108
Nodier, Charles 98, 150
Normand, Tom x, 138, 157
Notman, William 4-5, 130-131, 150

Pagan, James 50, 142-143
Paton, Noel 26-28, 133
Peel, Robert 29, 75
Pernot, François-Alexandre 49
Pichot, Amédée 49
Plutarch 108
Prasch, Thomas 103
Pritchard, H. Baden 130

Raeburn, Sir Henry 31-32, 40
Raphael 99, 129
Reid, John Eaton 50-52
Rejlander, Oscar 99
Rice, Shelley 51, 146, 152, 158, 160
Rigby, Elizabeth, Lady Eastlake 39, 136
Riis, Jacob 95-97, 103, 106, 149-150, 160-161
Robinson, J.C. 25
Rodger, Thomas 3-4, 40-41
Rosenblum, Naomi 161
Rosler, Martha 106
Ross, Horatio 5-6

Salgado, Sebastião 160
Sand, George 40
Sant, James 26
Sassoferrato, Giovanni Battista Salvi da 99
Scott, David 29
Scott, Sir Walter 4, 7, 31, 49, 50, 52, 53-55, 70, 75, 139
Simpson, James Young 5
Simpson, Roddy x, 132, 135, 154
Smith, Adam 89
Smith, Alexander 92
Smith, John Guthrie 68-72
Sontag, Susan 98, 104, 107, 125-126, 150, 151, 153, 158-159
Spring, Ian 96, 104, 150, 154
Stanley, Henry Morton 44, 131
Steichen, Edward 72, 94, 152
Stevenson, Sara 102, 129

Stieglitz, Alfred 72, 94, 104, 152-153, 158, 161
Stirling-Maxwell, Sir William 132
Stocking, George 157
Strand, Paul 129, 141, 153, 158
Strauss, David Levi 160
Sutcliffe, Frank 100, 151
Sutton, Thomas 99, 152
Swan, Joseph (engraver) 1, 49-50, 127-128, 137, 142
Swan, Sir Joseph Wilson (physicist and chemist) 6, 95
Symons, Jelinger 90, 144

Tacitus 108
Tagg, John 106-107
Talbot, William Henry Fox 2-3, 3, 6, 22, 25, 49, 52, 99, 126, 152, 162
Tavernier, Bertrand 105, 159
Taylor, Isidor Justin Séverin, Baron 98, 149
Tennant 142
Tennant, Charles 142
Thomson, John 4-5, 82, 103, 106, 148, 157
Thoré-Bürger, Théophile 25
Trumbull, John 30
Turner, Joseph Mallord William 28, 52, 102

Urie, John 131

Valentine, James 3, 54, 125, 130
van der Meulen, Adam Frans 150
Veitch, John 40
Victoria, Queen 3, 53, 54, 75, 139

Waagen, Gustav Friedrich 139
Wall, Alfred H. 152
Watt, James 75
Wellington, Duke of 29, 75
Wey, Francis 100, 153
Wiegand, Wilfried 93, 148
Wilson, George Washington 3-4, 29, 49, 52, 54, 125, 130
Woolf, Virginia 8

Young, William 94

Zoffany, Johan 31

This book need not end here...

At Open Book Publishers, we are changing the nature of the traditional academic book. The title you have just read will not be left on a library shelf, but will be accessed online by hundreds of readers each month across the globe. We make all our books free to read online so that students, researchers and members of the public who can't afford a printed edition can still have access to the same ideas as you.

Our digital publishing model also allows us to produce online supplementary material, including extra chapters, reviews, links and other digital resources. Find *Thomas Annan of Glasgow* on our website to access its online extras. Please check this page regularly for ongoing updates, and join the conversation by leaving your own comments:

      http://www.openbookpublishers.com/isbn/9781783741274

If you enjoyed this book, and feel that research like this should be available to all readers, regardless of their income, please think about donating to us. Our company is run entirely by academics, and our publishing decisions are based on intellectual merit and public value rather than on commercial viability. We do not operate for profit and all donations, as with all other revenue we generate, will be used to finance new Open Access publications.

For further information about what we do, how to donate to OBP, additional digital material related to our titles or to order our books, please visit our website: http://www.openbookpublishers.com

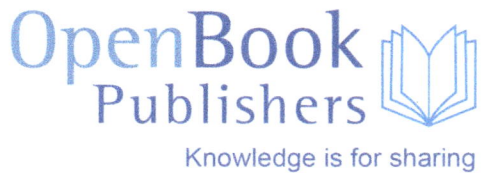

www.ingramcontent.com/pod-product-compliance
Lightning Source LLC
Chambersburg PA
CBHW071535220526
45469CB00003B/793